D0449670

Social Approaches to Communication

HM 258 .S58 1995
Social approaches to
                    211691

DATE DUE

JAN 0 1997	
JUL 1 6 1997	
APR _ 6 2002	
NOV 2 6 2002	
BRODART	Cat. No. 23-221

THE GUILFORD COMMUNICATION SERIES

Editors

Theodore L. Glasser, *Stanford University*

Howard E. Sypher, *University of Kansas*

Advisory Board

Charles Berger	Peter Monge	Michael Schudson
James W. Carey	Barbara O'Keefe	Linda Steiner

SOCIAL APPROACHES TO COMMUNICATION
Wendy Leeds-Hurwitz, *Editor*

PUBLIC OPINION AND THE COMMUNICATION OF CONSENT
Theodore L. Glasser and Charles T. Salmon, *Editors*

COMMUNICATION RESEARCH MEASURES: A SOURCEBOOK
Rebecca B. Rubin, Philip Palmgreen, and Howard E. Sypher, *Editors*

PERSUASIVE COMMUNICATION
James B. Stiff

MESSAGE EFFECTS RESEARCH:
PRINCIPLES OF DESIGN AND ANALYSIS
Sally Jackson

REFORMING LIBEL LAW
John Soloski and Randall P. Bezanson, *Editors*

COMMUNICATION AND CONTROL: NETWORKS
AND THE NEW ECONOMIES OF COMMUNICATION
G. J. Mulgan

CRITICAL PERSPECTIVES ON MEDIA AND SOCIETY
Robert K. Avery and David Eason, *Editors*

THE JOURNALISM OF OUTRAGE: INVESTIGATIVE
REPORTING AND AGENDA BUILDING IN AMERICA
David L. Protess, Fay Lomax Cook, Jack C. Doppelt, James S Ettema,
Margaret T. Gordon, Donna R. Leff, and Peter Miller

MASS MEDIA AND POLITICAL TRANSITION:
THE HONG KONG PRESS IN CHINA'S ORBIT
Joseph Man Chan and Chin-Chuan Lee

STUDYING INTERPERSONAL INTERACTION
Barbara M. Montgomery and Steve Duck, *Editors*

CASE STUDIES IN ORGANIZATIONAL COMMUNICATION
Beverly Davenport Sypher, *Editor*

VOICES OF CHINA: THE INTERPLAY
OF POLITICS AND JOURNALISM
Chin-Chuan Lee, *Editor*

OKANAGAN UNIVERSITY COLLEGE
LIBRARY
BRITISH COLUMBIA

Social Approaches to Communication

Edited by

Wendy Leeds-Hurwitz

Foreword by Robert T. Craig

The Guilford Press
New York   London

© 1995 The Guilford Press
A Division of Guilford Publications, Inc.
72 Spring Street, New York, NY 10012

All rights reserved

No part of this book may be reproduced, stored in a retrieval system,
or transmitted, in any form or by any means, electronic, mechanical,
photocopying, microfilming, recording, or otherwise, without written
permission from the publisher.

Printed in the United States of America

This book is printed on acid-free paper.

Last digit is print number: 9 8 7 6 5 4 3 2 1

Library of Congress Cataloging-in-Publication Data

Social approaches to communication / edited by Wendy Leeds-Hurwitz.
      p.   cm. — (The Guilford communication series)
   Includes bibliographical references and index.
   ISBN 0-89862-867-9 (hard). — ISBN 0-89862-873-3 (pbk.)
   1. Communication — Social aspects.   2. Interpersonal communication—
Research.   3. Interpersonal relations.   I. Leeds-Hurwitz, Wendy.
II. Series.
HM258.S58   1995   95-18761
302.2 — dc20   CIP

Foreword

The publication of *Social Approaches to Communication* should mark a turning point in the development of interpersonal communication research. The field has long been dominated by a rigorous but rather narrow behavioral science approach closely aligned with experimental social psychology. The history that led to this dominance is complex but can be sketched briefly in rough outline.

Interpersonal communication emerged as a distinct area within U.S. speech communication departments in the 1960s and '70s. From the start, most leading scholars in the field agreed that interpersonal communication research should adhere to the highest standards of scientific method, which for them implied the use of sophisticated statistical models and experimental designs. Quantitative methods do have certain real advantages, of course, but the field's early commitment to an exclusively quantitative approach had a decidedly militant quality that requires some additional explanation. I can suggest three possible reasons.

First, speech departments since as early as the 1920s had been polarized between humanistic and scientific approaches (Cohen, 1994). On the humanistic side were rhetoricians who conducted historical-critical studies of public discourse. For many rhetoricians, communication was always and forever a liberal art and could never be made into a science—which, of course, is precisely what the behavioral scientists generally proposed to do. For their part, many behavioral scientists believed that the entire historical-critical approach to rhetoric was simply outdated. Experimental research studies leading to formal scientific theories of communication were, they thought, the wave of the future. Interpersonal communication emerged on the "scientific" side of speech departments and was quite predictably shaped by the traditional conflict between scientists and humanists in those departments. Interpersonal scholars tended to think in terms of a dichotomy between scientific and humanistic approaches; they assumed that humanistic approaches had to be excluded or marginalized in order to establish interpersonal communication as a truly respectable scientific field.

Academic respectability was perceived to be an important problem for the field of interpersonal communication, and the desire for respectability offers a second explanation for the early emphasis on scientific method. Interpersonal communication courses began mushrooming in the late 1960s in part because of a trend in popular culture known as the human potential movement. Inspired by the thought of humanistic psychologists such as Carl Rogers and Abraham Maslow, adherents of this movement believed that more open, intimate interpersonal relationships were the key to improved psychological health and human relations throughout society. Influenced by this popular movement, interpersonal communication courses of the time frequently emphasized experiential exercises in group dynamics, interpersonal trust, and intimate self-disclosure. Such courses were controversial, and many interpersonal communication scholars were at pains to distance themselves from the academically disreputable, anti-intellectual, "touchy-feelie" image often associated with their field. An emphasis on rigorous scientific method was one way to improve the field's academic image.

A third explanation for the early emphasis on science arises from the fact that the field of interpersonal communication initially had no established theories or lines of research of its own. Early interpersonal researchers borrowed extensively from other fields, especially from experimental social psychology. Social psychologists for a long time had been studying such topics as persuasion and attitude change, group dynamics, self-disclosure, and interpersonal attraction, which seemed highly relevant to interpersonal communication. Not only were these topics relevant, but experimental psychology was considered a rigorous scientific field and thus a good model for interpersonal scholars to emulate. Behavioral scientists in speech departments had traditionally borrowed theories and methods from psychology, so it seemed quite natural to borrow from social psychology in order to get research under way in the new field of interpersonal communication. Lannamann (1991) has shown that the attractiveness of individualistic psychological approaches may also have deeper ideological roots. In any case, the habit of borrowing has persisted (Berger, 1991) and the mainstream of interpersonal communication research has continued to follow trends in experimental social psychology.

These are among the reasons why interpersonal communication research has been so closely identified with a quantitative, experimental, social psychological approach. From the beginning, interpretive social approaches to interpersonal communication were also available, but they held at best a marginal position in the field. Interpersonal scholars were well aware of the symbolic interactionist tradition in sociology. Erving Goffman's works were widely read (e.g., Goffman, 1959). So was Berger and Luckmann's (1967) *The Social Construction of Reality.* So were the cybernetics-influenced writings of Gregory Bateson and the Palo Alto Group (especially Watzlawick, Beavin, & Jackson, 1967). So were qualitative studies of nonverbal communication (e.g., Birdwhistell, 1970). And so, of course, were writings of the humanistic psychologists mentioned earlier. Such works were often read or discussed in communication theory and interpersonal courses, but they were not often followed as research models because their methods were unfamiliar or deemed insufficiently "scientific." Interpersonal scholars sometimes attempted to develop new lines of research by recasting ideas from these works in the mold of the prevailing methodological norms. For example, research on relational communication (e.g., Millar & Rogers, 1976) emerged in this way as an effort to operationalize concepts derived from the Palo Alto Group. Thus the orthodox approach maintained its central position and kept alternative approaches well to the margins of the field.

On the evidence of the present volume, interpretive social approaches to interpersonal communication are now poised to play a more central role. As Leeds-Hurwitz suggests in the introduction, the proliferating literatures of social constructionism, ethnography, critical theory, cultural studies, ethnomethodology, discourse analysis, and so on, despite important differences among them, also share important themes in common. "Social approaches" (plural) is a useful label for indicating both the convergence as well as the continuing diversity among these newly flourishing ways of studying interpersonal communication.

This book grew out of a two-part forum, "Social Approaches to Interpersonal Communication," published in *Communication Theory* (1992, 2, 131–172 and 329–356), coedited by myself and Wendy Leeds-Hurwitz. Leeds-Hurwitz has now assembled this larger collection of essays by leading scholars in the field. Included are six entirely new chapters along with revised and expanded versions of six of the original forum articles. Not all social approaches are represented here, but the reader will find a high-quality anthology presenting a broad range of views for contemplation. In conclusion, I would like to comment briefly on the conceptual, methodological, and practical implications of social approaches as I see them in contemplating these essays.

Conceptually, social approaches move away from exclusively psychologistic explanations of interpersonal behavior toward a fuller understanding of communication practices in their social and cultural contexts. Interpersonal communication research has tended to be isolated from areas such as cultural studies and mass communication, in part because of the erroneous assumption that interpersonal relationships are private interactions between individuals that can be understood entirely apart from broader sociocultural forms and processes. With the emergence of social approaches, interpersonal research will now be better equipped to understand patterns and address problems of communication in our increasingly complex, multicultural societies, and, in so doing, to join at last—and contribute to the articulation of a distinct communication perspective within—the vital conversation of interdisciplinary social theory.

Social approaches also imply a pluralistic understanding of research methods that flattens the methodological hierarchy of empiricist social science. Qualitative, interpretive, and critical methods are not inferior to quantitative empirical methods. They are not merely prescientific warm-up acts that only hold the stage until the big-name band of "Explanation, Prediction, and Control" is ready to make its entrance. They do not lack rigor; rather, they respond to different standards of rigor—standards such as cultural sensitivity, narrative coherence and fidelity to personal experience, comprehensive accounting for individual cases, critical awareness of ideology, and moral–political responsibility for the reflexive interactions involved with every act of observation, interpretation, or theorization. In my view, these new standards should not be taken to exclude the standards of traditional social science. Reliability, internal and external validity, theoretical scope and precision—the standards of traditional social science—do not cease to have value in their own terms just because other standards are now also recognized. Every methodological approach requires trade-offs that favor some standards over others. Every approach has its limitations. Statistics, experimental design, coding, measurement, and sampling methods continue to be useful for addressing certain questions. The implication of social approaches is not that we should no longer ask those questions but that we should ask them in conjunction with a broader range of questions about interpersonal communication.

Finally, social approaches imply that interpersonal communication research has an active role to play in cultivating better communication practices in society. The responsibility of such a role follows from the *reflexivity* inherent in our research practices. Reflexivity means that research necessarily involves a dialectical interplay between observer and observed, description and phenomenon described, and theory and practice. Interpersonal communication is not a set of objective facts just simply "out there" to be described and explained. Ideas about interpersonal communication disseminated by researchers, teachers, and other intellectuals circulate through society and participate in social processes that continually influence and reshape interpersonal communication practices. Our choice, as interpersonal scholars, is not ultimately *whether* to participate in those processes but rather *how* to participate. We should be asking not just what interpersonal communication *is*, but also what it *should* be. If we're going to help make it, let's at least try to make it better.

ROBERT T. CRAIG
University of Colorado at Boulder

REFERENCES

Berger, C. R. (1991). Communication theories and other curios. *Communication Monographs, 58,* 101–113.

Berger, P. L., & Luckmann, T. (1967). *The social construction of reality.* Garden City, NY: Doubleday.

Birdwhistell, R. L. (1970). *Kinesics and context: Essays on body motion communication.* Philadelphia: University of Pennsylvania Press.

Cohen, H. (1994). *The history of speech communication: The emergence of a discipline, 1914–1945.* Annandale, VA: Speech Communication Association.

Goffman, E. (1959). *The presentation of self in everyday life.* Garden City, NY: Anchor Books.

Lannamann, J. W. (1991). Interpersonal communication research as ideological practice. *Communication Theory, 1,* 179–203.

Millar, F. E., & Rogers, L. E. (1976). A relational approach to interpersonal communication. In G. R. Miller (Ed.), *Explorations in interpersonal communication* (pp. 87–103). Beverly Hills, CA: Sage.

Watzlawick, P., Beavin, J. H., & Jackson, D. D. (1967). *Pragmatics of human communication: A study of interactional patterns, pathologies, and paradoxes.* New York: W. W. Norton.

Contents

Part IV: Applications

Part V: Conclusion

Part I

Introduction

CHAPTER 1

Introducing Social Approaches

WENDY LEEDS-HURWITZ

Current thinking in the field of communication takes for granted that there are two main ways to approach the study of interpersonal communication, what are sometimes called the objectivist and the interpretivist positions (i.e., Montgomery & Duck, 1992). Yet no single book currently summarizes the theoretical assumptions of the interpretivist position. It is long past time to compile such a work. Surely this will be neither the only nor the last book on this topic, but it is hoped that it will make a significant contribution to the discussion.[1]

"Interpretivist" is a fuzzy word, and it is not always clear where the boundaries between this and other theoretical approaches should be drawn. Additional terms used to describe innovative approaches abound, including cultural studies, critical theory, structuralism, poststructuralism, postmodernism, symbolic interactionism, dialogism, semiotics, feminism, naturalistic inquiry, ethnography of communication, systems theory, rules theory, conversation analysis, discourse analysis, ethnomethodology, pragmatics, social constructivism or constructionism, coordinated management of meaning, critical sociology, social communication, and social interaction. Obviously these are not synonyms, and those who identify themselves with one or another of these approaches, schools, or methods do not necessarily read, pay attention to, or appreciate all the others' work.

Rather than offering a detailed historical consideration of the development and boundaries of each of these approaches, it will be more useful to indicate ways in which at least some of their assumptions or implications overlap, because their similarities are not widely acknowledged. The efforts to develop a new approach to the study of human communication behavior have tended to have at least a few common threads, though these generally go unnoticed in the frequent territorial battles over what form future research will take.

The fact that the majority of the approaches named originated outside the field of communication, or that they concern broader issues of social theory, does not excuse communication researchers from attending to them. Stuart Hall (1989) provides explicit rationale for the need to acknowledge social theory in general when he argues that work by communication scholars is "inextricably bound up with" (p. 43) more general social theories. Graham Murdock (1989) puts the matter even more forcefully: "Above all, we need to reconnect the study of communications with the cutting edge of contemporary social theory. This is not an option. It is an imperative" (p. 246).

I propose it is time we accept this imperative, applying it specifically to the study of interpersonal communication. The choice of emphasis on interpersonal interaction is simple: face-to-face communication is the beginning point and the exemplar, for it is the most obvious, the most central case of what constitutes communication.[2] Interactional sequences are at the heart of what we study. Before people invented either formal organizations or mass media, there was social interaction.[3]

SOCIAL APPROACHES AND THE FIELD OF COMMUNICATION

Interpretive or social approaches have been most successful to date in studies of organizational and mass communication. In organizational communication, the energizing work was *Communication and Organizations: An Interpretive Approach* by Linda Putnam and Michael Pacanowsky (1983). Introducing the interpretive perspective as an alternative to functionalism, Putnam (1983) defined interpretation as centering on the study of meanings, "the way individuals make sense of their world through their communicative behaviors" (p. 31). Today a major research topic of choice is "organizational culture" (Pilotta, Widman, & Jasko, 1988; O'Donnell-Trujillo & Pacanowsky, 1983), currently foregrounded in studies of organizational symbols (Carbaugh, 1986) and ideology (Mumby, 1988). In mass communication, the significant work was "A Cultural Approach to Communication" by James W. Carey (1975a, newly revised in Carey, 1989).[4] Carey (1989) deliberately borrowed the phrase "cultural studies" from the Centre for Contemporary Cultural Studies in Birmingham, England, describing the task not as seeking to discover laws but rather to understand human behavior, to diagnose human meanings (Hall, 1980).[5] In the case of both organizational and mass communication, the ultimate goals and assumptions are similar to those proposed here for interpersonal communication; only the settings in which people interact significantly differ.

Social approaches have influenced the larger body of communication theory (as reflected in Dervin, Grossberg, O'Keefe, & Wartella, 1989a, 1989b) yet have repeatedly touched interpersonal communication only at the periphery, never becoming mainstream.[6] This book, as well as the two *Communication Theory* forums that preceded it, is deliberately designed to change that. My point is not to raise social approaches above all other alternatives but rather to bring them more clearly into the realm of the accepted and possible. They should certainly be among the group of approaches deemed appropriate. One implication of the ongoing "ferment in the field" is that we must continuously reevaluate and reformulate our questions.[7] The questions that drive our research should precede our methodology. Yet, in communication as in many other fields, the opposite too frequently has been the case. As Fisher (1978) pointed out, when choosing between theoretical perspectives, "You cannot make the choice on the basis that one perspective is inherently superior but rather on whether it asks the questions you wish to ask" (p. 324).

In keeping with this spirit of openness and reevaluation, this book is about "social approach*es*" in the plural, indicating that even the few researchers grouped together here do not always agree and may not rest comfortably under a single label. As Rabinow (1988) pointed out in reference to anthropology, "Scientific debate does not imply agreement; it does imply civility, acceptance of difference, imagination, and risk taking" (p. 430). I did not require of contributors that they agree either with me or with each other. Rather, these are all people with whom I have had interesting discussions of theoretical issues. Plurality of viewpoints is seen, I think by all of us, as a positive, rather than a negative, characteristic. Indeed, I would argue that there is something inherently contradictory in a theoretical approach stressing polysemy and multiple interpretations which remains unable or unwilling to recognize the validity of alternative approaches.[8]

DEFINING SOCIAL APPROACHES

Approaches grouped together here under the umbrella term "social" have, in the recent past, been set in opposition to a "psychological" approach (Sigman, 1987; Zabor, 1978); described as an "organic" versus a "mechanistic" approach (Thomas, 1980); "ritual" as opposed to "transmission" (Carey, 1975b); "interpretive" as opposed to "scientific" (Delia & Grossberg, 1977). Pearce has often used the term "new paradigm" research (Pearce & Foss, 1987), contrasting the new with the old. Gergen (1993) has divided all the alternative intellectual movements into three strands: the ideological critique, the literary critique, and the social critique (obviously the latter is the most comparable to the research described here).

As has often been pointed out, names are less important than central themes. In keeping with this sentiment, the very real differences among the various approaches that might appropriately be termed "social" are not of concern here. That is not to say they do not exist, only that my preferred goal is to establish areas of overlap. Rather than emphasize a dichotomy between social approaches (as good, avant garde) and other possible approaches (as bad, outdated), this book will begin the more positive task of defining what social approaches attempt to accomplish. This introduction will outline a set of themes that seem to be taken for granted by the majority of those whose work fits under the social approaches heading, as a first step in recognizing the ways in which a wide variety of research can be seen as contributing to the same endeavor.

At the very least, these approaches I have labeled "social" share a willingness to question the assumption that researchers can ever be permitted to resume "business as usual," questioning whether the traditional theoretical assumptions and research methods followed in the field are still valid and appropriate. Beyond this starting point, there is wide acceptance of the major concepts outlined below. My intent here is to open up a discussion rather than close it down, so these are brief indications of the direction of thought, rather than hard and fast definitions.

1. Social approaches are first and foremost *social*. That is, they describe events occurring between people in the process of interacting rather than reporting how events are perceived through a single person's understanding. Communication is, in this view, "an inherently collaborative and cooperative activity" (Kellerman, 1992, p. 288). Thus there is generally an emphasis on visible behavior over cognition, on groups small or large, but rarely on individuals. Individuals can, of course, choose to follow, change, violate, or negotiate the expected structures and rules of interaction, but a social approach is likely to focus less on *why* they do this (which would be a cognitive question) than on *how* they do it (an interactional question). By "social" I intend to refer primarily to the emphasis on a larger sociocultural context for an understanding of communication behavior. There is no intent to refer specifically to the discipline of sociology, which may or may not be relevant to social approaches to communication.

2. Social approaches tend to accept a particular sort of definition of *communication*. This is variously stated, but in general it assumes a focus on process as well as final product. Carey's (1975a) definition of communication as "a symbolic process whereby reality is produced, maintained, repaired, and transformed" (p. 17) is more appropriate than most, though I hesitate to recommend any as the ultimate one, for each author must retain the right to begin with his or her own revision.[9]

This new definition of communication is likely to include an assumption that not all communication is intentional, and a consequent incorporation of nonverbal behavior with verbal for a more adequate understanding of what constitutes communicative behavior. As Kendon (1972) has pointed out, "It makes no sense to speak of 'verbal communication' and 'nonverbal communication.' There is only communication" (p. 443).

3. Though not always explicitly stated, some version of the *social construction of reality* (Berger & Luckmann, 1967; Gergen, 1985) is generally common to social approaches. In this view, social reality is not a fact or set of facts existing prior to human activity; it is created through human interaction. We create our social world through our words and other symbols and through our behaviors; thus these become research topics. As with all theoretical statements, there are important implications for research. Most basically, a social constructionist view of the world implies that we question the validity of traditional "scientific" experiments. As Anderson (1990) tells us: "For the interpretive social scientist (who is necessarily a constructionist), the business of inquiry is not to reveal the world to us but to create some part of the world for us. Inquiry is the professional practice of the social creation of reality" (p. 14).

The implication of social constructionism for the study of interaction is to put forth a view of interaction as a social accomplishment, a human creation, and, thus, emphasize the element of creativity in interaction, the interplay between new and old, the ways in which innovation mixes with tradition. Researchers look to determine how people manage their interactions, how they invent and display their various social identities and roles, and how they respond to the inventions and displays of others.

4. Social approaches often take as their central problematic the issue of *how social meanings* are created—how social actors construct meaning from incomplete bits and pieces of behavior.[10] Social approaches often focus on the connection between structure and action—or product and process, or theory and praxis, or tradition and change—on the ways people manage to do enough of what is expected that they will be understood while maintaining the flexibility to behave in some original and unique ways. The assumption here is that any adequate description of interaction "must take into account both the structure, that is, the social forms for that interaction, and the individual operating within that

structure" (Duncan & Fiske, 1977, pp. 10–11; see also Leeds-Hurwitz & Sigman with Sullivan, 1995). The focus is on people as rule makers, as creative individuals operating within social contexts, not on people as rule followers, who discover preexisting regulations (Shotter, 1980). Social approaches view people as active rather than passive agents.

5. Social approaches often emphasize the study of *identity*, treating identity as a social construction, with the self understood "not [as] an entity half-concealed behind events, but a changeable formula for managing oneself during them" (Goffman, 1974, p. 573; see also Fisher, 1983, pp. 126–127; Shotter & Gergen, 1989). Here the early psychological view of the self is understood to be outdated, replaced by a more appropriate cultural, socially constructed view of the self. In this view, identity is a subtle thing, which can be highlighted, deemphasized, or changed through specific use of language and behavior at particular moments in social interaction. The related concepts of *social role* and *cultural identity* are parallel topics of study. A focus on identity can lead to studies of *power*, investigations of what happens when particular identities are chosen or ascribed by others, and discussions of which identities are viewed more or less positively within particular groups.

6. Social approaches frequently make good use of the concept of *culture* (defined as all the knowledge members do not have in their heads at birth, but which must be learned in order to become appropriate members of a given society).[11] Culture is the widest context within which communication behavior occurs and can be understood to make sense. In organization and mass communication, a new understanding of the relevance of cultural frameworks already has been widely accepted. In keeping with this, Davis (1990) suggests "it now appears obvious that the recent era of communication research will be characterized by the emergence of a cultural analysis paradigm" (p. 546). Yet interpersonal communication has to date been remarkably untouched and so remains to be significantly influenced by an understanding of culture and the impact cultural differences can make on behavior. Recently several interpersonal communication books have utilized various approaches fitting readily under a "social" umbrella which make better use of the concept of culture (including Deetz & Stevenson, 1986; Haslett, 1987; Leeds-Hurwitz, 1989; Pearce, 1994; Pearce & Cronen, 1980; Sigman, 1987).[12] Recent research on discourse or conversation analysis and language is also relevant (Craig & Tracy, 1983; Pomerantz, 1989; Tracy, 1991), especially in the British transformations (Atkinson & Heritage, 1984).

It is particularly surprising to see the lack of change in interpersonal communication research, which most specifically studies interaction, when it is precisely interaction that serves as the new focus of interest in mass and organizational communication. Authors such as Erving Goffman (1983) and Clifford Geertz (1973, 1983) should have first and foremost something to say to interpersonal communication researchers, yet they are cited more often in articles written from other perspectives.[13] According to at least one recent description:

> Interpersonal communication is the foundation on which interpersonal and organizational structures are produced, maintained, and modified. It is through interpersonal communication that we construct various forms of social relationships, definitions of reality, and programs of action. (Burke & Miller, 1988, p. 21)

If this definition were broadly accepted by the field, the need for social approaches would be self-evident.

7. Acknowledgement of the centrality of the concept of culture assumes that no interaction takes place outside a particular cultural *context* (Duranti & Goodwin, 1992; Nofsinger, 1989). One part of cultural context is the *community* within which particular communicative behaviors occur, so there is often an increasing awareness of the need to base descriptions of behavior on the particular community within which these have a home, thus expanding from culture, which is quite large, to subcultures (or, to use the more recent term, "co-cultures"), which are generally smaller. As a result, interest in ethnicity, social class, and gender is increasing and will likely continue to increase, as these are all reasonable cultural divisions useful in researching communication.

8. Accepting the significance of context leads directly to understanding the need for *direct observation* of actual behavior. Acknowledging the influence of context on behavior has implications for choice of method. A more careful match of methodology to theory than has always been the case in the past is required. Any method that removes communication from its natural context becomes suspect.

Understanding the value of direct observation does not entirely preclude the use of techniques such as extended interviews because there is still information to be gained through their use. However, it does make a few traditionally accepted methods, such as questionnaires, highly unlikely choices. Some version of the ethnography of communication, despite its origins as an attempt to bridge the gap between linguistics and anthropology, has often been the tool used by communication scholars to meet this need. While far from the only possible social approach, it is a particularly useful one and thus has recently established a second home within communication.[14]

9. Social approaches frequently make use of the concept of *symbol* as a basic building block in the study of interaction, assuming that

"symbolization constitutes objects not constituted before, objects which would not exist except for the context of social relationships wherein symbolization occurs" (Mead, 1934, p. 78). Research focusing on exactly how we socially construct the world often entails the study of symbols because they play such an important role. In his attempt to isolate the one emphasis shared by all subfields, Gary Cronkhite (1986) proposed a new definition of communication as "the study of human symbolic activity" (p. 245), thus pointing to the centrality of symbols. The new focus on symbols may well involve a reconsideration of semiotic theory, examining what it has to offer the field of communication (Hodge & Kress, 1988; Leeds-Hurwitz, 1993, in press), since semiotics is traditionally the discipline devoted to the study of symbols and other signs.[15]

10. Equally significant to social approaches is accepting the need for *reflexivity* (Babcock, 1980; Cronen, Johnson, & Lannamann, 1982; Ruby, 1982; Steier, 1991). Reflexivity involves questioning the methodology used (and often results in a more careful choice of methodology to match theoretical questions posed); it involves questioning the validity of the results obtained as well as questioning what is done with those results. It also requires some attention to questions of genre (How will the results be presented? What form is most appropriate?), for research report writing is itself a genre of discourse with rules and conventions we can study. Reflexivity implies accepting a multiplicity of meanings in events, and of participants' viewpoints, acknowledging that any study is but a partial accounting, heavily dependent on the particular researcher's training, questions, and assumptions. Reflexivity requires understanding research as a process involving the researcher as much as the "subjects," questioning the researcher's results no less than the subjects' responses.[16] It accepts research as a complex process, with understanding emerging throughout rather than imposed once, securely, at the onset. It can lead to disturbing texts with multiple voices and discovery of the frequently hidden "I," the self of the researcher, no longer absent from the final reporting of results. In short, reflexivity implies the placement of inquiry into a particular social context (one that includes rather than excludes the researcher and the research report), rather than assuming our inquiry (alone) stands outside context (McNamee, 1988). Those who accept a reflexive approach feel it does no more than what is necessary.

11. In keeping with their reflexive stance, social approaches are most frequently *holistic*: The study of interaction requires an adequate picture of the whole event—understanding how multiple pieces are related and incorporating the researcher as one of the pieces. Tambiah (1985) pointed out that the tendency to divide fields of study into increasingly

smaller portions has led to gaps in our overall knowledge of human action, and he calls for greater synthesis. Social approaches often attempt great scope, incorporating a larger body of potentially relevant information in their analyses, on the grounds that this wider context is critical to an adequate understanding of the behavior being studied.

Together these 11 themes underlie much recent research, but they are not generally pointed out as the center of attention themselves. My goal here is to bring them forward, making them available for further discussion. None of the approaches mentioned at the beginning of this chapter has identified itself with all these themes, and no one theme runs through every single approach. But, as a group, adherents of most social approaches accept most of these themes. Thus I would argue that it is appropriate to bring them together into a single package for joint examination.

ORGANIZATION OF THIS VOLUME

Each of the authors brought together in this volume has been chosen because of a commitment to social approaches, though they may not always define their work in that way. The various chapters do not divide up the pie, with each author discussing one section of it (e.g., each describing or following what could be considered one social approach, or each discussing one theme of those outlined here), but rather they consider overlapping topics. This is not quite so neat and tidy, but it is far more realistic. Taken together, these chapters give the reader a variety of "takes" on the issues that social approaches address and their implications for conducting communication research. My idea is to unite those currently utilizing a variety of social approaches in their investigation of interpersonal communication (making a clear statement that these authors have something to say to one another), as well as to identify available options for those still considering, or reconsidering, their assumptions (opening the topic to others).

Although there is considerable overlap of interests and concerns, as would be expected, each chapter takes a quite distinct focus, responding to and extending different parts of the agenda as it has been laid out in this introduction. Aside from this introduction (serving as Part I), the book is divided into four main parts. Part II, "Philosophical Roots," contains a single chapter. In "Philosophical Features of Social Approaches to Interpersonal Communication," John Stewart grounds the remaining studies historically and conceptually, pointing out the ways in which they are not, after all, entirely new but based on a particular philosophical view of the relationship between person and world and of the adequacy of representational accounts of knowledge, language, and understanding.

Part III, "Basic Issues," includes four chapters. The first, "Quantitative versus Qualitative?," by Janet Beavin Bavelas, begins with a central issue, questioning the bases for the often assumed dichotomy of quantitative versus qualitative research. (For the uninitiated, social approaches are often casually equated with qualitative research.) She examines a series of what are generally assumed to be obvious dichotomies, concluding that all of the dichotomies are false because they inappropriately simplify the complex process of research.

Frederick Steier, in "Reflexivity, Interpersonal Communication, and Interpersonal Communication Research," presents one of the central issues for all social approaches, reflexivity. He is specifically concerned with adapting discussion of reflexivity to interpersonal communication research, explaining the implications if researchers begin to take it seriously.

"A Sailing Guide for Social Constructionists," by W. Barnett Pearce, provides a detailed examination of another central issue, social constructionism. Using the metaphor of a constellation, he supplies an overview of the various forms of social constructionism that have been proposed. His chapter will be particularly valuable for those who have never quite sorted out such details as the specific distinctions between constructionism and constructivism.

In "The Politics of Voice in Interpersonal Communication Research," John W. Lannamann examines the reasons why interpersonal communication research has traditionally emphasized the study of the individual, looking both at linguistic constraints and at the larger socio-historical context of communication research. He concludes with suggestions for more socially oriented research.

Part IV, "Applications," begins the task of applying the theoretical statements of Parts I and II to particular research contexts. Victoria Chen and W. Barnett Pearce begin this discussion in "Even if a Thing of Beauty, Can a Case Study Be a Joy Forever? A Social Constructionist Approach to Theory and Research." They specifically ask that we reconsider how to evaluate case studies as a form of research, suggesting that case studies are particularly useful and necessary following the assumptions of social approaches, but they must be evaluated according to a different set of criteria.

Jane Jorgenson, in "Re-relationalizing Rapport in Interpersonal Settings," looks to the implications of the co-construction of the research interview, deconstructing in particular the concept of rapport. She moves beyond simply stating that we must consider reflexivity, demonstrating how to take a more reflexive stance toward research, applying the general comments about reflexivity provided above. Her argument is that rapport must be understood as a joint production of interviewer and respondent. Viewing communication in context has implications for our understanding of research interviews, and she explores these implications.

"A Role for Communication Theory in Ethnographic Studies of Interpersonal Communication," by Donal Carbaugh and Sally O. Hastings, expands on the ways in which theorizing is central to our understanding of communication. Assuming ethnography to be an appropriate perspective for the investigation of cultural behavior, the authors pose a new question: Where lies the communication theory of that method?

Stuart J. Sigman, in "Order and Continuity in Human Relationships: A Social Communication Approach to Defining 'Relationship,' " argues that society and culture transcend any one moment of interaction, and that communication scholars must therefore consider the larger, ongoing sociocultural system of which face-to-face interactions are only subsidiary partials.

"Telling and Living: Narrative Co-construction and the Practices of Interpersonal Relationships," by Arthur P. Bochner and Carolyn Ellis, is the most specific extension of a social theoretical approach to a particular research example. Their work demonstrates the range of innovative texts of modern ethnography, inviting the reader to rethink old assumptions about genre conventions while simultaneously analyzing new data. There is a current move to grant greater consideration to the study of personal narratives (Langellier, 1989, provides some history of this); Bochner and Ellis move beyond a discussion of history and into the future, using personal narratives as a vehicle to combine theory and research in new ways.

Part V, "Conclusion," has again only a single chapter. In "Practical Theory and the Tasks Ahead for Social Approaches to Communication," Vernon E. Cronen provides readers with a synthesis of what has been presented throughout the chapters, directing attention to a few topics that seem as yet unfinished. After providing a clear sense of where the discussion so far has taken us, he moves on to a consideration of what needs to happen next, introducing the concept of practical theory.

CONCLUSION

The authors included in this book do not always make their assumptions explicit and do not attempt to describe the ideas they hold in common. This has been my task here. These contributions overlap in their concern for the social construction of self, other, and event; in their assumption that reflexivity requires acknowledging the involvement of the researcher in establishing not only the research questions but the research context; in their acceptance of a sociocultural grounding for the study of interaction; in their focus on instances of contact between individuals, the actual social transactions in which people engage; and in their concern that we seriously question the ways in which we have constructed our theories and research in the recent past. Together they demonstrate the ability to synthesize prior approaches and to disregard labels in pursuit of a common goal, the construction of a more adequate understanding of human interaction. The chapters in this book provide evidence that, although we must more often question our own assumptions, incorporating our questions into our research reports, we do at least have some good questions with which to begin and some good ideas about how to investigate these questions most productively.

NOTES

1. This topic was the subject of two forums published in *Communication Theory* in 1992, both presented under the title "Social Approaches to Interpersonal Communication." My thanks to Robert T. Craig, who was editor at the time, for opening that journal to the issues raised in the forums. Those prior publications laid the basic groundwork for this volume, with the addition of several authors who have been asked to continue the discussion and illuminate the topic further.

2. Burleson (1992) provides one recent discussion of this point.

3. A different, but complementary, effort would be simply to sidestep interpersonal communication, establishing a new name for a related, socially based study of human interaction. This is in fact now taking place, as the creation of the "Language and Social Interaction" (LSI) divisions within the Speech Communication Association (SCA) and the International Communication Association (ICA) attests (see Glenn, 1994, for specific discussion of the connections between the two areas). I have no problem with establishing separate spheres of influence and have participated actively in both LSI divisions. However, it is equally important to examine areas of overlap between the traditional field of interpersonal communication and the new field of social interaction.

4. A later book, less influential to date but potentially quite important, is Jensen and Jankowski (1991). In the introduction, Jensen (1991) argues that approaches they label qualitative "examine meaning production as a *process* which is contextualized and inextricably integrated with wider social and cultural practices" (p. 4), a position close to that taken here.

5. As Rogers (1989) suggests, interpersonal and mass communication are currently essentially intellectually separated, in addition to the separation evident in most academic departments. One implication of this discussion is that they need not remain so.

6. Earlier efforts to bring about this same change can be also documented (such as Benson & Pearce, 1977; Bochner & Krueger, 1979; Fisher, 1981; Pearce & Foss, 1987; Simons, 1978).

7. Obviously the implied reference here is to the 1983 special issue of the *Journal of Communication*, explicitly called "Ferment in the Field," but there have been later considerations as well, including a 1993 issue of the same journal devoted to a 10-year reevaluation of the same topic.

8. Grossberg (1989) put this nicely in his description of cultural studies, but it applies to most other approaches as well:

> Cultural studies is constantly renegotiating its identity and repositioning itself within changing intellectual and political maps. Its identity—as well as the significance of any position or concept within cultural studies—can only be defined by an always incomplete history of political engagements and theoretical debates in response to which alternative positions are constantly being taken into account and new positions offered. (p. 416)

Gusfield (1989) expands on this point of view, saying, "The dialogue of all voices is itself the answer and not a road to a consensus of voices around a unified conclusion" (p. 27). All this implies that theory is best seen as "a temporary construct" (Bourdieu, 1985, p. 11).

9. It is interesting to compare this definition with that for interpersonal communication by Burke and Miller (1988) presented earlier. The overlap is obvious and, I would argue, appropriate.

10. Rommetveit (1980) has some useful discussion here.

11. See Leeds-Hurwitz (1989, pp. 62–65) for elaboration of the connections between the definitions of culture and communication.

12. One of the best, *La Nouvelle Communication* [*The New Communication*] (Winkin, 1981), synthesized the basics of this approach for a French audience long before it had been done for (and by) Americans.

13. See Davis (1990) for discussion of Goffman; see Carey (1989) for the preeminent exemplar of Geertz used to good effect within mass communication.

14. The classic introductions to the field are Gumperz and Hymes (1972) and Saville-Troike (1982). See the articles in Winkin and Sigman (1984) and the new introduction by Philipsen (1992) for an introduction to the ethnography of communication particularly emphasizing the connections with the field of communication. Originally, there were two research centers where one could learn about the ethnography of communication, both within linguistic anthropology: the University of Pennsylvania (with Dell Hymes) and the University of California–Berkeley (with John Gumperz). Today, within communication, there is a new center at the University of Washington, where Gerry Philipsen has trained a large cadre of students, now publishing books using the ethnography of communication as their primary framework (Carbaugh, 1988; Katriel, 1986, 1991). Murray (1994) documents the development of the ethnography of communication, focusing particularly on the people involved.

15. See, however, Stewart's books (1995, in press) which reconsider the value of symbols and semiotic theory.
16. Tambiah (1985) puts this well:

> In the human sciences, the pretense that the observer is divorced from the thing observed does not accord with the fact that human consciousness and social representations are their ultimate subject matter, and the realities they deal with are the products of intersubjective interactions and conventions created in an open-ended historical process. (pp. 352–353)

REFERENCES

Anderson, J. A. (1990). Preface. In J. A. Anderson (Ed.), *Communication yearbook* (Vol. 13, pp. 11–15). Newbury Park, CA: Sage.

Atkinson, J. M., & Heritage, J. C. (1984). (Eds.). *Structures of social action: Studies in conversation analysis*. Cambridge: Cambridge University Press.

Babcock, B. (1980). Reflexivity: Definitions and discriminations. *Semiotica*, *30*(1–2), 1–14.

Benson, T. W., & Pearce, W. B. (Eds.). (1977). Alternative theoretical bases for the study of human communication: A symposium. *Communication Quarterly*, *25*(1), 1–73.

Berger, P. L., & Luckmann, T. (1967). *The social construction of reality*. Garden City, NY: Doubleday/Anchor.

Bochner, A. P., & Krueger, D. L. (1979). Interpersonal communication theory and research: An overview of inscrutable epistemologies and muddled concepts. In D. Nimmo (Ed.), *Communication yearbook* (Vol. 3, pp. 197–211). New Brunswick, NJ: Transaction Books.

Bourdieu, P. (1985). The genesis of the concepts of *habitus* and of *field*. *Sociocriticism*, *2*, 11–24.

Burke, J., & Miller, D. (1988). Part I: Interpersonal communication. In D. R. Maines & C. J. Couch (Eds.), *Communication and social structure* (pp. 21–22). Springfield, IL: Charles C. Thomas.

Burleson, B. R. (1992). Taking communication seriously. *Communication Monographs*, *59*, 79–86.

Carbaugh, D. (1986). Some thoughts on organizing as cultural communication. In L. Thayer (Ed.), *Organization–communication: Emerging perspectives I* (pp. 85–101). Norwood, NJ: Ablex.

Carbaugh, D. (1988). *Talking American: Cultural discourses on Donahue*. Norwood, NJ: Ablex.

Carey, J. W. (1975a). A cultural approach to communication. *Communication*, *2*, 1–22.

Carey, J. W. (1975b). Communication and culture. *Communication Research*, *2*, 173–191.

Carey, J. W. (1989). *Culture as communication: Essays on media and society*. Boston: Unwin Hyman.

Craig, R. T., & Tracy, K. (Eds.). (1983). *Conversational coherence: Form, structure, and strategy*. Beverly Hills, CA: Sage.

Cronen, V., Johnson, K. M., & Lannamann, J. (1982). Paradoxes, double binds, and reflexive loops: An alternative theoretical perspective. *Family Process, 21*, 91–112.

Cronkhite, G. (1986). On the focus, scope, and coherence of the study of human symbolic activity. *Quarterly Journal of Speech, 72*, 231–246.

Davis, D. K. (1990). Finding new models for mass communication research: Notes on surviving ferment in the field. *Communication Yearbook, 13*, 545–553.

Deetz, S., & Stevenson, S. L. (1986). *Managing interpersonal communication*. New York: Harper & Row.

Delia, J. G., & Grossberg, L. (1977). Interpretation and evidence. *Western Journal of Speech Communication, 41*, 32–42.

Dervin, B., Grossberg, L., O'Keefe, B. J., & Wartella, E. (Eds.). (1989a). *Rethinking communication: Vol. 1. Paradigm issues*. Newbury Park, CA: Sage.

Dervin, B., Grossberg, L., O'Keefe, B. J., & Wartella, E. (Eds.). (1989b). *Rethinking communication: Vol. 2. Paradigm exemplars*. Newbury Park, CA: Sage.

Duncan, S., & Fiske, D. W. (1977). *Face-to-face interaction: Research, methods, and theory*. Hillsdale, NJ: Erlbaum.

Duranti, A., & Goodwin, C. (Eds.). (1992). *Rethinking context: Language as an interactive phenomenon*. Cambridge: Cambridge University Press.

Fisher, B. A. (1978). *Perspectives on human communication*. New York: Macmillan.

Fisher, B. A. (1981). Implications of the "interactional view" for communication theory. In C. Wilder-Mott & J. H. Weakland (Eds.), *Rigor and imagination* (pp. 195–209). New York: Praeger.

Fisher, B. A. (1983). Introduction. In M. S. Mander (Ed.), *Communications in transition: Issues and debates in current research* (pp. 123–131). New York: Praeger.

Geertz, C. (1973). *The interpretation of cultures*. New York: Basic Books.

Geertz, C. (1983). *Local knowledge*. New York: Basic Books.

Gergen, K. J. (1985). Social constructionist inquiry: Context and implications. In K. J. Gergen & K. E. Davis (Eds.), *The social construction of the person* (pp. 30–180). New York: Springer-Verlag.

Gergen, K. J. (1993, February 10). *Science as social construction: Problems and prospects*. Lecture presented at Loyola University, Chicago, IL.

Glenn, P. (1994). LSI and IPC: Some political considerations. *LSI Notes, 7*(1), 1–2.

Goffman, E. (1974). *Frame analysis*. New York: Harper.

Goffman, E. (1983). The interaction order. *American Sociological Review, 48*, 1–17.

Grossberg, L. (1989). The circulation of cultural studies. *Critical Studies in Mass Communication, 6*, 413–421.

Gumperz, J. J., & Hymes, D. (Eds.). (1972). *Directions in sociolinguistics: The ethnography of communication*. New York: Holt, Rinehart & Winston.

Gusfield, J. R. (1989). Introduction. In K. Burke, *On symbols and society* (pp. 1–49). Chicago: University of Chicago Press.

Hall, S. (1980). Cultural studies and the Centre: Some problematics and problems. In Centre for Contemporary Cultural Studies, *Culture, media, language* (pp. 15–47). London: Hutchinson.

Hall, S. (1989). Ideology and communication theory. In B. Dervin, L. Grossberg, B. J. O'Keefe, & E. Wartella (Eds.), *Rethinking communication: Vol. 1. Paradigm issues* (pp. 40–52). Newbury Park, CA: Sage.

Haslett, B. (1987). *Communication: Strategic action in context.* Hillsdale, NJ: Erlbaum.

Hodge, R., & Kress, G. (1988). *Social semiotics.* Ithaca, NY: Cornell University Press.

Jensen, K. B. (1991). Introduction: The qualitative turn. In K. B. Jensen & N. W. Jankowski (Eds.), *A handbook of qualitative methodologies for mass communication research* (pp. 1–11). London: Routledge.

Jensen, K. B., & Jankowski, N. W. (Eds.). (1991). *A handbook of qualitative methodologies for mass communication research.* London: Routledge.

Katriel, T. (1986). *Talking straight: Dugri speech in Israeli sabra culture.* Cambridge: Cambridge University Press.

Katriel, T. (1991). *Communal webs: Communication and culture in contemporary Israel.* Albany: State University of New York Press.

Kellerman, K. (1992). Communication: Inherently strategic and primarily automatic. *Communication Monographs, 59,* 288–300.

Kendon, A. (1972). Review of *Kinesics and context* by Ray Birdwhistell. *American Journal of Psychology, 85,* 441–455.

Langellier, K. M. (1989). Personal narratives: Perspectives on theory and research. *Text and Performance Quarterly, 9,* 243–276.

Leeds-Hurwitz, W. (1989). *Communication in everyday life: A social interpretation.* Norwood, NJ: Ablex.

Leeds-Hurwitz, W. (1993). *Semiotics and communication: Signs, codes, cultures.* Hillsdale, NJ: Erlbaum.

Leeds-Hurwitz, W., & Sigman, S. J., with Sullivan, S. J. (1995). Social communication theory: Communication structures and performed invocations, A revision of Scheflen's notion of programs. In S. J. Sigman (Ed.), *The consequentiality of communication* (pp. 163–204). Hillsdale, NJ: Erlbaum.

Leeds-Hurwitz, W. (in press). A social account of symbols. In J. Stewart (Ed.), *Beyond the symbol model: reflections on the representational nature of language.* Albany: State University of New York Press.

McNamee, S. (1988). Accepting research as social intervention: Implications of a systemic epistemology. *Communication Quarterly, 36,* 50–68.

Mead, G. H. (1934). *Mind, self and society.* Chicago: University of Chicago Press.

Montgomery, B. M., & Duck, S. (Eds.). (1991). *Studying interpersonal interaction.* New York: Guilford Press.

Mumby, D. (1988). *Communication and power in organizations: Discourse, ideology, and domination.* Norwood, NJ: Ablex.

Murdock, G. (1989). Critical inquiry and audience activity. In B. Dervin, L. Grossberg, B. J. O'Keefe, & E. Wartella (Eds.), *Rethinking communication: Vol. 2. Paradigm exemplars* (pp. 226–249). Newbury Park, CA: Sage.

Murray, S. O. (1994). *Theory groups and the study of language in North America: A social history.* Amsterdam: John Benjamins.

Nofsinger, R. E. (1989). Collaborating on context: Invoking alluded-to shared knowledge. *Western Journal of Speech Communication, 53,* 227–241.

O'Donnell-Trujillo, N., & Pacanowsky, M. E. (1983). The interpretation of organizational cultures. In M. S. Mander (Ed.), *Communications in transition: Issues and debates in current research* (pp. 225–241). New York: Praeger.

Pearce, W. B. (1994). *Interpersonal communication: Making social worlds.* New York: HarperCollins.

Pearce, W. B., & Cronen, V. E. (1980). *Communication, action, and meaning: The creation of social realities.* New York: Praeger.

Pearce, W. B., & Foss, K. A. (1987). The future of interpersonal communication. *ACA Bulletin, 61,* 93–105.

Philipsen, G. (1992). *Speaking culturally: Explorations in social communication.* Albany: State University of New York Press.

Pilotta, J. J., Widman, T., & Jasko, S. A. (1988). Meaning and action in the organizational setting: An interpretive approach. *Communication Yearbook, 11,* 310–334.

Pomerantz, A. M. (1989). Epilogue. *Western Journal of Speech Communication, 53,* 242–246.

Putnam, L. L. (1983). The interpretive perspective: An alternative to functionalism. In L. L. Putnam & M. E. Pacanowsky (Eds.), *Communication and organizations: An interpretive approach* (pp. 31–54). Beverly Hills, CA: Sage.

Putnam, L. L., & Pacanowsky, M. E. (Eds.). (1983). *Communication and organization: An interpretive approach.* Beverly Hills, CA: Sage.

Rabinow, P. (1988). Comment on P. Steven Sangren, "Rhetoric and the authority of ethnography: 'Postmodernism' and the social reproduction of texts." *Current Anthropology, 29,* 429–430.

Rogers, L. E. (1989). Relational communication processes and patterns. In B. Dervin, L. Grossberg, B. J. O'Keefe, & E. Wartella (Eds.), *Rethinking communication: Vol. 2. Paradigm exemplars* (pp. 280–290). Newbury Park, CA: Sage.

Rommetveit, R. (1980). On "meanings" of acts and what is meant and made known by what is said in a pluralistic social world. In M. Brenner (Ed.), *The structure of action* (pp. 108–149). Oxford: Basil Blackwell.

Ruby, J. (Ed.). (1982). *A crack in the mirror: Reflexive perspectives in anthropology.* Philadelphia: University of Pennsylvania Press.

Saville-Troike, M. (1982). *The ethnography of communication: An introduction.* Baltimore: University Park Press.

Shotter, J. (1980). Action, joint action and intentionality. In M. Brenner (Ed.), *The structure of action* (pp. 28–65). Oxford: Basil Blackwell.

Shotter, J., & Gergen, K. J. (Eds.). (1989). *Texts of identity.* London: Sage.

Sigman, S. J. (1987). *A perspective on social communication.* Lexington, MA: Lexington Books.

Simons, H. W. (1978). In praise of muddleheaded anecdotalism. *Western Journal of Speech Communication, 42,* 21–28.

Steier, F. (Ed.). (1991). *Research and reflexivity.* London: Sage.

Stewart, J. (1995). *Language as articulate contact: Toward a post-semiotic philosophy of communication*. Albany: State University of New York Press.

Stewart, J. (Ed.). (1995). *Beyond the symbol model: Reflections on the representational nature of language*. Albany: State University of New York Press.

Tambiah, S. J. (1985). *Culture, thought, and social action: An anthropological perspective*. Cambridge, MA: Harvard University Press.

Thomas, S. (1980). Some problems of the paradigm in communication theory. *Philosophy of the Social Sciences, 10*, 427–444.

Tracy, K. (Ed.). (1991). *Understanding face-to-face interaction: Issues linking goals and discourse*. Hillsdale, NH: Erlbaum.

Winkin, Y. (Ed.). (1981). *La nouvelle communication*. Paris: Éditions du Seuil.

Winkin, Y., & Sigman, S. (Eds.). (1984). The ethnography of communication: Twenty years later [Special Issue]. *Papers in Linguistics, 17*(1), 1–88.

Zabor, M. R. (1978). *Essaying metacommunication: A survey and contextualization of communication research*. Unpublished Ph.D. dissertation, Indiana University, Bloomington, IN

Part II

Philosophical Roots

CHAPTER 2

Philosophical Features of Social Approaches to Interpersonal Communication

JOHN STEWART

S ome proponents of social approaches to interpersonal communication argue for the revolutionary status of this perspective. For example, in this volume, Leeds-Hurwitz (Chapter 1) emphasizes how significant the differences are between "interpretive," "ethnographic," "postmodern," "hermeneutic," and "social constructivist" approaches on the one hand and "psychological," "mechanistic," and "scientific" ones on the other (see also Leeds-Hurwitz, 1992). She describes 11 "major concepts" that characterize social approaches and are enabling interpersonal communication scholars to develop "a more adequate understanding of human interaction" (1992, p. 136). Elsewhere in this volume, Steier (Chapter 4) explores the concept of *reflexivity*, Lannamann (Chapter 6) examines communication scholars' understanding of *the individual*, Jorgenson (Chapter 8) scrutinizes the construct *rapport*, and Sigman (Chapter 10) underscores the importance to all communication of *sociocultural context*.

These writers and others acknowledge that the distinctive nature of social approaches is rooted in certain basic assumptions or general beliefs. But, primarily because they have other fish to fry, "the authors included in this book do not always make their assumptions explicit, and do not attempt to describe the ideas they hold in common" (Leeds-Hurwitz, Chapter 1, this volume, p. 13). As a result, it is less clear than it might be exactly what is "revolutionary" about this orientation. More important, a discussion of some central philosophical dimensions of social approaches may enable interpersonal scholars to assess which specific conceptual and methodological strategies embody this perspective and which reflect "psychological," "mechanistic," and "scientific" approaches. In other words, insofar as the philosophical claims are articulated, it may be easier to design and carry out research that carefully tests or faithfully applies this orientation.

Perhaps the most important single philosophical idea that distinguishes "social" approaches to interpersonal communication from their predecessors is the view of the relationship between "person" and "world" embodied in each. In a nutshell, most psychological and scientific approaches are grounded in what philosophers call the subject–object polarity and the epistemology that grows from it, whereas social approaches are responsive to philosophical critiques of this polarity and its epistemological focus. This means that the former approaches generally view persons as Cartesian–Kantian subjects who engage in various relations with elements of a more or less objective world, whereas the latter approaches integrate the conviction that the person is first and foremost being-in-the-world, not a "subject" relating to "world–objects." In the original forum, Lannamann (1992) focused in part on this issue but from a materialist cultural perspective, which left its ontological grounds unarticulated. Martin Heidegger did attempt to articulate these grounds, and he is the philosopher who has perhaps most influenced 20th-century thinking about this problematic. Thus, as a contribution to the conversation about social approaches, I briefly review Heidegger's critique of the subject–object polarity and the related reconceptualization of language as interpersonal communication developed primarily by Heidegger's student, Hans-Georg Gadamer. I then extend this analysis by clarifying how the Heideggerian–Gadamerian account of the relationship between person and world challenges the understanding of "the representational problem" that currently animates much interpersonal communication theorizing and research. I argue that because of difficulties generated by communication theorists' accounts of the person-and-world relationship and representation, there is a need to rethink current conceptualizations of several of the major concepts Leeds-Hurwitz discusses and the central constructs, "sign/symbol," "code," and "message." I hope in this way to demonstrate how some contemporary philosophy may inform interpersonal communication scholarship and also to suggest how some philosophers might profit from reviewing social theorists' research.

DASEIN AND THE SUBJECT–OBJECT SPLIT

Descartes's (1637/1962) *"Cogito, ergo sum"* directly announced the discovery of one irreducible, ultimate pole of reality and implied the other. Systematic questioning led Descartes to conclude that everything could be doubted except the existence of that which was doing the doubting, namely, the sovereign, rational subject or *cogito*. It followed, for him, that everything not *res cogitans* was *res extensa*, roughly the objective furniture of the world. From this perspective, the first business of philosophy became epistemology, the branch of the discipline that clarifies how subjects come to know objects, that is, how consciousness comes into relation with, or forms a representation of, *res extensa*. From the 17th century to the present this perspective has been developed by influential Western philosophers and appropriated by scholars and laypersons to constitute a multitude of "obvious" and "certain" beliefs. These include, for example, the convictions that each person is a unique individual, a singular concantenation of heredity and environment; that the study of these individuals and their relationships—psychology or social psychology—is thus the first of the human sciences; that the things around us—rocks and trees, institutions, and other individuals—exist separately from us; that persons can come to know these elements of the world best by forming distanced, "objective" mental representations of them; and that this knowledge can be verified by comparing the representations persons form with the things themselves.

Heidegger and other postmodern[1] thinkers have raised serious questions about these Cartesian–Kantian assumptions and the obvious and certain beliefs based on them (McCarthy, 1987; Stewart, 1991). But the presence of this volume and the two social approaches forums in *Communication Theory* illustrate that these critiques have not yet been assimilated into interpersonal communication scholarship. One reason may be that interpersonal scholars have not yet become familiar with the arguments against the subject–object dichotomy or with the alternative that Heidegger and other philosophers have proposed.

Heidegger's primary argument was that Cartesian–Kantian analyses of humans began one giant step too far into the problematic. As Hubert Dreyfus (1991) explains:

> Since Descartes, philosophers have been stuck with the *epistemological* problem of explaining how the ideas in our mind can be true of the external world. Heidegger shows that this subject–object epistemology presupposes a background of everyday practices into which we are socialized but that we do not represent in our minds. Since he calls this more fundamental way

of making sense of things our understanding of being, he claims that he is doing *ontology*, that is, asking about the nature of this understanding of being that we do not *know*—that is not a representation in the mind corresponding to the world—but that we simply *are*. (p. 3)

In other words, Heidegger noticed something about humans that precedes our operating as subjects on objects. It is that humans are immersed in what might be called *everyday coping*: For the most part "without thinking," we make our way about, inhabiting our residences; eating and grooming; avoiding or connecting with people on the street; operating familiar machinery such as keyboards, bicycles, and automobiles; engaging in mediated and face-to-face professional and personal transactions. These are all examples of our being-in-the-world. With the help of acculturation and socialization, we more or less successfully, and yet "mindlessly," *accomplish* everyday coping. Not infrequently, humans experience themselves as conscious subjects relating to the world around them via such intentional states as desires, beliefs, perceptions, or intentions. But Heidegger argues that this is "a derivative and intermittent condition that presupposes a more fundamental way of being-in-the-world that cannot be understood in subject–object terms" (Dreyfus, 1991, p. 5).

Heidegger coined the term "Dasein" to characterize the human as being-in-the-world. A literal translation of the German is "there-being," that is, a concrete instantiation ("there") of Being. Thus when the term is translated into English it is rendered "the person," but it clearly differs from the monadic consciousness Descartes envisioned. Dasein is characterized not by its "essential features" but by its mode of involvement, its engagement in a characteristic way of everyday coping. Dasein is not first and foremost a knower engaged in forming representations of the external world, but an involved doer. As Heidegger (1985) explained:

Knowing is now not a comportment that would be added to an entity which does not yet "have" a world, which is free from any relation to its world [i.e., a Cartesian *cogito*]. Rather, knowing is always a mode of being of Dasein on the basis of its *already* being involved with the world. The basic defect of epistemology is just that it fails to regard what it means by knowing in its *original* phenomenal datum as a way of being of Dasein, as a way of its in-being, and to take from this basic consideration all the questions which now begin to arise on this ground. (p. 161, emphasis added)

The point of Heidegger's argument is that the person is not first and foremost an isolated *cogito* employing reason to connect and disconnect with objects around it but is first and foremost a situated interpreter, understander, or "sense maker" engaged in everyday coping. Moreover, as situated interpreter, the person is irreducibly relational not individual, social not psychological. It is not the case that humans first "are" and then "behave in relation to" or "respond to" the people and things around them. Rather, Heidegger (1985) argued:

> The phenomenological statement, "Dasein as being-in-the-world is a being-with with others," has an existential–ontological sense and does not intend to establish that I in fact do not turn out to be alone and still other entities of my kind are on hand. If this were the intention of the stipulation, then I would be speaking of my Dasein as if it were an environmental thing on hand. . . . Being-with signifies a character of being of Dasein as such which is co-original with being-in-the-world. . . . This character of being-with defines the Dasein even when another Dasein is in fact not being addressed and cannot be perceived as on hand. Even Dasein's being-alone is only a deficiency of being-with. . . . (p. 238)

Thanks to almost three centuries of dominance in the West, the Cartesian picture appears almost utterly self-evident. What could be more obvious than that the human world is populated by individuals defined by cutaneous boundaries and idiosyncratic, ultimately unfathomable mental processes? What could be more obvious than the fact that rocks, rowboats, and tenure review committees objectively exist separate from the individuals who come into relation with them? And yet, many postmodern thinkers have challenged precisely this picture in ways that invite responses from communication scholars. To cite just one example, postmodern analyses raise questions about whether information-processing models of human cognition and communication misconstrue the relationship between person and world by positing a fundamental distinction between "processors" and "information."[2] The chapters by Bochner and Ellis (Chapter 11), Jorgenson (Chapter 8), and Carbaugh and Hastings (Chapter 9) in this volume address aspects of this problematic as they show how important features of everyday coping cannot be successfully explicated in information-processing terms.

But one disadvantage of many philosophical critiques of the subject–object polarity is that they do not work out a general theoretical alternative to the Cartesian picture. This occurs in part because such a project would be inconsistent with the insight it purports to develop. If it is the case that humans do not relate to things primarily by having an implicit theory about them, it is impossible to "have a theory of what makes theory possible" (Dreyfus, 1991, p. 1). One who would understand human beings should not begin by theorizing but, for example, by tracking persons in their everyday coping. As Bochner and Ellis clearly recognize, this tracking should not proceed from a detached, "objective" stance, but from one engaged with the very coping that is being interpreted. Moreover, the interpersonal scholar or other human scientist should not assume that the resulting interpretations will render human practices lucidly explicit. There is a "nonexplicitable background that enables us to make sense of things" (Dreyfus, 1991, p. 4) which remains after even the most detailed account. This context of coherence, parts of which Sigman (Chapter 10) discusses in this volume, frames human self-understanding, and "Dasein is what, in its social activity, it interprets itself to be. Humans do not already have some specific nature. . . . Human being is essentially simply self-interpreting" (Dreyfus, 1991, p. 23; Taylor, 1985).

Dasein and Interpersonal Communicating

Serendipitously for communication scholars, the paradigmatic site of everyday coping and self-interpretation is linguistic–communicative. This is the primary point of Heidegger's (1977) often-cited claim that "Language is the house of Being. In its home [the hu]man dwells. Those who think and those who create with words are the guardians of this home. Their guardianship accomplishes the manifestation of Being insofar as they bring the manifestation to language and maintain it in language through their speech" (p.193). But as his mention of "speech" suggests, Heidegger did not mean by "language" the *system* that de Saussure (1983) investigated or that Wittgenstein (1961) attempted to describe in the *Tractatus*. As Richard Rorty (1991) notes, attempts to account for language as a system "reify" their object of study and need to be replaced with the recognition that, in Donald Davidson's (1986) words, "there is no such thing as a language, not if a language is anything like what philosophers . . . have supposed. . . . We must give up the idea of a clearly defined shared structure which language users master and then apply to cases" (p. 446). Rorty (1991) shows how Heidegger and the Wittgenstein of the *Philosophical Investigations* basically agreed on this point. When Heidegger claimed that "language" is the paradigmatic site of everyday coping and self-interpretation, he meant that Dasein accomplishes these projects in what communication scholars call events of interpersonal communicating. *So the "object of study" of interpersonal communication scholarship is precisely at the center of the philosophical enterprise that occupied both Heidegger and the later Wittgenstein and that occupies many of their conceptual progeny.* As Heidegger (1985) put it, "Discourse as a mode of being of Dasein qua being-with is essentially *communication*" (p. 263). Moreover, he continued, communication is emphatically "not a matter of transporting information and experiences from the interior of one subject to the interior of the other one. It is rather a matter of being-with-one-another becoming manifest in the world, specifically by way of the discovered world, which itself becomes manifest in speaking with one another" (p. 263).

Heidegger's ontological, social, and communicative view of the relationship between person and world has been developed and extended by Hans-Georg Gadamer. Gadamer (1989a) argues that the main reason subject–object analyses of language are inherently distorted is that "language is not just one of [the hu]man's possessions in the world; rather, on it depends the fact that [the hu]man has a *world* at all" (p. 443). In other words, Gadamer emphasizes that humans do not simply "possess" or "use" language, we *inhabit* it. If we are in a subject–object relationship with something, we can distance ourselves from it; like a tool, we can pick it up when we need it and put it down when it has done its service. But this is clearly not the relationship we have with our native tongue. We are born into a world shaped by culturally distinctive speech communicating, and we develop our sense of ourselves and our place in it primarily in verbal–nonverbal address and response. As Gadamer (1976) summarizes, "Learning to speak does not mean learning to use a preexistent tool for designating a world already somehow familiar to us; it means acquiring a familiarity and acquaintance with the world itself and how it confronts us" (p. 63). Thus the infant's or child's development as a linguistic being is synonymous with its development as a being involved in everyday coping. The processes are coterminous: Language (speech communicating) is the human's way of being-in-the-world (everyday coping).

Gadamer (1989a) explains the connection between everyday coping and discourse or dialogue this way[3]:

> On the other hand, however, it must be emphasized that language has its true being only in dialogue, in *coming to an understanding*. This is not to be understood as if that were the purpose of language. Coming to an understanding is not a mere action, a purposeful activity, a setting up of signs through which I transmit my will to others. Coming to an understanding as such, rather, does not need any tools, in the proper sense of the word. It is a life process in which a community of life is lived out . . . for language is by nature the language of conversation; it fully realizes itself only in the process of coming to an understanding. (p. 446)

From this perspective, it is not the case that (already) human beings use language in a subject–object way as an instrument or tool for the purpose of reaching understanding. Rather, to be human is to engage in the life process of coming to an understanding (everyday coping), a process that paradigmatically occurs in conversation. Humans co-construct and negotiate their worlds in verbal–nonverbal address and response.

THE REPRESENTATIONAL PROBLEM

This radically altered understanding of the relationship between person and world affects other philosophical constructs with important implications for communication theorizing. One of the most significant is the understanding of representation. Historically, both cognition and language have been treated as forms of representation, and the perennial representational problem concerns how one phenomenon of a given ontological status—for example, a cognition or electrico-organic episode—can stand for or present again a phenomenon of a radically different ontological status—for example, an object. Thomas McCarthy (1987) is one of several philosophers who argue that a central feature uniting many postmodern thinkers is their approach to this problem. As McCarthy (1987) points out, many of these philosophers reject the "picture of *knowledge as representation,* according to which the subject stands over against an independent world of objects that it can more or less accurately represent" (p. 5). If Heidegger's analysis of Dasein is plausible, humans are always actively coping with the entities they are allegedly representing. Thus, as Charles Taylor (1987) explains, "The notion that our understanding of the world is grounded in our dealings with it is equivalent to the thesis that this understanding is not ultimately based on representations at all, in the sense of depictions that are separately identifiable from what they are of" (p. 477).

The 10 articles that made up the April/July 1988 special issue of the journal *Human Studies* demonstrate how representation is one of the most basic constructs underlying the natural and especially the human sciences. As these essays illustrate, scholars of many different persuasions understand themselves to be manipulating and analyzing entities and theoretical relationships that are made visibly present—that is, represented—in, for example, electron micrographs, autoradiographs of systematically prepared tissue, numerical aggregations displayed in tables and graphs, and/or labels for constructs. As they do so, these scholars work from certain assumptions about (1) the extent to which their representational devices (RDs) (graphs, diagrams, models, etc.) are socially constructed, interpreted, and deployed; (2) the ontological status of the represented object (RO); and (3) the relationship between RD and RO, especially the accuracy with which RD *represents* RO (Tibbetts, 1988, p. 117). All three sets of assumptions foreground aspects of the representational problem.

Historically scholars have dealt with the problem by developing one of two fundamentally different accounts of representation. The realist version stipulates that ROs exist separately from the persons studying them and that the primary initial task of the scientist is to arrive at RDs that correctly, accurately, veridically, and verifiably represent their ROs. The interpretivist or constructivist version of this process stipulates that, as Barnes (1977) puts it, the phenomena commonly thought of as representations are actually more constructions, in that they

> are actively manufactured renderings of their referents [ROs], produced from available cultural resources. The particular forms of construction adopted reflect the predictive or other technical cognitive functions the representation [RD] is required to perform when procedures are carried out, competencies executed, or technologies applied. Why such functions are initially required of the representation is generally intelligible, directly or indirectly, in terms of the objectives of some social group. (p. 6)

Few natural scientists and almost no human scientists still subscribe to the straightforward realist version of representation. Instead, taking cues from Heidegger, the later Wittgenstein, Kuhn (1962), and Hesse (1974), sociologists of science (e.g., Barnes, 1977; Barnes & Shapin, 1979; Bloor, 1976) and other theorists underscore the agenda-driven, context-dependent, constructed, and interpreted nature of such basic research constructs as "data" and "evidence."

Some ethnographers of science have undertaken empirical studies that extend these philosophers' and sociologists' arguments to clarify how data and evidence are not just constructed but are collaboratively constructed in discourse or conversation. For example, as part of a larger research program (Amann & Knorr-Cetina, 1988a, 1988b, 1988c; Knorr-Cetina, 1983; Lynch & Woolgar, 1988), one empirical study of work at the Center for Molecular Genetics in Heidelberg (Amann & Knorr-Cetina, 1988c) concludes that as scientists work with autoradiograph film, data are the product of conversational *talk*, in that the primary perceptual mode of "looking" or "seeing" is "interactively accomplished. Thus the process [of 'seeing what is on the film'] is not just a semiotic process, in the sense of involving a translation into a generalized system of signs. Nor is it mainly a cognitive or interpretative process in the sense of involving individual conceptual decoding. Instead, the process has . . . particularly a *dialogical* or *interactive* structure" (p. 138). One of the goals of this research program is to analyze the distinctive features and interactional organization of this talk that constitutes "the machinery of seeing" (p. 140).

Studies such as these lead philosohers of inquiry and sociologists of knowledge to conclude that the "contents" of scientific and human scientific research are not simply representations of "natural objects" formed independent of cultural processes and literary forms. Instead, they are culturally and socially embedded and communicatively co-constructed, "a rich repository of 'social' [trans]actions" (Lynch & Woolgar, 1988, p. 103).

IMPLICATIONS FOR INTERPERSONAL
THEORIZING AND RESEARCH

None of these claims, either about person-and-world or about representation, is strikingly new to many interpersonal scholars familiar with social approaches to communication. From their perspective, it may be reassuring to know that some philosophers and sociologists of knowledge agree with, for example, Berger and Luckmann (1967), Geertz (1983), Goffman (1974, 1983), and Hymes (1962, 1972). But, these scholars might ask, what is new? How can these philosophical analyses contribute to interpersonal communication theorizing and research? I believe there are at least four responses to this question.

First, it is helpful to recognize that at least since the 1920s, several careful thinkers have been grappling with ideas central to what some scholars now call social approaches to interpersonal communication. As Leeds-Hurwitz (1992) suggests, the "revolution" has been going on for more than half a century. These works make up an important part of the intellectual history of concepts currently central to interpersonal theorizing, and as such, they deserve close attention. Most analyses by philosophers and sociologists of knowledge lack the precision and specificity present in interpersonal scholars' empirically anchored descriptions. But, as I hope to illustrate next in my comments about "symbol," "code," and "message," each enterprise can inform the other.

Second, even a cursory review of some postmodern philosophy can clarify why it has taken so long for these ideas to become assimilated. This perspective clearly constitutes a paradigm shift which requires theorists and laypersons to rethink some of Western humanity's most entrenched beliefs. We are asked to revise our understanding of what it means to be a person, how humans fit into what is taken to be the human "world," and whether we can continue to understand verbal and nonverbal language as simply "about" the "reality" it "represents." Human scientists across disciplines are also asked to alter both their definition of "who" they study (see Lannamann, Chapter 6, this volume) and their research methods (see Jorgenson, Chapter 8; Carbaugh & Hastings, Chapter 9; and Bochner & Ellis, Chapter 11, this volume).

Third, as I have already noted, this revolution places the basic problematic of interpersonal communication at the center of the human sciences. Insofar as persons are fundamentally relational or social beings who work out their self-interpretations in interpersonal address and response or conversation, the phenomenon of interpersonal communicating becomes focal for anthropology, political science, psychology, sociology, and the other human sciences.[4] This recognition can contribute to communication theorists' understanding of how our work relates to that done in neighboring disciplines.

Fourth, and most important, these philosophical analyses can enrich and increase the precision of interpersonal scholars' understanding of several central constructs. In the remainder of this chapter I briefly consider five: "the social construction of reality," "reflexivity," "sign/symbol," "code," and "message."

Social Construction of Reality

The third "major concept" characterizing social approaches that Leeds-Hurwitz highlights in this book's introduction is a commitment to "the social construction of reality" (also see Berger & Luckmann, 1967). Unfortunately, it is possible to understand this phrase as a description of a subject–object process. From a Cartesian–Kantian perspective, to say that reality is socially constructed is to say that individuals informally and formally form dyads and groups that develop construals of salient elements of the objective world into what counts for the individual or group as "reality." This understanding could guide a reader's interpretation of such statements as, "We create our social world through our words and other symbols, and through our behaviors; thus these become research topics" (Leeds-Hurwitz, 1992, p. 133). The philosophers quoted earlier clarify why and how such an interpretation of either Berger and Luckmann or Leeds-Hurwitz would be inaccurate, because it would constitute a subject–object reading of an insight that revises subject–object thinking. In fact, insofar as the "construction" metaphor is understood to characterize a process of subjects ("builders," "carpenters") operating on objects, it is *inherently* misleading.

What, then, would constitute a postmodern interpretation of the social construction of reality theme that avoided any subject–object connotations? This is not a simple question; both the subject–verb–object structure of English and the pervasiveness of Cartesianism make this problem difficult to solve. Heidegger employed the locution "being-in-the-world" and other German neologisms, many of which are virtually untranslatable. Gadamer (1989a) writes of "being played by the game," distinguishes between experience as *Erlebnis* and experience as *Erfahrung*, and describes the differences between the nonhuman animal's *Umwelt* and the human *Welt*. Philosopher Calvin Schrag (1986) favors the term "decentered subject" (Lannamann, 1992). And communication scholars have attempted to manage this difficulty with such phrases as "situated accomplishment" (Stewart & Philipsen, 1984), "conversational" versus "literary" referring (Clark & Wilkes-Gibbs, 1986), "worlding in talk" (Stewart, 1991, 1994a, 1995) or "Interactants World, as culturally shaped" (Pomerantz, 1989). The challenge is to discuss this basic feature of humans as pre-reflective, framed by negotiated self-interpretations, discursive, and productive of *world*. I cannot offer a simple substitute for the phrase "social construction of reality," which avoids all potential ambiguities. As I note below, in Stewart (1995) I lay out an account of language as "constitutive articulate contact" that affirms the Heideggerian–Gadamerian picture of the relationship between person and world and attempts to avoid the representational problem. But there is clearly room for additional work linking postmodern philosophy with communication theory and research.

Reflexivity

Another central concept that Leeds-Hurwitz (Chapter 1, this volume) and Steier (Chapter 4, this volume) discuss is "reflexivity," which Leeds-Hurwitz characterizes as a process of "questioning," "accepting a multiplicity of meanings in events," and the potential "discovery of the frequently hidden 'I,' the self of the researcher, no longer absent from the final reporting of results" (Chapter 1, this volume, p. 10). Here again, relevant philosophical discussions can head off potential misinterpretations. One could conceivably understand this notion as a call for researchers to add a reflexive step or stage to their research design, data gathering, analysis, and/or writing. But the philosophers cited clarify that something more basic is at stake. The point is not to "add" reflexivity but to acknowledge explicitly that reflexivity is inescapable and pervasive. Because humans are inherently self-interpreting, all human projects—including research—both affect and are affected by these self-interpretations (Steier, 1991). So reflexivity is not an option; as Leeds-Hurwitz (Chapter 1, this volume) notes, "Those who accept a reflexive approach feel it does no more than what is *necessary*" (p. 10, emphasis added).

Sign/Symbol

Leeds-Hurwitz also mentions as one of 11 common themes "use of the concept of *symbol* as a basic building block in the study of interaction" (Chapter 1, this volume, p. 9). She cites with approval Cronkhite's (1986) definition of communication as "the study of human symbolic activity" and urges interpersonal scholars interested in social approaches to explore semiotic theory. I would argue, to the contrary, that semiotic characterizations of language and communication embody the very misunderstandings that postmodern critiques of subject–object thinking and representation so helpfully illuminate. In fact, I believe that *one of the primary implications of the postmodern understanding of the relation between person and world sketched here is that communication theorists and researchers should fundamentally reconsider their commitment to semiotic thinking.*

Since ancient times, language has been characterized as a semiotic system. Aristotle (ca. 330 B.C./1941) laid down the view that "spoken words are the symbols of mental experience and written words are the symbols of spoken words" (p. 40). Although scores of classical, medieval, and renaissance theorists modified and elaborated this Greek insight, its basic form persisted through John Locke's (1690) explanation of the semiotic relationship between "articulate sounds" and the "ideas" which they are "signs" of and therefore "represent." Today, influential accounts of language in philosophy, linguistics, and many other human sciences continue to foreground the claim that, as Kenneth Burke (1978) put it, language is "a conventional, arbitrary symbol system" (p. 809), and, in sociologist Norbert Elias's (1991) words, "communication by means of symbols . . . is one of the singularities of humankind" (p. 4; cf. Cronkhite, 1986; Motley, 1990).

Some postmodern philosophers warn their readers to beware of these semiotic characterizations of language, in part because they maintain representational thinking and thereby contribute to the reification of language and to an exclusive focus on language as *system* rather than *event*. Heidegger (1971) contended that "the essential being of language is Saying as Showing," and that "Its showing character is not based on signs of any kind" (p. 123), including "symbols." Gadamer (1976) also emphasizes that from his perspective, "as long as [language] is even conceived as a symbolic form, it is not yet recognized in all its true dimensions" (p. 76). Extending these claims, I argue (Stewart, 1991, 1995) that these and other postmodern philosophical works challenge what Michael Motley (1990) calls communication theory's "symbol postulate." And in Stewart (1995), I demonstrate the vulnerability of semiotic accounts of the nature of language to postmodern critiques of representionalism and subject–object thinking.

This work begins by tracing the history of semiotic views of language and laying out the five theoretical commitments common to these accounts. Its survey of pre-Socratic through late 20th-century works demonstrates that whether theorists use sign or symbol vocabulary, they assume, first, that there is some fundamental distinction between two realms or worlds, the world of the sign and the signified, symbol and symbolized, name and named, word and thought or meaning, *aliquid* and *aliquo*. The four remaining commitments follow from this one. The second commitment is the belief that the linguistic world consists of identifiable units or elements (phonemes, morphemes, words, utterances, speech acts) which are its atoms or molecules. The third is the claim that the relationship between these units of language and the units that make up the other of the two worlds is some sort of representational relationship. Commitment four is the belief that these ontologically distinct, representationally functioning units make up a system, the system called language. And the final commitment asserts that language is a tool or instrument that humans more or less consciously use to accomplish their goals. Some version of these five commitments to two worlds, atomism, representation, system, and instrumentality, follows as a consequence of characterizing language semiotically.

After demonstrating the manifest inability of semiotic models to explain the paradigmatic instance of language-in-use, face-to-face conversation, *Language as Articulate Contact* then proposes a postsemiotic account of the nature of language grounded in the Heideggerian–Gadamerian perspective between person and world outlined in this chapter. With the help of philosophers Mikhail M. Bakhtin (1986) and Martin Buber (1965, 1965/1970), I argue that (1) language should be treated first and foremost as event, not system (as "languaging"); (2) this event embodies the distinctive dynamic of human being, which is understanding; (3) this ongoing process of understanding-via-languaging is the human's way of constituting world ("world-building-and-rebuilding" or simply "worlding"); (4) this understanding occurs in contact between persons, that is, the event is irreducibly dialogical or social; and (5) this understanding-in-contact is articulate, which means both that it accomplishes differentiation or categorization and that it occurs paradigmatically as oral–aural contact. The final chapters of this book trace parallel arguments about the nature of language found in postmodern hermeneutics, artificial intelligence, and deaf education and then apply the postsemiotic account as a critical tool to works by V. N. Vološinov, Kenneth Burke, and Calvin O. Schrag.

There is no space to elaborate these arguments or support these claims here. But I hope it is apparent that a case can be made that communication theorists who find postmodern critiques of representationalism and postmodern accounts of the relationship between person and world to be plausible need at least to reconsider any residual commitment they might maintain to the essentially semiotic character of language. From a postmodern perspective, language cannot be adequately understood as a system of signs or symbols. This is perhaps one of the most far-reaching implications of this philosophical work for interpersonal communication theorists and researchers.

Code

In communication theory, the constructs of encoding and decoding are almost as pervasive as semiotic characterizations of the nature of language. One reason for this parallel is that the constructs are parasitic on the semiotic assumptions outlined above. A code is generally defined as a system that uses "long and short sounds, light flashes, colored flags, or the like, to *symbolize* [emphasis added] letters, words or phrases," or "a word, letter, number, or other symbol used in a code system to represent or identify something." To encode is to "convert into code," and to decode is to translate back into "the original form" (*Random House College Dictionary*, 1984, pp. 259, 345, 435). All these descriptions presume the existence of two systems, realms, or worlds, the code and that which is translated into or out of it. Elements of a code are viewed as symbols—representations—of "something else."

Clearly the foreign language translator and military cryptographer often deal with a linguistic "something" and a linguistic "something else." Here, the two-worlds assumption sketched above need not necessarily apply. But in communication theory, encoding and decoding are generally used to label processes that translate cognitions into language units, for example, or meanings into words. So the two-worlds assumption *is* clearly operative in many communication theorists' accounts of encoding and decoding. When these theorists describe language as a code, they typically treat it as a system that people use to transform, preserve, perhaps alter, and, above all, to *transmit* ideas, meanings, thoughts, concepts, or messages to someone else. These treatments of encoding and decoding embody at least two implicit claims that reveal the presence of the two-worlds assumption. One is that the code is more manageable or efficient than are the phenomena that it codifies. Another is that encoding permits transmission because the precoded phenomena are assumed to be internal, idiosyncratic, or in some other way resistant to being transmitted. Communication models that highlight encoding and decoding often focus attention on problems that inescapably arise when we try to transform one sort of phenomenon into another while maintaining representational fidelity.

It is difficult to make the constructs of encoding and decoding coherent when we adopt the perspectives on language and communication outlined earlier. In the first place, a code is a *system* alleged to be used by subjects to somehow *represent* that which is codified, a view consistent with a subject–object analysis of the relationship between person and world. I have already noted Gadamer's (1976, 1989a, 1989b) arguments that humans do not "possess" or "use" language as we use tools but that we *inhabit* and are *subject to* the tongues we speak. In this view, we are used by language at least as much as we use it, not because we have yet to "master" this "resource" but because it is incoherent to set as a goal the development of a mastery over one's *way of being*. Such a project would involve an ontological version of lifting oneself by one's own bootstraps. Thus, attempts to apply the labels "encoding" and "decoding" to describe central features of the event of languaging or communicating commit a kind of category mistake analogous to the attempt to specify the height of a football game or the density of a promise. In order to study how to put something into or take it out of a code, one would have to assume a type of separation between thought and language, for example, or between language and meaning that is challenged by a wide range of critics. These critics agree that we cannot coherently employ subject–object terminology to characterize a non-subject–object process.

So how might we talk about that which many theorists characterize as "code" or "encoding–decoding"? From this postmodern perspective, our vocabulary or expertise with a certain language or jargon, for example, would not be treated as a code but as a set of abilities that facilitate or obstruct our involvement in the processes of negotiating and coconstituting worlds. So our grasp of technical terms and sophisticated syntactic rules would not be thought of as constitutents of a code but as aspects of our competence to engage in specialized understanding–events.

This perspective also offers another set of reasons to revise the continuing tendency among some communication theorists to talk and write about "nonverbal codes." Research programs designed to identify the atoms or molecules that make up the nonverbal "system" would be abandoned. Scholars would acknowledge the recent claims that "it is impossible to study either verbal or nonverbal communication as isolated structures. Rather, these systems should be regarded as a unified communication construct" (Higginbotham & Yoder, 1982, p. 4), and "there is now a current body of literature devoted to rejoining the two" (Leeds-Hurwitz, 1989, p. 102). In research influenced by this perspective, neither verbal elements nor nonverbal ones would be isolated and treated as parts of a code, that is, as surrogates or representations of something else. Instead, efforts would be made to provide more synoptic accounts of relationships among the context-dependent, situated elements of communication events and to articulate what the events enact and accomplish.

Message

The term "message" is obviously problematic in some similar ways. When this term appears in communication research, it is virtually universally employed to identify the linguistic (and sometimes paralinguistic) product that an individual communicator creates, a product that is assumed to embody—or sometimes to represent—the communicator's purposes and goals. One currently influential line of research focuses on "message design logics" (O'Keefe, 1988; O'Keefe & McCornack, 1987; O'Keefe & Shepherd, 1987). Interestingly, O'Keefe's (1988) primary theoretical outline of this program carefully defines all her central constructs but this one. She distinguishes "messages" from "their goals or functions" (p. 80), reviews "message analysis systems" (p. 82), and states that "messages are organized and produced through a rational process of deriving means to serve communicative goals" (pp. 81–82). But only when she reports on empirical work does she clarify that what she means by message is a response to the researcher's request that the subject "write out what they should say, [for example,] to Ron; that is, they [were] asked to provide a message and not just a general description of the approach they would take" (p. 93). So "message" in this research means a written self-report of what one would say in a certain situation. The appendix to O'Keefe's (1988) study reveals that the messages produced ranged from "You asshole. I knew you wouldn't do your work. I'm going to see that you are fired" (p. 100) to 10-sentence attempts to save everyone's face and rescue the troubled project outlined in the research scenario. In a report of another study (O'Keefe & Shepherd, 1987), much is made of the importance of "exchanges" between interlocutors, but the actual data analysis is performed on "lines of action within arguments" (p. 403), which consist of utterances that one person produced.

The perspective outlined here indicates why this treatment of the construct "message" is conceptually problematic. One primary problem is that O'Keefe and her colleagues' work studies written data and thus omits all the paralinguistic and physical phenomena that are included in actual conversation. Another problem, as critics of constructivist research have noted, is that these studies focus not on the event of communicating but on one interlocutor's actions. Thus, they generate information of psychological and protocommunicational interest, but they do not focus directly on the event that engages *both* communicators. The study of "lines" within "exchanges" (O'Keefe & Shepherd, 1987) definitely moves in this direction. But little of the researchers' analysis attempts to articulate how individual "lines" build on or undermine what precedes and follows them. This appears primarily to be the result of the decision to focus the research program on the "*logics* of *message* design" and to assume that conversation consists essentially of individual utterances strategically configured and instrumentally performed to accomplish individual goals. This way of approaching communication can clearly generate some important insights. But it is also limited by its structurally monologic, instrumental, and rationalistic biases.

Under the perspective outlined here, if the term "message" survived as an important construct, it would be part of the theorist's or researcher's discussion of the precipitate of an interpersonal transaction. "Message," like its even more problematic counterpart, "meaning," would be considered a collaborative, negotiated product, an outcome of verbal–nonverbal engagement about some subject matter. On this view, there would be no single or final account of any given message, any more than one can provide for a single or final reading of a text. The definition of the message produced in any communication event would change with the person(s) asked to define it (one participant, all participants, a participant–observer, a distanced observer) and the context (time, place, constraints) of the request. Such an approach to this central and common construct would clearly require changes in many currently influential accounts of human communication.

CONCLUSION

Several additional constructs central to communication theorizing and research could fruitfully be reexamined in light of the accounts of representation and of the relationship between person and world outlined here. Two that immediately come to mind are "intent" and "validity." Research by the philosophers cited here raises serious questions about some communication scholars' accounts of both these constructs (Stewart, 1991, 1994). Moreover, I have emphasized here only Heidegger's, Gadamer's, Bakhtin's, and Buber's writings. As other authors of the original forum note, heuristic insights are also available in the works of Merleau-Ponty (1974), Foucault (1978, 1979), Derrida (1976), and other philosophers. In addition, secondary sources (e.g., Bernstein, 1985; Bleicher, 1980; Hekman, 1986; Madison, 1990; Palmer, 1969; Rorty, 1979, 1991; Theunissen, 1984; Warnke, 1987) can clarify the significance of some primary works and the applicability of philosophical analyses to the concerns of communication scholars. But I hope enough has been said to demonstrate that some postmodern philosophy can inform interpersonal communication theorizing *and* that there are genuine opportunities for cross-pollination. Philosophers centrally interested in communicative praxis (Schrag, 1986, 1992), the hermeneutics of intersubjectivity (Madison, 1990), and similar phenomena might usefully review descriptions by authors in this volume of communication as a social process.

NOTES

1. Since it first emerged in discourse about architecture, the term "postmodern" has taken on an unfortunately broad range of meanings. Even in the single discipline of philosophy it is now applied to a range of projects from deconstruction through radical feminism, to cultural studies and philosophical hermeneutics. Moreover, Habermas (1987), Schrag (1992), and others develop philosophical programs situated *between* modernity and postmodernity. Elsewhere (Stewart, 1991) I have sketched my sense of the term as it may inform communication theorizing. In my view, the most important development of postmodern thought is the shift from viewing language as a semiotic system to acknowledging language or linguisticality as world constituting. I develop these ideas below and in Stewart (1995).
2. Dreyfus (1991) discusses Heidegger's critique of information-processing models on pages 2 to 3.
3. It should be clear that for Gadamer, "dialogue" has a different meaning than it had for Martin Buber (1965, 1965/1970). See Stewart (1986).
4. Some scholars in each of these disciplines recognize this. See, for example, works by political scientist Fred Dallmayr (1989) and anthropologist Dell Hymes (1962, 1972).

REFERENCES

Amann, K., & Knorr-Cetina, K. (1988a). Thinking through talk: An ethnographic study of a molecular biology laboratory. In R. A. Jones, L. Hargens, & A. Pickering (Eds.), *Knowledge and society: Studies in the sociology of science past and present* (Vol. 8, pp. 98–126). Greenwich, CT: JAI Press.

Amann, K., & Knorr-Cetina, K. (1988b). Werkstattsgesprache in der Wissenschaft: Am Beispiel der Molekularbiologie. In H. G. Soeffner (Ed.), *Sprache und Gesellschaft* (pp. 47–66). Frankfurt: Campus Verlag.

Amann, K., & Knorr-Cetina, K. (1988c). The fixation of (visual) evidence. *Human Studies, 11*, 133–169.

Aristotle. (1941). *The basic works of Aristotle* (R. McKeon, Ed.). New York: Random House. (Original work published ca. 330 B.C.)

Bakhtin, M. M. (1986). *Speech genres and other late essays* (V. W. McGee, Trans.). Austin: University of Texas Press.

Barnes, B. (1977). *Interests and the growth of knowledge.* Boston: Routledge & Kegan Paul.

Barnes, B., & Shapin, S. (Eds.). (1979). *Natural order: Historical studies of scientific culture.* London: Sage.

Berger, P. L., & Luckmann, T. (1967). *The social construction of reality.* Garden City, NY: Doubleday/Anchor.

Bernstein, R. J. (1985). *Beyond objectivism and relativism: Science, hermeneutics, and praxis.* Philadelphia: University of Pennsylvania Press.

Bleicher, J. (1980). *Contemporary hermeneutics: Hermeneutics as method, philosophy and critique.* London: Routledge & Kegan Paul.

Bloor, D. (1976). *Knowledge and social imagery.* London: Routledge & Kegan Paul.

Bochner, A. P., & Ellis, C. (1992). Personal narrative as a social approach to interpersonal communication. *Communication Theory, 2,* 165–172.

Buber, M. (1965). Dialogue. In *Between man and man* (M. Friedman, Ed. & R. G. Smith, Trans.). New York: Macmillan.

Buber, M. (1970). *I and Thou* (W. Kaufmann, Trans.). New York: Charles Scribner's Sons. (Original work published 1965)

Burke, K. (1978). (Nonsymbolic) motion/(symbolic) action. *Critical Inquiry, 4,* 809–838.

Clark, H. H., & Wilkes-Gibbs, D. (1986). Referring as a collaborative process. *Cognition, 22,* 1–39.

Cronkhite, G. (1986). On the focus, scope, and coherence of the study of human symbolic activity. *Quarterly Journal of Speech, 72,* 231–246.

Dallmayr, F. (1989). Hermeneutics and deconstruction: Gadamer and Derrida in dialogue. In D. P. Michelfelder & R. E. Palmer (Eds.), *Dialogue and deconstruction: The Gadamer–Derrida encounter* (pp. 75–92). Albany: State University of New York Press.

Davidson, D. (1986). A nice derangement of epitaphs. In E. LePore (Ed.), *Truth and interpretation: Perspectives on the philosophy of Donald Davidson* (pp. 49–73). Oxford: Basil Blackwell.

Derrida, J. (1976). *Of grammatology* (G. C. Spivak, Trans.). Baltimore: Johns Hopkins Press.

Descartes, R. (1962). *Discourse on method* (J. Veitch, Trans.). Chicago: Open Court. (Original work published 1637)

Dreyfus, H. L. (1991). *Being-in-the-world: A commentary on Heidegger's Being and Time, division I.* Cambridge, MA: MIT press.

Elias, N. (1991). *The symbol theory.* London: Sage.

Foucault, M. (1978). *The history of sexuality.* New York: Random House.

Foucault, M. (1979). *Discipline and punish: The birth of the prison.* New York: Vintage.

Gadamer, H. -G. (1976). *Philosophical hermeneutics* (D. Linge, Ed., Trans.). Berkeley: University of California Press.

Gadamer, H. -G. (1989a). *Truth and method* (2nd rev. ed.) (J. Weinsheimer & D. G. Marshall, Trans.). New York: Crossroad.

Gadamer, H. -G. (1989b). Text and interpretation (D. J. Schmidt & R. Palmer, Trans.). In D. P. Michelfelder & R. E. Palmer (Eds.), *Dialogue and deconstruction: The Gadamer–Derrida encounter* (pp.21–51). Albany: State University of New York Press.

Geertz, C. (1983). *Local knowledge: Further essays on interpretive anthropology.* New York: Basic Books.

Goffman, E. (1974). *Frame analysis.* New York: Harper.

Goffman, E. (1983). The interaction order. *American Sociological Review, 43,* 1–17.

Habermas, J. (1987). *The philosophical discourse of modernity* (F. Lawrence, Trans.). Cambridge, MA: MIT Press.

Heidegger, M. (1971). *On the way to language* (P. D. Hertz, Trans.). San Francisco: Harper & Row.

Heidegger, M. (1977). *Basic writings* (D. F. Krell, Ed.). New York: Harper & Row.

Heidegger, M. (1985). *History of the concept of time* (T. Kisiel, Trans.). Bloomington: Indiana University Press.

Hekman, S. J. (1986). *Hermeneutics and the sociology of knowledge*. Notre Dame, IN: University of Notre Dame Press.

Hesse, M. (1974). *The structure of scientific inference*. Berkeley: University of California Press.

Higgenbotham, D. J., & Yoder, D. E. (1982). Communication within natural conversational interaction: Implications for severe communicatively impaired persons. *Topics in Language Disorders, 2*, 3–11.

Hymes, D. (1962). The ethnography of speaking. In T. Gladwin & W. Sturtevant (Eds.), *Anthropology and human behavior* (pp. 99–135). Washington, DC: Anthropological Society of Washington.

Hymes, D. (1972). Models of the interaction of language and social life. In J. Gumperz & D. Hymes (Eds.), *Directions in sociolinguistics: The ethnography of communication* (pp. 35–71). New York: Holt, Rinehart & Winston.

Knorr-Cetina, K. (1983). The ethnographic study of scientific work: Towards a constructivist interpretation of science. In K. Knorr-Cetina & M. Mulkay (Eds.), *Science observed: Perspectives on the social study of science* (pp. 109–133). London and Beverly Hills: Sage.

Kuhn, T. (1962). *The structure of scientific revolutions*. Chicago: University of Chicago Press.

Lannamann, J. W. (1992). Deconstructing the person and changing the subject of interpersonal studies. *Communication Theory, 2*, 139–148.

Leeds-Hurwitz, W. (1989). *Communication in everyday life: A social interpretation*. Norwood, NJ: Ablex.

Leeds-Hurwitz, W. (1992). Forum introduction: Social approaches to interpersonal communication. *Communication Theory, 2*, 131–139.

Locke, J. (1690). *Essay concerning human understanding*. London: Elizabeth Holt for Thomas Basset.

Lynch, M., & Woolgar, S. (1988). Introduction: Sociological orientations to representational practice in science. *Human Studies, 11*, 99–116.

McCarthy, T. (1987). General introduction. In K. Baynes, J. Bohman, & T. McCarthy (Eds.), *After philosophy: End or transformation?* (pp. 1–18). Cambridge, MA: MIT Press.

Madison, G. B. (1990). *The hermeneutics of postmodernity: Figures and themes*. Bloomington: Indiana University Press.

Merleau-Ponty, M. (1974). *The phenomenology of perception* (C. Smith, Trans.). London: Routledge & Kegan Paul.

Motley, M. T. (1990). On whether one can(not) not communicate: An examination via traditional communication postulates. *Western Journal of Speech Communication, 54*, 1–20.

O'Keefe, B. J. (1988). The logic of message design: Individual differences in reasoning about communication. *Communication Monographs, 44*, 80–103.

O'Keefe, B. J., & Shepard, G. J. (1987). The pursuit of multiple objectives in face-to-face persuasive interaction: Effects of construct differentiation on message organization. *Communication Monographs, 54,* 346–419.

O'Keefe, B. J., & McCornack, S. A. (1987). Message design logic and message goal structure: Effects on perceptions of message quality in regulative communication situations. *Human Communication Research, 14,* 68–92.

Palmer, R. T. (1969). *Hermeneutics.* Evanston, IL: Northwestern University Press.

Pomerantz, A. M. (1989). Epilogue. *Western Journal of Speech Communication, 53,* 242–246.

Random House College Dictionary (Rev. ed.). (1984). New York: Random House.

Rorty, R. (1979). *Philosophy and the mirror of nature.* Princeton, NJ: Princeton University Press.

Rorty, R. (1991). *Essays on Heidegger and others.* Cambridge: Cambridge University Press.

Saussure, F. de (1983). *Course in general linguistics* (R. Harris, Trans.). LaSalle, IL: Open Court.

Schrag, C. O. (1986). *Communicative praxis and the space of subjectivity.* Bloomington: Indiana University Press.

Schrag, C. O. (1992). *The resources of rationality: A response to the postmodern challenge.* Bloomington: Indiana University Press.

Steier, F. (1991). *Research and reflexivity.* London: Sage.

Stewart, J. (1986). *Dimensions of dialogue in Gadamer's theory and practice.* Paper presented at the Speech Communication Association, Chicago.

Stewart, J. (1991). A postmodern look at traditional communication postulates. *Western Journal of Speech Communication, 55,* 354–379.

Stewart, J. (1994a). Structural implications of the symbol model for communication theory. In R. L. Conville (Ed.), *Uses of "structure" in communication studies* (pp. 125–153). New York: Praeger.

Stewart, J. (1994b). An interpretive approach to validity in interpersonal communication research. In K. Carter & M. Presnell (Eds.), *Interpretive approaches to interpersonal communication* (pp. 45–81). Albany: State University of New York Press.

Stewart, J. (1995). *Language as articulate contact: Toward a post-semiotic philosophy of communication.* Albany: State University of New York Press.

Stewart, J., & Philipsen, G. (1984). Communication as situated accomplishment: The cases of hermeneutics and ethnography. In B. Dervin & M. J. Voigt (Eds.), *Progress in communication sciences, V* (pp. 177–218). Norwood, NJ: Ablex.

Taylor, C. (1985). *Human agency and language: Philosophical papers* (Vol. 1.). New York: Cambridge University Press.

Taylor, C. (1987). Overcoming epistemology. In K. Baynes, J. Bohman, & T. McCarthy (Eds.), *After philosophy: End or transformation?* (pp. 459–488). Cambridge, MA: MIT Press.

Theunissen, M. (1984). *The other: Studies in the social ontology of Husserl, Heidegger, Sartre, and Buber.* Cambridge, MA: MIT Press.

Tibbetts, P. (1988). Representation and the realist–constructivist controversy. *Human Studies, 11,* 117–132.

Warnke, G. (1987). *Gadamer: Hermeneutics, tradition and reason.* Stanford, CA: Stanford University Press.

Wittgenstein, L. (1961). *Tractatus logico-philosophicus.* (D. F. Pears & B. F. McGuiness, Trans.). London: Routledge & Kegan Paul.

Wittgenstein, L. (1963). *Philosophical Investigations.* (G. E. M. Anscombe, Trans.). London: Blackwell.

Part III

Basic Issues

CHAPTER 3

Quantitative versus Qualitative?

JANET BEAVIN BAVELAS

One of the most useful vestiges of my undergraduate education has been an alertness for false dichotomies, that is, for putative opposites such as democracy versus socialism, heredity versus environment, individual versus society. Each of these is, at the very least, likely to be a continuum rather than a dichotomy and is even more likely to be a complex combination of several continua. For example, democracy versus socialism confounds political and economic systems. If we separate the two, we have democracy versus dictatorship and socialism versus capitalism, which create four possible combinations (all of which occur in the modern world). Given especially the prevalence of mixed economies, many more combinations also exist. So much for democracy versus socialism.

The inventor Edwin Land (1962) added to my skepticism about prefabricated choices by suggesting that, when faced with a polarity on which one seems required to choose, there is always the option of thinking orthogonally. That is, rather than being limited to positions along a one-dimensional line, it is possible to cut across it, strike out in another direction, and even create another dimension.

These practical and comfortable old ideas have remained useful, and I admit they shaped my initial reaction to rumblings about quantitative versus qualitative research: Here is another false dichotomy that is best handled by ignoring it and going in a direction completely independent of either side. (Indeed, my primary credentials for writing this chapter are that, over my career, I have been equally criticized from both sides.) It did not take long, however, to realize that it was a mistake to dismiss the issue, because people were taking it very seriously. Soon, I had to admit that, like everything else since I was an undergraduate, this issue had become much more sophisticated and that there had been massive inflation as well. The qualitative-versus-quantitative debate could now be described, not entirely whimsically, as a series of concatenated false dichotomies, having expanded in scale and complexity to the status of (equally false) isomorphisms.

In mathematical logic, an isomorphism is "a one-to-one relation onto the map between two sets, which preserves the relations existing between elements in its domain."[1] For example, the set of all odd numbers can be mapped onto the set of all even numbers because, within each set, the elements have exactly the same relations to each other (namely, an ascending difference of two). The set of quantitative versus qualitative research is usually constructed as consisting of only two elements in a relationship of opposition. Moreover, debates about quantitative and qualitative research have explanded to co-opt several other sets and mapped them onto the original. An example is experimental versus nonexperimental: Quantitative research is experimental, whereas its polar opposite, qualitative research, is nonexperimental (the polar opposite in the new domain).

Another way to visualize this way of thinking is to imagine a child's stacking toy that consists of short rods with a round cup at one end and a square cup at the other. The starting piece is white, its square cup is called quantitative and its round one is called qualitative. Another piece is red; its square cup is called experimental and its round cup is called nonexperimental. If there is a way to stack the red piece smoothly into the white one (like egg cartons), an isomorphism exists. I propose that a lot of people believe that the experimental end of one piece fits smoothly into the quantitative end of the other, and that the nonexperimental cup also fits smoothly into the qualitative cup.

What surprises me is that there are so many proposed isomorphies in the debate over quantitative versus qualitative research. Table 3.1 summarizes 13 domains that have been stacked neatly into the basic quantitative-versus-qualitative piece. The only disagreement is which way the last piece fits: Is it good to be quantitative/experimental/statistical/deductive (etc.) or is it good to be qualitative/nonexperimental/nonstatistical/inductive (etc.)? That is, researchers seem to agree to let themselves be lined up neatly on opposite sides of these dichotomies; they only disagree about which side it is better to be on.

The purpose of this chapter is to suggest that these are all *false* isomorphies, that diverse aspects of a complex process such as research cannot be simplified into a child's stacking toy. These differences are socially constructed, and to the extent that we insist on maintaining them, we will severely limit the number of approaches we can invent to explore

Table 3.1. False Isomorphies

Quantitative research	Qualitative research
Numbers	No numbers
Parametric	Nonparametric
Statistics	No statistics
Empirical	Not empirical
Objective	Subjective
Deductive	Inductive
Hypothesis testing	Exploratory
Experimental	Nonexperimental
Laboratory	Real world
Artificial	Natural
Not generalizable	Generalizable
Internal validity	External validity
Good guys	Bad guys
or	
Bad guys	Good guys

our common interests. A highly restricted choice of methods inevitably stunts the growth of theory as well. On the other hand, if we reject polarization we may discover new, previously unexplored combinations of both approaches. In the following pages, I am going to defer my deconstruction of the obvious distinctions between quantitative and qualitative research (the use of numbers and statistics) until we have examined the other dichotomies listed in Table 3.1; these may be considered less central and defining, but they are equally important in practice.

EMPIRICAL VERSUS NONEMPIRICAL

One of the most extreme isomorphisms can be dealt with quickly. Sometimes a quantitative approach is equated with empirical research whereas qualitative research is treated as nonempirical. It is usually implicitly bad to be nonempirical, but I have also heard quantitative resarch dismissed as "merely" or "trivially" empirical, so (as usual) the good guys–bad guys mapping is open. However, empirical simply means "derived from or guided by experience," which fits any communication researcher from the most dedicated conversation analyst to an equally hard-core multivariate devotee. The alternatives to empirical conclusions are those based on intuition, authority, faith, or some other means of knowing without recourse to data. Clearly, all researchers do empirical research (unless they ignore the data and draw their own conclusions, which unfortunately is not unusual).

OBJECTIVE VERSUS SUBJECTIVE

An initially more plausible mapping characterizes quantitative research as objective and qualitative research as subjective. This isomorphism suggests that the two kinds of researchers deal in inherently different kinds of data or at least take dramatically different stances toward their data (e.g., detached vs. interpretive). The question is whether there are ever any inherently objective data.

In a research context, the best working definition of objective is *intersubjective agreement*. All measurement is subjective in the sense of requiring some human inference; even reading the weight on a scale is a human perceptual and cognitive operation. Reading a weight or (more relevant here) which number someone chose on a rating scale is a subjective operation, albeit one that is very likely to yield the same result regardless of who does the reading. Many people would call these objective data because of presumed intersubjective agreement, but to do so creates a misleading dividing line by imposing a dichotomy onto a continuum.

A more accurate approach would be to examine the degree of agreement. Measurements on which people cannot agree well might be called subjective; I would prefer simply to call them unreliable. If we take this approach, there are a couple of surprises waiting. First, objectivity is usually equated with physical, noninferential measures, yet in my experience these are not the most likely to yield high agreement. For example, Ekman and Friesen's (1976, 1978) Facial Action Coding System is purely physical, describing various muscle groups in the face rather than their meaning. Interrater reliability for these "objective" descriptions is often quite low. In contrast, our research group always analyzes the *meaning* of the communicative act, and our reliabilities are consistently high. For example, Chovil (1991/1992) developed a highly reliable system that captured the meaning of each facial display (e.g., as portraying someone else's reaction or as looking quizzical). Coates (1994) assessed the meaning of the entire communicative act at the moment (verbal and nonverbal) and whether this was a mock or serious meaning, again with good intersubjective agreement. I believe that high reliabilities for phenomena that are usually eschewed as subjective are possible because analysts are people who, in their ordinary daily interactions, respond to the meaning of their interlocutors' acts rather than to the physical components. Thus, what is usually considered subjective is quite natural for us; what is presumed to be objective is often quite unnatural. To capture this knowledge is admittedly more work than creating a 7-point scale but well worth the investment.

A second surprise is the benefit of pursuing high intersubjective agreement. There are many qualitative researchers who would be insulted if someone asked whether others could interpret their data in the same way as they do. This attitude can imply that intersubjective reliability is only for trivial phenomena and that complex and interesting phenomena do not lend themselves to such mechanical approaches. In contrast, we have found that trying to explicate what we are seeing or hearing is a goal worth having. When analyzing communication, we are each isolated individuals. Some may take pride in their apparently unique ability to interpret what others do not notice, but I suspect that they, too, have the occasional nagging fear that what they interpret is not really there. Facing this fear by asking others to analyze the same data can lead to the euphoric discovery that others can in fact see it as well. Every time we achieve high intersubjective agreement in our research, we feel a profound sense of intellectual confirmation. In addition to the personal payoff, there is a more concrete reward for seeking inter-subjective agreement: To do so requires a set of written, highly explicit rules of interpretation, which cover all possible instances and problems (Coates, 1993). These guidelines are themselves an outcome of the research and constitute an important part of the subsequent research report, that is, *exactly* what the authors mean by the phenomenon. In our experience, abandoning our comfortable but vague intuitive judgments in favor of a set of rules often results in better analyses; newcomers applying our rules and unemcumbered by our preconceptions can do a better job than we did.

INDUCTIVE VERSUS DEDUCTIVE

One of the most misunderstood notions in social science research is the aristocratic ideal of formal deductive research, which conjures an image of a highly sophisticated intellectual (obviously a quantitative type) who has such a grand theory of communicative phenomena that he or she can easily spin off predictions about how people will behave. In contrast, the pedestrian, lower-class inductive researcher rummages around in the detritus, trying to come up with something that will never achieve the urbane generality of the deductivist's theory. The radical inductivist takes pride in being a street person, dealing with day-to-day reality far from the ivory tower.

As usual, the dictionary destroys this constructed contrast by showing that neither term fits what we do:

Deductive and inductive refer to two distinct logical processes. *Deductive reasoning* is a logical process in which a conclusion drawn from a set of premises contains no more information than the premises taken collectively. All dogs are animals; this is a dog; therefore, this is an animal: The truth of the conclusion is dependent only on the method. All men are apes; this is a man; therefore, this is an ape: The conclusion is logically true, even though the premise is absurd.

Who would want to play such silly games? No empirical researcher uses deductive reasoning in this way, much less relies on it entirely, because the data play no role at all.

Inductive reasoning is a logical process in which a conclusion is proposed that contains more information than the observations or experience on which it is based. Every crow ever seen was black; all crows are black: The truth of the conclusion is verifiable only in terms of future experience and certainty is attainable only if all possible instances have been examined. In the example, there is no certainty that a white crow will not be found tomorrow, although past experience would make such an occurrence seem unlikely.

This process is somewhat closer to empirical research in that it includes actual data, some reasoning to and from the data, and especially the inevitable amount of uncertainty. But it is not all that we do.

What the dichotomy misses is that virtually all researchers engage in a *sequential process* that includes aspects of both forms of reasoning at various points. We get an idea inductively, usually from our own observations or from reading the literature (i.e., others' observations), and then apply deduction: If my hunch is correct, I should see more supporting instances in my data, or if my theory is correct, I should be able to predict the outcome of a formal study. If we are wrong or if new possibilities emerge from the data, we construct a new hypothesis (inductively) and go on to deduce how to tell whether this new idea works better, and so forth. This common process is obscured by the fixed deductive format of the research article. Students often think that the way published research results are presented is the way (and the only way) they are obtained (Bavelas, 1987). More experienced researchers know better but may still act as if the way they report the results is also how they got to them.

HYPOTHESIS TESTING VERSUS EXPLORATORY RESEARCH

Closely related to the deductive-versus-inductive dichotomy is another construction that divides (in one view) the elite hypothesis testers from the mere triflers, who are perhaps too intellectually limited or too cowardly to scale the heights and play for big stakes. Or, seen from the other side, the intellects of hypothesis testers are, if not actually in rigor mortis, at least severely anal retentive: Hypothesis testers are permanently imprisoned inside their own paradigms, whereas the explorers go boldly (and qualitatively) where no one has gone before. Obviously, if we again reject class systems and look at the *process* of any particular research project, these stereotypes quickly stop working.

For example, the moment a quantitative, hypothesis testing researcher adds more variables than he or she has clear and firm hypotheses to cover, the research becomes exploratory. Given the current popularity of multivariate research, this approach is rapidly becoming the norm. The exploration is done by the statistic of choice rather than by the researcher, but it is just as preliminary and subject to confirmation as any other exploratory approach. Classical hypothesis testing research should have few variables and simple statistics, sometimes just a single one-tailed test.

Researchers who identify themselves as qualitative often do not recognize the important role hypothesis testing plays in their analyses. They probably start with hypotheses about a certain kind of data being particularly rich, or about their method being more appropriate than others. And, fortunately, they cannot avoid hypotheses about what they begin to find. Inductive researchers do not simply describe the data; they move from specific instances to some level of generality that subsumes these instances. There is a very exciting point in such research when one begins to see a pattern and looks eagerly to find out whether it will hold up. This is hypothesis testing of a kind that needs to be legitimized as a valuable tool but also honed to remove some of its potential defects.

EXPERIMENTAL VERSUS NONEXPERIMENTAL

No self-respecting qualitative researcher would even fantasize about an experiment, much less consciously commit one. Yet the generic meaning of experiment is very inclusive: "A test, trial, or tentative procedure; an act or operation for the purpose of discovering something unknown or of testing a principle, supposition, etc."

This definition reveals a common root with the simple term "experience" and requires only that we try something out, with or without hypothesis, whether to explore or to test. The degree of formality is not prescribed.

In scientific parlance, the *true experiment* is formally defined by its purpose and method. The purpose of a true experiment is to seek information about causality; the method is random assignment of sub-

jects to conditions that have been created ("manipulated") by the experimenter, which is only possible with certain kinds of data. Nothing in the
definition of a true experiment requires that the independent or dependent variable have to be quantitative. Actually, experimental conditions are
usually qualitative categories, and the outcome can also be categorical or
frequency data. That is, the experimenter is free to ask not only "how
much" something happened but, alternatively, "how often," "whether,"
or "what sort." For example, we (Bavelas, Black, Lemery, & Mullet, 1986)
varied experimentally whether eye contact occurred or not and measured
the pattern of facial expression that resulted. Thus, both the independent
and dependent variables were qualitative.

A great deal of communication research is quasi-experimental in that
the key variable is neither manipulated nor manipulable (e.g., friendship,
gender, marital status, or any other personal characteristic). Although
these designs can be very good and can approximate a true experiment,
they are technically not experiments, especially if we insist on an experimental–nonexperimental dichotomy. Moreover, "nonexperimental" includes a lot of methodological territory, such as correlational, observational, archival, or case studies. The answer, obviously, is not to
dichotomize but rather to talk about kinds of control or intervention and
consequent degrees of causal inference that can be made. If the goal is
not causal inference, or if the phenomenon of interest is not amenable to
experimentation, nonexperimental work is the better choice. If the goal
is to get from point A to point B as fast as possible and a highway exists,
a car is the best option. But if the goal is more leisurely, or if the terrain
is rough and roadless, hiking may be a better choice.

Even a true experiment does not exist simply because the researcher
intended to conduct one. I see a surprising number of supposed experiments where (if one reads the procedure section carefully) subjects were
not actually randomly assigned or where the conditions differed in more
ways than the level of the independent variable. These are not true
experiments but failed experiments; they cannot serve their purpose and
can only mislead us about causality.

THE LAB VERSUS THE REAL WORLD; ARTIFICIAL VERSUS NATURAL DATA

After years of hearing people talk about the "real world," I think I have
finally located it: It is anywhere off a university campus, as far as possible
from a research laboratory (where the world is presumably not real). As
a keen science fiction fan, I only wish it were true that the lab is not the
real world. It would be wonderful to encounter unreal worlds just by

conducting experiments. I keep peeking hopefully into our lab, but it remains just a pleasant, well-equipped room with no paranormal properties. Our lab is different from (and I behave differently in) my office, my kitchen, a movie theater, or the nearby park. But these places are also different from each other, and I behave differently in each of them as well. So which of them is the *real* real world?

The pastoral variation on this theme is to bless all research outside the lab with the label "natural"—or with the more common but questionably derived term "naturalistic." In contrast, lab/experimental/quantitative research, and indeed any behavior that occurs in the presence of an experimental psychologist, is characterized as "artificial" (though only in the negative senses of that term, i.e., not acknowledging its origin as "created by art"). The radical eco-methodological view is that *any* observation renders data artificial or even not real. It is ironic to hear this position supported by a lofty appeal to experimental (lab) physics via the Heisenberg principle, a demonstrably spurious and false analogy (Bavelas, 1984).

Critics of lab research have raised valid questions about the experimentalists' implicit assumption that the behaviors they study somehow occur in a sterile vacuum, unaffected by the messy contexts of everyday life. But the key point of the criticism surely must be that *all* behavior is situationally grounded, that there is always a context that affects behavior, and that context can be hidden but not eliminated by being held constant. It is therefore completely inconsistent to imply that all nonlaboratory behavior has the special quality of being real and natural by virtue of occurring outside the lab. The logical consequence of these critical questions would be to pursue the specifics of how different contexts affect different behaviors, not to propose that some contexts for behavior are real and others are artificial. I know of few people pursuing these questions.

GENERALIZABLE VERSUS NOT GENERALIZABLE

The concept of generalizability can be a more useful way of posing the above questions than is a prejudgment about the physical location of the research. Generalizable conclusions come from a proper sample of a defined population of people, settings, and events—an ideal virtually no researcher achieves. Our question is usually: to which other people/settings/events are my ad hoc results generalizable? Notice that I ask "to which" rather than "whether" the results will generalize or "how much" they might. We cannot sensibly ask whether or not results will generalize because generalizability is not a single property of research, a sort of one-size-fits-all quality that some studies have and others do not. It is probably not even a quantitative ("how much") continuum, although this is often implied, ironically, by qualitative researchers who argue that their results are "more generalizable" than other kinds of data. Such statements imply that the researcher has systematically inventoried all people/settings/events, created a dimension that ranges from "like few others" to "like most others," and has a method by which particular configurations of people/settings/events can be validly placed on this dimension. A more modest and realistic approach is to consider closely the features of the data one is committed to studying: In what concrete and abstract ways are these data like data in which other other settings?

INTERNAL VERSUS EXTERNAL VALIDITY

The final variation on this particular theme is the claim that quantitative research maximizes internal validity whereas qualitative research maximizes external validity. The implication that we can pursue quite different goals in different studies is a useful one (and even better if we are open-minded about which goals other people are pursuing).

If a study has, because of the above analysis of its generalizability, some claim to being similar to something else, it has some degree of external validity. However, any researcher is entitled to be indifferent to this goal if he or she has a different passion. Some of us can be quite taken from time to time with the links between events that are usually put under the stuffy rubric of *causality*. The measure of understanding we achieve in these efforts is often called internal validity. In my view, discussions of internal validity are usually far too narrow and puritanical, aimed mainly at showing us how hopeless it is to aspire to demonstrate that X causes Y. This narrow focus neglects all the other fuzzy and interesting relationships between X and Y that we might wish to explore, such as "somehow leads to," "accompanies," "precludes," "mutually influences," and so forth. Some students in my research methods courses are invariably distressed when I explain these two kinds of validity and propose that they cannot pursue both in a single study—unless that single study is going to be the only one they do in their life. Realistically, they must choose a priority and pursue it, conceding weakness in the other area. In any case, whenever one of these two broad goals dominates my research, I find the rewards and demands far too great to permit any time for disparaging those who pursue other goals.

NUMBERS VERSUS NO NUMBERS

Finally, the obvious and accepted distinction between quantitative and qualitative research is that quantitative researchers seek, use, and even worship numbers, whereas qualitative researchers avoid them and may treat them as unholy.

This debate is an old one. Many quantitative researchers agree with the scornful opinion of William Thomson (Lord Kelvin), the English physicist and mathematician:

> When you can measure what you are speaking about, and express it in numbers, you know something about it; but when you cannot measure it, when you cannot express it in numbers, your knowledge is of a meager and unsatisfactory kind; it may be the beginning of knowledge, but you have scarcely, in your thoughts, advanced to the stage of *science*. (Thomson, 1891–1894, cited in *Bartlett's Familiar Quotations*, 1968, p. 723)

George Miller (1962), one of the pioneers of mathematical psychology and of applications of information theory to human communication, had his own view of Lord Kelvin's dictum:

> In truth, a good case could be made that if your knowledge is meager and unsatisfactory, the last thing in the world you should do is to make measurements. The chance is negligible that you will measure the right things accidentally. Nevertheless, many social and behavioral scientists, assured that measurement is the touchstone of scientific respectability, have rushed out to seek numbers before they knew what the numbers would mean. (p. 79)

Thus, we might ask whether it is "unquantitative" to use meaningless numbers—unreliable, invalid, questionable, or superficial numbers. If so, a lot of quantitative research is in big trouble.

To give equal time to criticism of both sides, we might also ask whether it matters how many numbers one uses, whether more and more numbers are less and less qualitative. If so, quantitative–qualitative would become a quantitatively defined continuum, which hardly seems fair. The alternative, purist approach is to treat even the slightest hint of quantity as an impurity. This dichotomy would require that all words such as "many," "often," "several," "usually," and so on, be expunged from the word processors of qualitative researchers. One can hardly argue that these terms are acceptable because they are used loosely, with no attempt at precision.

PARAMETRIC VERSUS NOMINAL MEASUREMENT

A more sophisticated distinction than the simple numbers–no numbers dichotomy is between different levels of measurement (i.e., nominal, ordinal, interval, and ratio) (Stevens, 1946). Note that the term "levels" and the order in which these four kinds of measurement are always introduced make it clear (to quantitative researchers) that this is an evolutionary scale. One emerges from the swamp of nominal measurement and struggles toward the pinnacle of evolution, a ratio scale. In this view, nominal measurers are not yet *Homo sapiens*; they are Lord Kelvin's poor beknighted protoscientists.

Qualitative researchers would probably order the levels in the opposite direction, on a moral dimension. The identification and discovery of new kinds of phenomena are their ultimate goals. Qualitative researchers see nominal description as "natural" for communicative phenomena, and their reaction to Arabic numerals (other than as page numbers) resembles the impassioned prejudice of the Crusaders. To convert their categories into numbers is heresy; ratio and interval scales are a descent into the "black arts."

Seldom in this debate does a simple question arise: Which kind of measurement best captures what the researcher wants to know? I would give absolute primacy to the researcher's immediate goals and to the data he or she is working with, rather than to membership in a particular school of numbers. Two illustrations from our team's research may be useful.

In our work on equivocation (e.g., Bavelas, Black, Chovil, & Mullett, 1990), we began like earlier observers who had described the phenomenon categorically—a message was clear or not; it was evasive or not. However, when we began collecting such messages systematically, nominal measurement alone became unsatisfactory because these fascinating messages clearly varied among themselves in both degree and kind. To draw an arbitrary line would be to continue to construct a two-dimensional world of good and bad messages, ignoring the very subtlety we were interested in. Therefore, we used both quantitative and qualitative approaches to the same messages. The reactions to our hybrid approach were puzzling: One communication journal cut out our qualitative analyses and would publish only the tables of numbers. Another communication journal published a review that was scathing about our use of numbers.

Our measurement of motor mimicry (e.g., wincing at someone else's injury) (Bavelas, et al., 1986) went in another direction. In our experiments, people did not react in degrees of motor mimicry; rather they displayed *patterns* of increase, decrease, or no change. Therefore, in this experimental, hypothesis-testing lab study, our measurement was strictly nominal because trying to make it otherwise would have been inappropriate to the phenomenon.

STATISTICS VERSUS NO STATISTICS

The fastest way to identify an author as quantitative or qualitative is to rifle the pages rapidly under your thumb looking for statistical tables (vs. transcripts). Depending on your preference, you can then decide whether to read the article or not. This is an excellent way to avoid being influenced by new ideas.

To deconstruct this difference, recall that there are the two broad kinds of statistics, *descriptive* and *inferential*. Descriptive statistics are used for data reduction (e.g., I tell my class their average on the midterm rather than reading all the individual marks out to them). One may then go on to inferential statistics, which recognize and assess the possibility of chance outcomes (e.g., whether women really did better than men on the midterm). Let us consider each of these in turn.

If the essence of statistics is data reduction, a great deal of quantitative analysis is nonstatistical because it generates *more* rather than fewer numbers. (One of my students, originally trained in this tradition, was worried that she did not have "enough" tables after her planned, simple analysis.) In contrast, most qualitative research definitely does achieve data reduction: Any transcription is selective and reduces the original conversations to a new form. The author's summary of the process or phenomenon discovered in these transcripts is another bite of the apple.

Clearly, quantitative researchers use inferential statistics, often lots of them. Tables and tables of inferential statistics actually create the paradox of *increasing* the probability of chance conclusions: Without appropriate protection of alpha levels and especially without replication of findings, the more inferential statistical analysis the researcher conducts, the greater the possibility of spurious findings. Equally clearly, one will never find a p-value in a qualitative research paper. However, one does find another p-word, *patterns* in the data, that is, descriptions of events that are interesting precisely because they seem systematic (nonrandom).

At this point, the reader may feel I am playing a shell game, but I am not sure where the peanut is either. It does appear that, in many instances, quantitative research achieves less data reduction and a less accurate assessment of the role of chance than does qualitative research.

This confusion is an appropriate note on which to end, because my goal has been to shake up all the neatly aligned pieces and let them fall in new combinations. Even better, imagine letting your data find their own best fit. In my view, all of us should focus on empirical data, aim for nontrivial objectivity, and make thoughtful choices about numbers and other possibilities: Is it time more for exploration or for hypothesis testing? *Which* real world is of interest? Is an experiment desirable or appropriate? How much generalization is possible? All these should be dictated by respect for the phenomenon and the state of our knowledge about it.

NOTE

1. Unless otherwise indicated, all definitions are from the second edition of the *Random House Dictionary* (1993).

REFERENCES

Bartlett, J. (1968). *Bartlett's familiar quotations* (14th ed., E. M. Beck, Ed.). Boston: Little, Brown.

Bavelas, J. B. (1984). On "naturalistic" family research. *Family Process, 23,* 337–341.

Bavelas, J. B. (1987). Permitting creativity in science. In D. N. Jackson & J. P. Rushton (Eds.), *Scientific excellence: Origins and assessment* (pp. 307–327). Beverly Hills, CA: Sage.

Bavelas, J. B., Black, A., Chovil, N., & Mullett, J. (1990). *Equivocal communication.* Newbury Park, CA: Sage.

Bavelas, J. B., Black, A., Lemery, C. R., & Mullett, J. (1986). "I *show* how you feel": Motor mimicry as a communicative act. *Journal of Personality and Social Psychology, 50,* 322–329.

Chovil, N. (1991/1992). Discourse-oriented facial displays in conversation. *Research on Language and Social Interaction, 25,* 163–194.

Coates, L. (1993). *Methods for developing scoring systems and calculating reliability in discourse analysis.* Unpublished manuscript, University of Victoria, Victoria, British Columbia, Canada.

Coates, L. (1994). *"Just Kidding." Spontaneous ironic humour in dialogue.* Unpublished manuscript, University of Victoria, Victoria, British Columbia, Canada.

Ekman, P., & Friesen, W. V. (1976). Measuring facial movement. *Journal of Environmental Psychology and Nonverbal Behavior, 1,* 56–75.

Ekman, P., & Friesen, W. V. (1978). *The Facial Action Coding System: A technique for the measurement of facial movement.* Palo Alto, CA: Consulting Psychologists Press.

Land, E. H. (1962). Unpublished commencement address, Stanford University.

Miller, G. A. (1962). *Psychology: The study of mental life.* New York: Harper & Row.

Random House unabridged dictionary (2nd ed.). (1993). New York: Random House.

Stevens, S. S. (1946). On the theory of scales of measurement. *Science, 103,* 677–680.

CHAPTER 4

Reflexivity, Interpersonal Communication, and Interpersonal Communication Research

FREDERICK STEIER

REFLEXIVITY AND INTERPERSONAL COMMUNICATION

Origins and Shepherding

A shepherd's staff, or crook, is distinguished by its bowed shape, curving, as it does, back onto itself. As Siegle (1986) notes, the Romans, focusing on that shape as a key feature of the shepherd's crook, took the Greek word for crook and adopted it to refer to the shape itself, the bowing, or curving back onto itself. It was the form that they admired, the "flex," or later, "flecto." Siegle continues by pointing out that the "re," added to form *reflex*, was thus a redundancy that nevertheless served to emphasize the recursive nature of a process of bending back onto a self. What is often lost in translation is that the idea of reflexivity has its origins in referring not to a thing but to a pattern—in particular, a pattern that is embedded in a relationship. (It is interesting to note that the shepherd's crook was itself embedded in the "shepherding" process of closing a circle, albeit a loosely defined one, through which a flock of sheep maintained its "flockness.") Reflexivity, thus meaning a bending back onto a self, can encompass many diverse processes, depending on what manner of connection, or relationship, is accomplishing the bending back. The relationship can be one of "pointing" or "referring," which we often associate with reflexivity, but it can also be one of "applying to" or "experiencing" (as Mead, 1962, has noted).

Indeed, mathematicians, in particular, algebraists, define a relationship as being reflexive if, within a set, a member of that set stands in that relationship to itself, for all members of that set (cf. Birkhoff & MacLane, 1968). In other words, a relationship such as "equals" is reflexive if we can say that a number equals itself, for a given group of numbers. As this is usually the case, we say that equality is a reflexive relationship. "Less than," on the other hand, is ordinarily not reflexive since a number is not less than itself. Extending this definition of reflexivity to social relationships, we can see that, at least for the Internal Revenue Service, "is a dependent of" can be a reflexive relationship whereas "is the mother of" is not. In the world of social processes, "agrees with" can be a reflexive relationship, whereas "speaks after," in the sense of turn taking, ordinarily is not, depending, however, on how one defines the elements that define a turn. For intrapersonal communication researchers, "communicates with" is clearly a reflexive relationship.

What is critical here is that reflexivity is a property of a relationship and not of the individuals. Further, reflexivity, as a relationship, is tied to a particular context and not a property of that relationship apart from that context. Reflexivity is thus relational-in-a-context.

It would seem as though a recognition of reflexive relationships and processes would be an important topic for communication researchers, given the concern of communication with connections and relationships. Yet, it has been a rather problematic topic. Indeed, Wittgenstein (1968) referred to reflexivity as a concept with blurred edges. Reflexive relationships have posed difficulties in communication processes, and for the most part, these difficulties have been dealt with either by admiring the problem as a problem (as is often the case with the recognition of logical paradoxes) or by attempting to create a world in which reflexivity is seen as irrelevant. Although the relationships that create concerns with reflexivity are different in different interpersonal domains, there are similar process issues that cut across these domains.

A key behind the difficulties is that inherent in any bending back onto a self, a circuit is completed. A circularity results, and we, at least we in the West, immersed in conversations of linearity, do not have comfortable ways to deal with circularities. One form of circularity that has been particularly problematic results from what might be called a logico-linguistic relationship of self-reference—that is, statements that refer to themselves.

Self-Reference

Ever since the Cretan Epimenides noted that "all Cretans are liars," self-reference has plagued those who look to language as referring to (rather than, for example, constituting) an external world. Indeed, it was particularly with regard to these kinds of statements and their ensuing paradoxes that Wittgenstein referred to reflexivity as a concept with blurred edges. For if the statement "All Cretans are liars" is true, Epimenides is telling the truth, which makes the statement false. If it is false, Epimenides is lying, which makes the statement true. And so on. One description of the problem is that we have a statement that is doing two things at the same time—it is about other statements (i.e., about a world apart from itself) but is simultaneously about itself, as it is being said by a member of the group being described. Recognizing the difficulty, Bertrand Russell tried to "ban" the making of statements about themselves, or being a member of their own class, as a way to deal with the potential for seemingly irresolvable paradoxes. Yet others (cf. Herbst, 1987) have noted that we cannot really ban these self-referential statements since, after all, we can actually make them (and need a way to deal with them). Further, their recognition can point to the frameworks that we put around situations that make them paradoxical.

Indeed, Spencer-Brown (1979) and Herbst (1976) have developed logics centered on the necessity of self-reference. In particular, Herbst has developed what he refers to as a behavioral, or, later, contextual logic (Herbst, 1987, 1993; Rasmussen, 1987). Their logics recognize that in seeing self-reference solely as a problem rooted in paradox, we make the assumption that our statements are exclusively about an observer-independent world, and hence are strictly other-referential. If we relax this assumption, we recognize that we construct the worlds in which we live. Further, this constructing process, rooted in language, is a social one (cf. Gergen, 1985; Shotter, 1984), with our statements referring not to a "ready-made" external world but back to our constructing processes. Austin (1975), in developing the concept of speech acts, pointed us in that direction when he noted that with words, we may often be performing those acts as we speak them rather than describing an independent world. His "performatives," such as a minister stating to a couple (in a socially satisfactory setting), "I now pronounce you man and wife," are self-referential but do not pretend to be strictly about a world other than the one they are creating.

The paradox inherent in some notions of self-reference derives from the idea that our statements refer to an independent world and thus have a truth value based on their "correspondence" to that world. Austin has shown this not to be the case. Further, this truth value is rooted in an either–or logic (something is either true or false), which itself is "true" only if we insist on and agree to this assumption. Spencer-Brown's and Herbst's logics do not; instead, they permit oscillating and/or contextual truths. Thus self-reference, as a kind of reflexivity, is problematic only if we insist on staying within an unquestioned frame, instead of recognizing its liberating or creative quality of pointing to the frame itself so that it may be changed.

Self-Reference in Everyday Life

At the 1983 meeting of the American Society for Cybernetics, there were several sessions focusing on the issue of self-reference. Given the central-ity of the notion of circularity and issues of closure and openness to cybernetics, this was not surprising. As chair of the 1984 meeting, I spent much of the conference reflecting on the various emerging themes, trying to parlay them into a snappy title for that 1984 meeting. At one point, during a session on self-reference and reflexivity, Ranulph Glan-ville, a British architect and something of an authority on the issue, stated that, to him, *everything* was paradoxical—we just did not consider how statements point to or close on themselves. (A relevant question here would be whether his statement itself was thus also paradoxical, and what would that mean?) Later, after settling on a choice of the conference theme for 1984, "Autonomy, Intervention and Dependence," I related this choice to him, noting proudly its potentially paradoxical quality, which I felt would force us to deal more seriously with issues of autonomy. Much to my surprise, Ranulph looked at me quizzically and said that he did not see anything paradoxical in that title.

Now how was sense to be made of this interaction? Here is an authority stating that everything is paradoxical but yet our title is not. After some initial consternation, I decided that I did not have to assume that Ranulph was lying in either case, but yet there was no contradiction there. He was simply "being Ranulph," which meant being provocative in relationships. My relationship to him permitted that reframing, indeed, encouraged it, while simultaneously encouraging me to take his comments seriously (and he, mine). Thus, his statements, both self-referential and contradictory within a universal two-valued logical system, lose their paradoxical quality when understood as being about our context-bound relationship.

As we move from questions about whether "'everything is paradoxical' refers to itself," to being in a conversation where "everything is paradoxical" and "this is not paradoxical" are both "not false," we also have moved from a one-step loop (something referring directly to itself) to a two-step loop (something referring to something else that refers back—a mutual self-ref-erence). This distinction becomes critical, as we shall see shortly, when acknowledging, as we must, the content *and* relationship (or, report and command [Bateson, 1968]) aspects of all messages.

We could imagine that a resolution of the Ranulph paradox is my feeling that what he is "really" saying is, "I always contradict myself."

Interestingly, this statement in itself, if taken literally, is also paradoxical. Yet it did not pose a problem for me and for Ranulph (and would not, I suspect, for others). Literalness is itself a context within which participants in a conversation may choose to operate, but it is only one such context.

Thus, many "literal" paradoxes are not problematic in everyday life simply because in that interpersonal relationship, we do not assume, at some level, statements to self-refer. "I contradict myself" is thus often taken to exclude the statement itself. Indeed, as Lawson (1985) notes, an insistence on a frame of the literalness of self-reference can appear "irritatingly pedantic" (p. 17) and the interactor who insists on such a frame unnecessarily legalistic. Thus, all statements of and involving self-reference (including this one) require a social setting within which they may be interpreted as such. It is my contention here that it is not the presence of reflexivity in the form of self-reference that is a problem, but rather it is the lack of reflexivity. More specifically, the problem is a lack of awareness, on the relational level, of how statements that assume a frame point back to the framing and the framers. Such lack of reflexivity can indeed have severe consequences in interpersonal relationships.

Self-Reference and Interpersonal Relationships

In my relationship with Ranulph, a new frame for understanding was proposed, even if implicitly, and accepted. Yet there are many situations in which those who are faced with the task of responding to self-referential, potentially paradoxical messages do not have the ability to comment on or change the frame within which those "paradoxes" are indeed paradoxical. The recognition of the double-bind situation (Bateson, Jackson, Haley, & Weakland, 1956) is such a case. Here, Bateson et al. offered insight into, for example, how the behavior of a person labeled "schizophrenic" might make "sense" if understood in a system riddled with paradoxes, with no available way out of that system. Bateson et al. relied on the recognition that although content and relationship aspects of messages (or, in his terms, report and command) mutually frame each other, the nonverbal cues that may form the core of a relationship aspect may contradict the verbal content. The frame created by the relational aspect negates or disqualifies the "usual" meaning of the content. A supervisor rolling her eyes while saying "nice work" to a supervisee and a father sneering while saying "I love you" to a child can be examples. In a history of interaction where one is hierarchically subjected to the authority of another, being placed in such a situation and not being able or allowed to comment on that situation can be paralyzing. Self-reference in these situations takes on the qualities of a "vicious circle." These vicious circles are, in a sense, examples of two-step self-reference, where the relationship aspect of a message in the form of a frame refers to the content which refers back to the frame (but contradicts it, having been referred to in this particular way). Thus, we have an illustration of how self-reference can be problematic in everyday life.

Yet it is not the literalness of logical self-reference that makes this situation so difficult for those immersed in it. Indeed, it is this issue that was at the heart of the "pragmatics of communication" (Watzlawick, Beavin, & Jackson, 1967). Another view of the difficulty rests on the power relationships of authority and submission of those who do not look at the frames they have created for those stuck in the vicious circle. A question emerges of whose interests are served, and what systems are maintained, by those relationships that disqualify metacommunicative statements about frames that may be problematic to at least one of the participants in a relationship.

Extending and modifying this work, Cronen, Johnson, and Lannamann (1982) point out that it is not reflexivity in the form of self-reference that is itself the problem. They note that many two-step self-referential sequences do not appear as problematic, vicious circles (or "strange" loops) but as positive, or "charmed," loops. What is critical is that both strange and charmed loops are self-referential. Cronen et al. (1982) posit that the distinction between them rests on an understanding of transitivity, by which they mean "whether one social perception can reasonably be the context for another perception" (p. 100). When two levels of meaning, each of which may be the frame for an interpretation or construction of meaning of the other, contradict, they can be said to have an intransitive relationship. Cronen et al. go on to propose that it is the intransitivity at the core of these mutual, or two-step, self-referencing statements, that is a problem—not the self-referencing. Intransitivity of mutually referring messages, whether verbal or nonverbal, can result in mutually exclusive interpretations, which can, in turn, affect the relationship between the participants as a whole. A key for them is how to transform, through a relational reframing, strange loops into charmed loops. This reframing may involve a mutual awareness of intransitivities at the heart of the participants' self-referencing meaning–constructing processes and an ability to act on that awareness. Interestingly, it is this kind of awareness of self-reference in relationships that was the basis for the work of Laing, Phillipson, and Lee (1966) in the development of their interpersonal perception method. Their concern was with metacognition and relational perception in interpersonal relationships—that is, the understanding of the experience of selves and others in relationships. What we have is a shift from reflexivity as a problem tied to an insistence on a univalued truth to a problem rooted in the authority of those defining the frames within which those truths are true, often disqualifying the self-experience of an other in a relationship.

Self-Experience

G. H. Mead (1962) noted that "it is by means of reflexiveness—the turning-back of experience of the individual upon himself—that the whole social process is thus brought into the experience of the individuals involved in it" (p. 134). Reflexivity is then moved to a domain of experience, where experience is a social process, for Mead goes on to note that reflexiveness is "the essential condition, within the social process, for the development of mind" (p. 134). (We can note a similar reflexive-based and yet social and ecological concept of mind in Bateson, 1972a). In building on Mead's work to link reflexivity as self-experience to concerns of semiotics, Babcock (1980) claims that "all collective representations or systems of signification are reflexive" (p. 4). Although at first glance this might seem, without a social understanding of a self, to promote a world of narcissism, Babcock notes that, paradoxically, the tragedy of Narcissus was that he was not narcissistic enough—"he is conscious of himself as an other, but he is not conscious of being self-conscious of himself as an other" (p. 2).

This social form of turning inward is at the heart of a shift from a modern to a postmodern identity (Gergen, 1991). Indeed, Taylor (1989) marks this distinction as one between, in his terms, taking a reflexive stance (as found in injunctions such as "take care of yourself") and taking a radically reflexive stance. In the latter, he focuses on the "way the world is *for* us" (p. 130) and our own agency in creating meaning of and in our worlds. Radical reflexivity, as Taylor notes, offers a stark contrast to the "view from nowhere" offered by nonradically reflexive science. This latter concern will have tremendous import, in the next section, on the self-experience of interpersonal communication researchers whose findings are densely connected to their "research relationships," becoming views from an often unacknowledged "somewhere."

REFLEXIVITY AND INTERPERSONAL COMMUNICATION RESEARCH

Self-Applicability

Whereas "problems" of reflexivity in interpersonal relationships have been shown to be tied to an externalization of "truth," or of authority, an extension to reflexivity in the form of self-applicability is problematic when a speaker/researcher denies responsibility for his or her observations.

Leeds-Hurwitz (Chapter 1, this volume) raises the issue of reflexivity as a key in the development of social approaches to interpersonal communication. We have seen thus far that much of what are typically seen as logical problems in reflexivity, including self-reference, look rather different when viewed from a social and relational perspective. Indeed, we have seen that reflexivity need not be a problem in everyday life, but, rather, its absence can be. Yet there are other implications of reflexivity in understanding interpersonal communication, and these are not trivial implications. They pertain to the activities of those of us engaged in doing interpersonal communication research, and, in particular, an awareness that the interpersonal situations we study should rest on a radical contextualization of any "findings" in terms of the frames through which such findings are created. These frames, rather than being unseen or unfelt background, necessarily include the processes by which *we* generate any findings. *These processes are themselves interpersonal communication situations.* Moreover, they are themselves researchable issues. In bringing reflexivity to the domain of interpersonal communication research, the very idea of reflexivity (as a turning back of one's experience upon oneself) can be understood as the very pointing action linked in languaging (Maturana, 1987) to social interpretive processes.

And yet, as Potter and Wetherell (1987), in their work on discourse, and Steier (1991a) have noted, reflexivity can emerge as a concern in communication research in many ways. First, there can be, as at the core of Garfinkel's (1967) ethnomethodology and the conversational analysis that developed from it, a reflexivity in the sense of talk or conversation being both about situations and part of those very situations. Much of the earlier part of this chapter deals with a recognition of reflexivities of this kind. Second, reflexivity can emerge as a concern with how research about communication, or indeed, about anything or any process, gets produced. This concern centers on the recognition that what gets reported as "fact" (cf. Fleck, 1979) is subject to scrutiny with regard to those very processes that allow those facts to emerge as such, whether in the field or in the scientific laboratory. For example, scientists are accountable (to other scientists as well as to themselves and, it is hoped, to a "larger community"), for the communication processes through which science gets done, and which traditionally are left hidden from research reports. These latter issues have come to form the core of research programs in the sociologies of science and knowledge (e.g., Knorr-Cetina, 1981; Latour & Woolgar, 1986), which seek to understand how knowledge is constructed through the communicative practices of persons acting (jointly) as scientists, and so on. Obviously, the same point can be made about communication researchers.

However, it is still possible to take a "constructed" position about knowledge and yet distance oneself from one's claims through the rhetoric of the "objective" observer of an independently existing world, albeit a world of others' constructions. It is an attempt to counteract this "naive" constructivism (Steier, 1991a)—of claiming to objectively know others' communicative constructing processes—that leads us to a third kind of reflexivity. This reflexivity, which is needed to complete the "circuit" of communication research, is one that recognizes that the idea that *worlds are constructed through our everyday interactions*, both in the field and through the discourse practices of our profession, applies to *us* as communication researchers—not just to others. In short, the reflexivity in which I am here interested forces us to see that our study of interpersonal communication hinges on our own interpersonal communication processes, neglect of which renders any "findings" markedly de-contextualized.

We need to devise programs of interpersonal communication research that allow for reflexivity to be the starting point for a radical re-contextualization of interpersonal communication. Interestingly, both the discourse work of Potter and Wetherell (1987) and several works in the sociology of science (e.g., Latour & Woolgar, 1986) confront, or work with, these issues, while varieties of constructivism emanating from communication, where it should most clearly be a concern, have not—this in spite of the plea, over a decade ago, by Hawes (1978), and by Pearce, Cronen, and Harris (1982), to have notions of self-reflexivity at the core of a new methodology for human communication research and theory.

Interpersonal Communication Research as Multiple Reflexive Conversations

As Ruesch and Bateson (1949) note, all observation can be understood as participatory, with the formal methodology of "participant observation" but one way of recognizing this constructing activity. This is so even if we "unobtrusively" observe and then construct, or specify, the "world" of those observed [in our language]. (*That* we, as observers, participate is not an issue, but to what extent those others, whom we "observe," is.) It is this reflexive awareness of our participation in the professional discourse of interpersonal communication research that helps form the scaffolding of our understanding of interpersonal communication.

Instead of recognizing the reflexivity of interpersonal communication research as a stopping point, we need to consider what space such a recognition opens up to us. As a starting point, I feel it is crucial that we understand what conversation we are in. The broad notion of conversation used here is congruent with the general sense of a "turning with (an other)" implied by its etymological roots. It happens when we engage and are engaged with others in interaction and is parallel to Wittgenstein's (1968) notion of a language game. I am here concerned with broadening conversational understanding rather than a particular form of analysis, such as conversation analysis or speech act theory. Indeed, my whole argument rests on multiple hearings. My argument is also guided by Pask's (1976) notion, central to his conversation theory, of the maintenance of difference through mutual understanding, rather than conversation as only guided toward consensus in the sense of agreement (in fact, con-sensing here might be understood as sensing together rather than agreeing).

In interpersonal communication research, we approach the groups through which we seek to address our research questions in different ways. Through the discourse of different methods and methodologies, we may call those persons subjects, informants, respondents, and so forth. To emphasize the participative role of these others, grounding interpersonal communication research in a mutual process, rather than an input–output mode, I prefer to refer to these "others," following Ortega (1957), as *reciprocators*. Of course, we could also use the term, as some interpersonal researchers do, "interlocutors." The idea of interlocutor is embedded in the notion of a conversation as one who speaks "in between." The important thing here is to mark the choice as a way of changing our orientation to those "others," and one way of accomplishing this is by recognizing the importance of the terms of address we choose (Leeds-Hurwitz, 1989). A new term, such as "reciprocator," rooted in a mutual process, may make my intentions more clearly marked than simply using "interlocutor," since many who refer to "others" as interlocutors have merely used it as a substitute for "subject" without changing their relationship to those same "others." In attempting to make interpersonal communication research more inter-personal, we must create a more relational discourse of method, recognizing that it is only by "their" hearing us and addressing us that we can emerge as a "we" doing interpersonal research.

We have a wide variety of methods for obtaining the material through which our claims about interpersonal communication are guided. We may get responses to a questionnaire that we have developed, make direct observation (either participant or "distant," in the standard sense), interview reciprocators, and make direct observation followed by interviews with those observed, and these may be recorded by notes, audiotapes, videotapes, and so forth. Many of these methods directly involve interpersonal processes (cf. Cicourel, 1964; Briggs, 1986). Whether the interview is a structured questionnaire or an open-ended conversation, recognition of such processes forces the interviewer to try to understand to whom reciprocators are addressing their responses and questions. That is, a large part of understanding the conversation in which material is generated involves an understanding of who "we" are as constituted by social others or "yous" (Shotter, 1989) in those conversations (Jorgenson, 1991). We are never neutral in a social setting, but neither are we reducible to variables (e.g., female or male) to be factored into a researcher bias equation, even though such characteristics can certainly be relevant to understanding our participation in that social setting. Indeed, we may be, to our reciprocators, many "you's" in the same setting. Note that this issue of understanding to whom responses are offered also applies to survey reciprocators, but such a situational and conversational understanding of ourselves is unattainable by this method (even if we boldly ask such an item in a questionnaire)—we thus remain somewhat unclear to whom responses are offered, at best reducing ourselves to an aggregate "you."

For example, in his work on interpersonal communication in organizational settings, Tom Robinson, a doctoral student at Old Dominion University, sought to interview people within a particular division of a defense-related organization about perspectives on organizational identities. He had been given permission to conduct his interviews, and the division members had been instructed to cooperate with Tom. When, after introducing himself, Tom would thank the division member for agreeing to participate, the reply would typically be, "I didn't agree to participate." Tom would tell them they did not have to participate if they did not want to (he wanted them to participate because they wanted to, as he was well aware of the context-bound nature of any information he might gather), to which they would reply that he did not understand—they *had* to participate (i.e., they were commanded to). And further, Tom could not (i.e., did not have the authority to) give them permission not to participate.

Taking a reflexive position allowed Tom to understand the setting as a clash of frames that would make interpretation of his interviews problematic, at least from a dialogical standpoint. However, he was also able to see what ensued in his interviews not as "bad data," because they were offered to a "you" he did not want to be, but as important comments, at another level, about their relationship (Steier, in press). (How a jointly stipulated frame could be created in these organizational interviews has become part of his dissertation work.) This example is a forceful reminder that information is *relationally* constructed. Statements about the goodness of data can be more clearly understood as about the relationship within which they are gathered; however, this relational quality generally remains unacknowledged.

Researchers have typically referred to data gathered as "good" if it is felt that the data are being offered to the "her" or "him" whom the researcher wanted to be in that situation. Conversely, reseachers often describe data as "bad" if it is felt that they were not offered to the person we would like ourselves to be in that research relationship. We may be tempted to say that informants withheld information, or "gave us the party line" (but not what they *really* felt). As Jorgenson (1991) noted, in her research on the construction of families' self-definitions, we may be many different selves (e.g., expert or someone to whom advice is to be given) to those others we are interviewing, even in the course of one interview. This recognition, that statements about the quality of information are about our relational selves, remains unacknowledged, concealed in the language game of objective knowledge. This socially situated understanding may take place in the "actual" setting, or it may take place upon reflection when examining the material generated in those interpersonal settings, whether those materials are videotapes or transcribed interviews.

What is often going on in the interpersonal settings in which interpersonal communication research is gathered is a mutual framing of the situation. Earlier (Steier, 1991b) I referred to this process as a "framing mirroring," and as one kind of reflexive issue to be considered in contextualizing our "findings." In previous works, I have presented issues that emerge when research becomes a reflexive enterprise (Steier, 1989, 1991b). After summarizing some of these below, I should like to develop the notion of interpersonal communication research as translation—especially as it relates to the emerging themes of this chapter.

Issues in Reflexive Research

Research as Both Invention and Intervention

What emerges as a key issue at first glance might appear paradoxical. It is that we, as researchers, guided by our own assumptions, specify the questions that characterize the domain in which our reciprocators' relationship, be it family-ness or team-ness, is displayed; we invent "order" from the (other) orderly world of their system. Yet, our reciprocators may also make inventive distinctions in the course of engaging in interactions that make up their "system" or world (even if this world is "informed" by ours through newspaper reports of our findings). Thus, our research can be seen as an intervention into a system insofar as the very questions we ask in trying to understand a relationship or system create possibilities for change. A way of reconciling this apparent paradox is to see research as a co-constructive process. "The system" is one that emerges in the investigative process and includes the researcher and his or her modeling processes (making research autobiographical), co-constructing that system in conversation with an "other(s)." This also forces us as researchers to develop clinical sensitivity.

Emotioning in Research

Our research activities involve an "emotioning" that values some things, making them "real" (as Vickers, 1965, noted in his appreciative system) and may include such elements as our own anxiety (Devereaux, 1967) concerning the entire process. This emotioning allows us to become engaged with certain stories, or surprised by others. Yet often our own engagement with what we call our data may not involve a rationalistic process, as the *stories through which we see* may get *lost in translation*. Reflexive research requires an awareness of this emotioning and feeling, although it need not be expressed in the traditional professional language.

Research as Mutual Mirroring

In making research reflexive, one issue that stands out across encounters is a reflecting, or mirroring, of various research relevant processes between reciprocators and researchers. We, as researchers, engage in what might be thought of as reciprocator-like activities (i.e., tied to what the research questions are "about") and reciprocators in research-like processes. I refer to mirroring not in the sense of one image being the real one that is reflected onto another surface but rather in the mutual sense where each image serves as a basis for the other.

In addition to the "framing mirroring" discussed earlier, mirroring may take other forms. For example, the reseachers' communication processes may mirror those of the groups they study. In investigating the internal dynamics of action research teams, Smith, Simmons, and Thames (1989) noted what they refer to as *parallel processes*, as the teams were observed to display "a parallel enactment of the system dynamics the researchers are seeking to understand" (p. 13). Thus, those relationships in which a research team engages can be seen to mirror and be mirrored by those relationships that a team studies "in others"—a kind of mirroring of which we should be aware, as a crucial way of providing a context for understanding how our "results" become results. In a family therapy team (Steier, 1991b), the metaphoric recognition that the team was a "family" engaging in similar family-like activities provided a frame within which other behaviors of the team made sense, and even provided for a discussion of what the families that they were treating were doing to their [the therapy] family, as well as what my interview was doing to their family-like relationships (bearing in mind that I too was a member of the family) that proved useful in understanding the "others." It allowed them (us) to see how what they saw and acted upon in the families that they were treating in many ways mirrored and grew out of their (our) own interactions.

Still another version of mirroring might be termed "figural mirroring." In my own research I have been concerned with the interpersonal processes that allow members of systems (organizations, families, etc.) to construct identities of those systems, or of objects of value in those systems, particularly with *how* groups elevate relevant features or processes to the status of "relevant features or processes." This "figuring" process (of marking a figure from a ground) must reflexively be turned back on the research process itself, as I, in order to say something of the constructing process, must elevate some aspect of a situation to the status "feature," while other streams remain as background. How I do this, which may involve a "feeling" process and my own predispositions, is certainly part of any claims that I offer. Thus, an awareness is required of *how* those (figural) constructing activities that we attempt to understand in our reciprocators are mirrored by our own constructing activities in research.

With these issues as background, we can now consider an additional reflexive issue, research as translation, which should be of particular importance to the interpersonal communication research community.

Interpersonal Communication Research as Translating

In doing research into human systems, we are engaged in different conversations, based on different activities. These conversations include those of our reciprocators among themselves, those of our reciprocators directly with us (as in interviews), and those of ourselves with our professional community. The crucial point is that *no one represents the way it really is*. This issue builds on an awareness of these different conversations as ways of structuring and sustaining realities and requires an attempt to see a world or worlds in others' terms but then to reflexively acknowledge that we are often translating reciprocators' conversations into the language of our professional community.

To this point, I have noted some of the multiple conversations involved in doing interpersonal communication research. These include conversations in which our reciprocators are engaged (i.e., the ones our research is purportedly about, or better, the ones about which we pose our initial questions), and the ones, such as interviews, used to generate the materials we use. These are interwoven with the conversations we have with our own materials (the transcripts, videotapes, self-reported logs, etc.). Yet there is another set of conversations in interpersonal communication research that needs to be understood to fully contextualize any claims we offer. This is the conversation we have with ourselves as researchers, usually in research teams prepared for an intended professional audience through the discourse of that audience. This conversation is also constituted by interpersonal communication processes, and will, if we are serious about hearing our reciprocators, involve processes of translation.

Why a "translating" conversation should be an issue at all must be made clear, since, for most interpersonal communication research, it does not even have the status of being an issue. First, we must understand that the conversations of interpersonal communication researchers, in our or their own language, are not trivial and are based on a history of interactions tied to distinctions that have come to matter to us as interpersonal communication researchers, "in our own language." However, our own language, constituted by conversations about others, can have no privileged claim to being "what is really going on." Second, there must be a desire to allow reciprocators to "talk back" and give voice to their way of understanding their interpersonal situation. This is usually expressed as a desire to hear reciprocators in their own terms, or "language." Third, we must also acknowledge that understanding another group in its own terms, while respectful of the integrity of any "culture," is nevertheless impossible. Any interpretation moves through the presuppositions embedded in the researchers' language and way of seeing, as well as the researchers' experiences. Even creating a written transcription from taped discourse, as Ochs (1979) has noted, involves assumptions about its interpretation and organization.

We are thus faced with the dilemma of wanting to understand how others understand their interpersonal communication, while recognizing that we are members of a community of researchers who have a particular language with which this (research) community demands to be addressed, and that these two views involve languages that are not the same. Karp and Kendall (1982) have noted this movement from the language of a local culture to the language of one's research community to be a key element in seriously linking reflexivity to fieldwork method, and this has also been a key theme in recent thinking by anthropologists about how anthropologists "write culture" (Clifford & Marcus, 1986).

I am suggesting that interpersonal communication research be looked upon as a translation process, recognizing that our conversations with our reciprocators, their conversations among themselves, and our conversations with our colleagues are simply different conversations or, in Wittgenstein's (1968) terms, different language games. In order to move from one to another, a translation is required. The need for the translation may not be so immediately noticeable, as it is in translating a distant text. However, this nonimmediacy can make assumed shared interpretations all the more problematic.[1]

Indeed, even if we choose not to attempt to understand our reciprocators in their terms, but instead see their *inter*personal worlds strictly in our terms, what I argue here is relevant. Yet more important here is that even so, *the processes by which this orientation to doing interpersonal communication research get accomplished still involve researchable interpersonal communication processes.*

"Translating" conversations are themselves social processes, researchable by the very kinds of procedures we use to understand other conversations. Thus, I am not speaking here of a one-to-one translation but one marked by recursive hermeneutic processes. As such, there are several guides to orient ourselves to this translating conversation to which I would like to call attention.

First, there is Ortega's (1957) recognition, at the heart of his "new linguistics," that "translation is a matter of saying in a language precisely what that language tends to pass over in silence" (p. 246), and his articulation of the "exuberances" and "deficiencies" of all utterances. For Ortega (1959), every utterance says less than it wishes to say (it is deficient) and, yet, conveys much more than it plans (it is exuberant). These ideas form the heart of Becker's (1989a, 1989b) work on the translation process. For us as interpersonal communication researchers, they may serve as guideposts for how we (co)create what others' interactions are "doing" or "about," whether it be in the form of tacit rules that we claim structure their interpersonal interactions or the implicit meanings we "find" in what they say to each other.

Added to this awareness, we might try to relax some of the distinctions and presuppositions of our professional language and allow ourselves to become, in Becker's (1989a) term, "defamiliarized" in our translating conversations. A refamiliarization that might then be necessary to converse with other colleagues external to our research team becomes a more enriching experience, as we look to see *if*, for example, our categories do indeed fit our experiences, instead of assuming that they do. Our de- and refamiliarization are processes central to a richer translation.

In addition, Tedlock (1983) recognizes the importance of the translation of *style*. The issue of how this gets accomplished, if it even becomes a concern (as it should), is yet another conversation to be understood. It is a dialogue of a critical bridging between cultures whose connectedness rests on the very processes it seeks to link.

WHEN IS A SOCIAL APPROACH
TO INTERPERSONAL COMMUNICATION?

Earlier, we have seen how "problems" of self-reference are often located in how we frame situations as either–or, which, in a reframing can become a both–and situation (without that particular problem). This reframing can also be extended to allow for a reexamination of the question of understanding what conversation we are in, and who we are in that conversation. For example, in many conversations within the community of interpersonal communication scholars, a social approach is often taken to imply a "naturalistic" approach (which is taken to be in opposition to many different things, depending on what aspect or feature of naturalism is chosen). Framing this as an either–or choice unnecessarily constrains the range of social approaches, particularly with regard to an insistence on understanding the relational contexts that create interpersonal situations. Indeed why "social" might, for many, imply a naturalism could be a researchable question into our own conversations as a community of interpersonal communication researchers. I submit that in order to deal adequately with questions of "What conversation are we in?" and "Who are we in that conversation?" two distinctions that have been taken as hard and fast rules need to be reexamined as both–and situations.

Both Naturalistic and Nonnaturalistic:
Contextual Understanding

Historically, we have had to choose whether to describe our research as naturalistic or not. Nonnaturalistic approaches have ranged from experimental (often taken to indicate that the researcher, in an effort to control what might be observed, specifies the situation and its constraints) to laboratory (often taken to indicate in what surrounding the research is conducted), depending on what aspect of "natural" is being emphasized. With regard to standard criteria of external validity, the various forms of "nonnaturalistic" research will be inferior to naturalistic research. Because of this validity, naturalistic is often equated to real-world-like. However, from any social approach, recognizing the criticality of multiple perspectives, this assumption needs to be further examined—whose "real" world?

In a classic article dealing with this dilemma, Bavelas (1984) points out several difficulties that ensue when such assumptions of naturalism are left unexplored. In her discussion of assumptions underlying naturalistic interaction research in families, she examines different ways that "naturalistic" is implied by interaction researchers by looking at what is offered as a contrast. Thus, in interpersonal communication research, naturalistic can mean "typical" (as in what persons might be doing anyway, were the researcher not there, such as arguing), or "relevant" (as in the topics persons might be discussing , had not the researcher given them a topic to discuss). However, as Bavelas points out, issues such as relevance are often defined as such by the investigator. In addition, the features that mark conversation as being about this or that, or doing this or that, are features of the investigator's repertoire of observational practices. What these features of relevance are depends on whether the observers are interpersonal communication researchers utilizing their own professional discourse (including the discourse of "naturalistic" interpersonal observation) or counselors or bartenders. Thus, the distinction between naturalistic and nonnaturalistic family research often presupposes an interpersonal "nature" that exists apart from researchers' concerns and ways of knowing. Although we recognize the need for a professional discourse as a way that we may jointly stipulate concerns that matter to us as interpersonal communication researchers, we must also acknowledge that this discourse does not in any way give us a privileged view of "one reality."

Whereas some naturalistic interpersonal studies may have limited the range of contextual understanding, nonnaturalistic studies often have ignored the social contexts of interpersonal research almost completely—based, as they are, on an unnecessary assumption of an orderly interpersonal world into which researchers might get a context-free glimpse, through a laboratory study or field experiment, for example. I say unnecessary, because one need not, and cannot, ignore the interpersonal context in which such research is conducted, a context that often leaves unexplored precisely what experiences and relationships experimenters must deny or control in order to render their subjects "comparable"—part of the context often is an unexplored conversation of control. Indeed, one of the outstanding features of social approaches, as Leeds-Hurwitz (1992) points out, is such an attention to context in *all* interpersonal settings.

Both naturalistic and nonnaturalistic situations can be seen to have frames that are constructed, although the constructions may take place in very different ways. As Bavelas (1991) points out, we must deal with the "anomaly of labeling some discourse, namely *methodological discourse,* as not-discourse" (p. 124). The social interactions that produce interpersonal communication research may include the social participants jointly making sense of the situations in which they are observed—whether in a laboratory or in the field. Yet it may also include interviewer–interviewee interactions, as Jorgenson (1992) notes, or researcher conversations as they create their stories, as illustrated by Bochner and Ellis (1992). These are all ways of marking contexts in which interpersonal research is generated. What is important for a social approach is not only the choice of settings in which to view and hear interpersonal communication but also attention to the multifarious *social* situations (as Goffman, 1964, has noted as "the neglected situation") that mark those interactions within those settings as interactions of a particular kind and render them intelligible to the participants, including the researchers.

Interestingly, while recognizing that the discourse in interviews (or questionnaires) that produces interpersonal communication research is also (presumably, researchable) discourse, Bavelas (1991) states that she does not wish to raise the "specter of recursiveness and self-reflexivity" (p.124). Yet her concerns are precisely those of reflexivity. If we are to concern ourselves with context in all its social entailments, as Bavelas admonishes us to do, reflexivity is already an issue.

We cannot assume that experiment translates to real life. However, we must also question what our own assumption of real life is and how it may differ from that of those we seek to understand, and through whom we derive and test our theories. What is missing is an examination and understanding of the diverse interpersonal contexts within which interpersonal research is done. From this point of view, a legitimate question becomes: What frames for understanding interaction do non-naturalistic, or naturalistic, observers impose upon a system, and how do those compare with those of our reciprocators? Focusing on these questions allows us to begin to understand what conversation we are in. There remains, however, the nagging question of who we are in that conversation, and how we cannot legislate that.

Both Researcher *and* Caregiver: Relational Stances

In *With a Daughter's Eye*, Mary Catherine Bateson (1984) describes how her parents, Margaret Mead and Gregory Bateson, systematically photographed and recorded her behavior as an infant. She notes how this fit in with their lives as researchers of interpersonal patterns of childrearing in different cultures, which in turn informed Mead's notions of her own mother–daughter relationship. In recalling reviews of her book, Bateson (1991) remarks how a reviewer was "appalled" by this anecdote, calling it "a perfectly horrible thing for a mother to do to a daughter" (p. 13). In trying to make sense of the reviewer's horror, Bateson states that he (the reviewer) had an image of scientists as cold and manipulative and uninvolved, whereas mothers were supposed to be caring and loving and responsive (and she understandably links the reviewer's maleness to the history of ways of doing "good" research, giving rise to a male-created scientific method). Mead, and indeed Mary Catherine Bateson, who herself does research on mother–infant communication and photographed and studied her own daughter, must, in the eyes of this not atypical reviewer, choose between being a mother and being a researcher. Yet Bateson points out this was not the choice that Mead saw—to her "the process of knowledge and the process of caring attention were identical" (p. 13).

The point is that here again, in creating an interpersonal context for ourselves as interpersonal communication researchers, we are often forced to choose between the position of a researcher and the position of someone who stands in a "feeling" relationship to the other(s) whose interpersonal communication processes we seek to understand. This choice is often unnecessarily recast as that between distant scientist and engaged person—perhaps to mark the distinction even more. But Mead's, and Bateson's, point is that this is not an either–or choice. It is a both–and situation. Nowhere is this clearer than in interpersonal communication research, where, in order to properly contextualize anything we might claim, we need to understand our own interpersonal relationships with our reciprocators.

Reflexive approaches thus move us to develop an awareness of the multiple conversations, contexts, and relationships in which we and our reciprocators interactively participate. As Bateson's story illustrates, they move us to develop a clinical sensitivity as interpersonal researchers.

REFLEXIVITY AS A SOCIAL APPROACH

By taking reflexivity seriously, we have seen how many new issues and questions are raised, particularly about our own interpersonal engagement to the research process. Some have taken this as an opportunity to include, in their research work, autobiographical material on the self (or selves) they are or become through the course of doing research (see Kondo, 1990, for a wonderful illustration of this, as a Japanese American anthropologist understanding a Japanese shop-floor organization). From a traditional viewpoint, a focus on the self (as in *self*-reflexivity) can be seen to rest on a bed of narcissism. Indeed, this is precisely a criticism (e.g., Patai, 1994) that has, wrongly I believe, been leveled at this reflexive turn. Yet what is often misunderstood here is that self-reflexivity is a relational process, as stated at the outset. The selves through which we see our research are social selves, continually adjusting to a variety of contexts we participate in creating.

What is most important here is that, as Becker (1989b) so eloquently notes in discussing translation, *self*-corrections of this hermeneutic sort "should not be confused with subjectivism, as some have suggested, for it is just the opposite—a respect for another voice, not an obsession with one's own" (p. 282). Thus, by becoming aware of our awareness of our own voice, reflexivity becomes, rather than a cognitive stance, a social process, allowing more space for others. It encourages different stances toward those whose communication processes we seek to understand, a point echoed by Hawes (1994) in his revisiting of his comments on reflexivity made 15 years earlier.

Of course, all that I have written here applies to my own work as well. This chapter is, after all, about affording recognition to a self-reflexiveness and "inter-personal"–autobiographical character of our interpersonal communication research, while allowing for the nonnarcissistic consequences of this same reflexiveness. My own research is constituted by these very same multiple and reflexive conversations of which I claim we must develop an awareness. It is important to note that many of the arguments I offer here emanate from several research settings in which I became interested in interpersonal processes involved in the construction of "organizations," "families," and even "objects." Concerns emerged within these projects that did not fit with traditional methodologies and yet guided what I wanted to say, but whose saying involved essentially investigating our own research group as it produced those very questions. To me, these self-findings, produced by recursive and oscillating processes of immersion and distancing, must somehow be offered alongside and interwoven with those of the groups about which our initial questions were posed.

To do this has not been and is still not easy. It forces us to recognize, as others who have written on reflexivity and knowing in other domains have also noted, how traditional forms of writing research constrain the very possibility of properly contextualizing our research (cf. Woolgar & Ashmore, 1988) . That is, our forms make it difficult for our claims to display the interpersonal processes that produced them.

What is clear, however, is that by allowing ourselves to render problematic the various interpersonal communication processes in which *we* participate to create our interpersonal communication research, many conversations become researchable communication issues. These conversations are consequences of taking seriously issues of reflexivity. They provide for a stronger contextualization of our understanding of interpersonal communication and allow our interpersonal research to become more a program of what Bateson (1972b) called "second order learning."

A concern for reflexivity thus moves us simultaneously in several directions. It forces us to develop an awareness of how we recursively and interactively construct our claims of interpersonal communication processes of others and thus encourages us to point to ourselves as the active observers and interpreters that we are. However, rather than solely "closing the circle," it allows us to open outward toward other forms of this self-expression, and toward an awareness of the multiple conversations in which we and our reciprocators participate.

NOTE

1. The idea of translation "within a language," or an internal translation, is certainly not a new one, although its salience across domains is often neglected. Zurbuchen (1989) writes of the importance of this idea in an "intralingual recasting" in the performance of Balinese poetry, and how this applies whether the text is an ancient one or one written in modern Balinese. She builds on Steiner's (1975) notion of internal translation, but marks internal here as tied to social process, rather than an individually based activity.

REFERENCES

Austin, J. (1975). *How to do things with words* (2nd ed., J. O. Urmson & M. Sbisa, Eds.). Cambridge, MA: Harvard University Press.

Babcock, B. (1980). Reflexivity: Definitions and discriminations. *Semiotica, 30,* 1–14.

Bateson, G. (1968). Information and codification: A philosophical approach. In J. Ruesch & G. Bateson, *Communication: The social matrix of psychiatry.* New York: W. W. Norton.

Bateson, G. (1972a). *Steps to an ecology of mind.* New York: Ballantine.

Bateson, G. (1972b).The logical categories of learning and communication. In *Steps to an ecology of mind.* New York: Ballantine.

Bateson, G., Jackson, D. D., Haley, J., & Weakland, J. H. (1956). Toward a theory of schizophrenia. *Behavioral Science, 1,* 251–264.

Bateson, M. C. (1984). *With a daughter's eye.* New York: William Morrow.

Bateson, M. C. (1991). Multiple kinds of knowledge: Societal decision-making. In M. J. McGee-Brown (Ed.), *Diversity and design: Studying culture and the individual.* Athens: University of Georgia Press.

Bavelas, J. B. (1984). On "naturalistic" family research. *Family Process, 23,* 337–341.

Bavelas, J. B. (1991). Some problems with linking goals to discourse. In K. Tracy (Ed.), *Understanding face-to-face interaction: Issues linking goals and discourse.* Hillsdale, NJ: Erlbaum.

Becker, A. L. (1989a). Introduction. In A. L. Becker (Ed.), *Writing on the tongue*. Ann Arbor: Center on South and Southeast Asia.

Becker, A. L. (1989b). Aridharma: Framing an old Javanese tale. In A. L. Becker (Ed.), *Writing on the tongue*. Ann Arbor: Center on South and Southeast Asia.

Birkhoff, G., & MacLane, S. (1968). *A survey of modern algebra*. New York: Macmillan.

Bochner, A. P., & Ellis, C. (1992). Personal narrative as a social approach to interpersonal communication. *Communication Theory, 2*, 165–172.

Briggs, C. L. (1986). *Learning how to ask: A sociolinguistic appraisal of the role of the interview in social science research*. New York: Cambridge University Press.

Cicourel, A. (1964). *Method and measurement in sociology*. New York: Free Press.

Clifford, J., & Marcus, G. E. (Eds.). (1986). *Writing culture: The poetics and politics of ethnography*. Berkeley: University of California Press.

Cronen, V. E., Johnson, K. M., & Lannamann, J. W. (1982). Paradoxes, double binds, and reflexive loops: An alternative theoretical perspective. *Family Process, 21*, 91–112.

Devereaux, G. (1967). *From anxiety to method in the behavioral sciences*. The Hague: Mouton.

Fleck, L. (1979). *The genesis and development of a scientific fact* (F. Bradley & T. J. Trenn, Trans.). Chicago: University of Chicago Press.

Garfinkel, H. (1967). *Studies in Ethnomethodology*. Englewood Cliffs, NJ: Prentice Hall.

Gergen, K. J. (1985). The social constructionist movement in modern psychology. *American Psychologist, 40*, 266–275.

Gergen, K. J. (1991). *The saturated self: Dilemmas of identity in contemporary life*. New York: Basic Books.

Goffman, E. (1964). The neglected situation. *American Anthroplogist, 66*, 133–136.

Hawes, L. C. (1978). On the reflexivity of communication research. *Western Journal of Speech Communication, 42*, 12–20.

Hawes, L. C. (1994). Revisiting reflexivity. *Western Journal of Communication, 58*, 5–10.

Herbst, D. P. (1987). *What happens when we make a distinction* (Paper No. 37, Einar Thorsrud Memorial Symposium). Oslo: Work Research Institute.

Herbst, D. P. (1993). What happens when we make a distinction: An elementary introduction to co-genetic logic. *Cybernetics and Human Knowing, 2*, 29–38.

Herbst, P. G. (1976). *Alternatives to hierarchies*. Leiden, The Netherlands: Martinus Nijhoff.

Jorgenson, J. (1991). Co-constructing the interviewer/co-constructing family. In F. Steier (Ed।)., *Research and reflexivity*. London: Sage.

Jorgenson, J. (1992). Communication, rapport and the interview: A social perspective. *Communication Theory, 2*, 148–156.

Karp, I., & Kendall, M. B. (1982). Reflexivity in field work. In P. Secord (Ed.), *Explaining human behavior*. Beverly Hills, CA: Sage.

Knorr-Cetina, K. (1981). *The manufacture of knowledge*. Elmsford, NY: Pergamon Press.

Kondo, D. K. (1990). *Crafting selves: Power, gender and discourses of identity in a Japanese workplace*. Chicago: University of Chicago Press.

Laing, R. D., Phillipson, H., & Lee, A. R. (1966). *Interpersonal perception: A theory and a method of research*. London: Tavistock.

Latour, B., & Woolgar, S. (1986). *Laboratory life* (2nd ed.). Princeton, NJ: Princeton University Press.

Lawson, H. (1985). *Reflexivity*. LaSalle, IL: Open Court.

Leeds-Hurwitz, W. (1989). *Communication in everyday life*. Norwood, NJ: Ablex.

Leeds-Hurwitz, W. (1992). Forum introduction: Social approaches to interpersonal communication. *Communication Theory, 2*, 131–139.

Maturana, H. R. (1987). Everything is said by an observer. In W. I. Thompson (Ed.), *Gaia: A way of knowing*. Great Barrington, MA.: Lindisfarne Press.

Mead, G. H. (1962). *Mind, self and society* (C. W. Morris, Ed.). Chicago: University of Chicago Press.

Ochs, E. (1979). Transcription as theory. In E. Ochs & B. B. Schieffelin (Eds.), *Developmental pragmatics*. New York: Academic Press.

Ortega y Gasset, J. (1957). *Man and people*. New York: Norton.

Ortega y Gasset, J. (1959). The difficulty of reading. *Diogenes, 28*, 1–17.

Pask, G. (1976). *Conversation theory: Applications in education and epistemology*. Amsterdam: Elsevier.

Patai, D. (1994, February 23). Sick and tired of scholars' nouveau solipsism. *Chronicle of Higher Education (Point of View)*, p. A52.

Pearce, W. B., Cronen, V. E., & Harris, L. M. (1982). Methodological considerations in building human communication theory. In F. X. Dance (Ed.), *Human communication theory*. New York: Harper & Row.

Potter, J., & Wetherell, M. (1987). *Discourse and social psychology*. London: Sage.

Rasmussen, P. (1987). *A contribution to contextual logic and a discussion of possible psychological implications*. Unpublished master's thesis, University of Oslo, Oslo, Norway.

Ruesch, J., & Bateson, G. (1949). Structure and process in social relations. *Psychiatry, 12*, 105–124.

Shotter, J. (1984). *Social accountability and selfhood*. Oxford: Basil Blackwell.

Shotter, J. (1989). The social construction of "you." In J. Shotter & K. J. Gergen (Eds.), *Texts of identity*. London: Sage.

Siegle, R. (1986). *The politics of reflexivity*. Baltimore: Johns Hopkins University Press.

Smith, K. K., Simmons, V. M., & Thames, T. B. (1989). "Fix the women": An intervention into an organizational conflict based on parallel process thinking. *Journal of Applied Behavioral Science, 25*, 11–29.

Spencer-Brown, G. (1979). *Laws of form*. New York: E. P. Dutton.

Steier, F. (1989). Toward a radical and ecological constructivist approach to family communication. *Journal of Applied Communication Research, 17*, 1–26.

Steier, F. (1991a). Introduction: Research as self-reflexivity, self-reflexivity as social process. In F. Steier (Ed.), *Research and reflexivity*. London: Sage.

Steier, F. (1991b). Reflexivity and methodology: An ecological constructionism. In F. Steier (Ed.), *Research and reflexivity*. London: Sage.

Steier, F. (in press). Relational understanding in organizations: Dilemmas of multiple description and joint participation. In H. P. Dachler & K. J. Gergen (Eds.), *From methodological individualism to relational formulations*. London: Avebury.

Steiner, G. (1975). *After Babel: Aspects of language and translation*. New York: Oxford University Press.

Taylor, C. (1989). *Sources of the self*. Cambridge, MA: Harvard University Press.

Tedlock, D. (1983). *The spoken word and the work of interpretation*, Philadelphia: University of Pennsylvania Press.

Vickers, G. (1965). *The art of judgment*. London: Chapman & Hall.

Watzlawick, P., Beavin, J. H., & Jackson, D. D. (1967). *Pragmatics of Human Communication*. New York: W. W. Norton.

Wittgenstein, L. (1968). *Philosophical investigations* (3rd ed.). New York: Macmillan.

Woolgar, S., & Ashmore, M. (1988). The next step: An introduction to the reflexive project. In S. Woolgar (Ed.), *Knowledge and reflexivity*. London: Sage.

Zurbuchen, M. S. (1989). Internal translation in Balinese poetry. In A. L. Becker (Ed.), *Writing on the tongue*. Ann Arbor: Center on South and Southeast Asia.

CHAPTER 5

A Sailing Guide for Social Constructionists[1]

W. BARNETT PEARCE

S ocial constructionism is one of many approaches[2] to under-standing and engaging with processes of communication. It has recently become a major focus of such work. In addition to the volume in which this chapter appears, Sage Publications has a lengthy list of titles in its Inquiries in Social Constructionism series; an international conference on the topic was held at the University of New Hampshire in Summer 1993; it has been the topic of a special issue of *Human Systems* (1992, *3* [3 and 4]) and of two "Forum" sections in *Communication Theory* (1992, *2* [2 and 4]); and HarperCollins has published two textbooks that take an explicit social constructionist perspective (Pearce, 1994; Powers, 1994).

Like those who develop any "new paradigm," social constructionists have a heady sense of excitement about their work. In this case, they believe that they are developing a paradigm "marked by a far greater charity toward disparate voices, sharpened by a sensitivity to the processes by which knowledge claims are made and justified, with a heightened moral concern, and a keener appreciation of the communal character of understanding" (Shotter & Gergen, 1989, p. x).

Social constructionism scarcely suffers from overly precise defini-tions. In this, it fits its intellectual *milieu*. Bernstein (1992) offered the metaphor of a "constellation" as a way of conceiving contemporary social and political theories. He declared that "we can no longer responsibly claim that there is or can be a final reconciliation ... in which all difference, otherness, opposition and contradiction are reconciled" (p.

8). The metaphor "constellation" depicts a situation that "defies and resists any and all attempts of reduction to 'a common denominator, essential core, or generative first principle'" (p. 8).

Although social constructionism in its current form is new, it certainly is not without precedent. One story of Western intellectual history features a recurring dialogue between two voices, one that earnestly seeks certainty in a representation of reality by means of propositions and the other that sees itself engaged in a process, simultaneously playful and serious, by which reality is both revealed and concealed, created and destroyed by our activities (Pearce & Foss, 1990). Framed this way, social constructionism is the contemporary version of this second venerable voice. However, the present is a moment of great innovation and creativity. While most versions of social constructionism stand as alternatives to scientific or positivistic approaches (see, e.g., Harré & Secord, 1972; Gergen, 1994), there are rich differences among them. Articulating some of these differences will facilitate good conversations in which these perspectives can be elaborated.

When there were still uncharted seas and navigation was an uncertain art, mariners would keep a record of where they had been as a way of finding their way home—and as guides for their next voyage. These "logs" described a retracable route through otherwise unknown waters. As a "sailing guide," this chapter is such a crude but perhaps useful log; it is not a precise navigational chart. Its method is split between presenting an array of social constructionist voices and providing a running commentary on them. I am not ashamed of its incomplete nature; my intent is to provoke, not end, discussion.

COMMONALITIES AMONG SOCIAL CONSTRUCTIONISTS

Constructionists delight in repudiating cherished virtues of "mainstream" ways of dealing with social life, in appealing to a new canon of virtues, and in making virtues of a new set of practices. We enjoy demonstrations that the verities of our own culture are the product of historically contingent social processes and that the variety of human cultures have in common these contingent social processes of constructing social realities.

We find ourselves inevitably twisted into reflexive loops, describing the process of social action from the "inside." We see research as both *about* socially constructed events and objects and as a specific instance *of* the social construction of events and objects. Constructionists share "a certain vision of the world and of our knowledge of it, that both consist of *activities* of various kinds ... and also a certain stance towards the conduct of research into such activity—that of investigating its nature from a position of active involvement in it, rather than contemplative withdrawal from it" (Shotter, 1989, p. 132).

Shotter and Gergen (1994) offered a series of "instructive statements" of a social constructionist "account of various crucial aspects of conversational exchanges" (pp. 14–24).

1. Accounts of "reality" originate in the contingent, indeterminate, and historical flow of continuous communicative activity between human beings.
2. An utterance has no meaning in itself but only as a constituent of ongoing dialogue; its meaning is generated by its use within dialogue.
3. Responsive utterances work both to create meaning and to constrain further meaning in the continuously developing context of a conversation.
4. It is in terms of "social languages" and "speech genres" that we can account for our ways of talking as working to hold social groups together as dynamic, relational wholes—they hold together as "behavioral and lived ideologies."
5. As linguistically coordinated social relationships acquire a history and become ordered or ranked, so we develop "official" ways of accounting for ourselves and our world, that is, local ontologies and social sanctions for their maintenance.
6. Particularly in Western cultural settings, the local ontologies and moralities are individuating.
7. Our psychological talk—supposed to be "about" our "perceptions," "memories," "motives," "judgments," and so on—does not refer to an already existing, inner reality of mental representations but consists in claims formulated on the basis of one's position in a conversational context.

Harré (1989, p. 23) argued that language "is our medium for being as persons." He noted that "we English-speaking heirs of Judaeo-Christian civilization and the schism between Protestant and Catholics" have a particular set of beliefs (centered on autonomy, agency, and histories) which make possible "certain kinds of lives" which are "closed" to people who are heirs to a different heritage. "The social constructivist line on all this," Harré explains, "is that what I call 'beliefs' are carried by the learning of grammar. Or to put the matter clearly, we could express in the rhetoric of belief part of the grammar of certain kinds of discourses."

"Social approaches" to interpersonal communication, Leeds-Hurwitz (1992, pp. 131–132) said, have in common (1) "an acceptance of the social construction of reality"; (2) "the implied need for taking a reflexive stance in research"; (3) "a sociocultural, rather than an individual, focus for the study of communication"; and (4) "investigation of symbols." Referring specifically to social constructionism in the tradition of pragmatism, Cronen (in press-a) identified five "commitments": (1) Communication is the primary social process, not a means of doing other things or a process in which the more important things are before, behind, or after. (2) The primary units of observation are, in Harré's (1984) term, "persons in conversation." Cronen notes that "persons in conversation" is a single entity, not three (e.g., *not* one person plus another person plus the conversation between them). (3) Social actions have an imminent rationality or, in Wittgenstein's term, "grammar" that organizes them. (4) Social constructionism is realistic but not objectivist. Persons in communication are embodied, material entities in a real world. (5) Certainty is possible *within* the grammar of particular language games as a matter of "experience" (as Dewey used the term), but not as general propositions or intrapsychic cognitions.

In its current form, social constructionism is about two decades old, and the preceding paragraphs summarize mature (or at least "young adult") statements of its philosophical commitments. However, the astute reader will have noticed that the *content* of these statements sharply circumscribes the *function* of statements such as these in giving an account of social constructionism. Statements are ways of *doing* things rather than describing things, and social constructionists have little interest in polishing particular propositions against the whetstones of data until they are suitable for "mounting" in the prongs of theory. This disinterest does *not* deny the value of data; rather, it devalues polished propositions as the form of theory.

DIFFERENCES AMONG SOCIAL CONSTRUCTIONISTS

Social constructionists—or those grouped under this label at its most inclusive—are not all alike. Perhaps because they often chose to emphasize their commonalities in distinction from the dominant paradigm, or because their disinterest in propositions precludes semantic logic chopping, these differences have been more often felt than articulated. For example, Sigman (1992) claims that Leeds-Hurwitz's (1992) statement of commonalities among "social approaches" is so abstract that it "obscures important conceptual and methodological distinctions among, say, symbolic interactionism, ethnomethodology, cultural analysis, social-structural realism, and ethnography of speaking/communication" (p. 348). In a similar vein, Cronen (in press-a) claimed that "confusion reigns" among those embracing the term "social constructionists." "At the 1993 New Hampshire conference on Creating Social Realities," he reports, "I even heard that Freud was a social constructionist. Other participants consistently confused Cartesian doubt about physical reality with social constructionism."[3] Strange bedfellows are being discovered: "Social constructionism is the keystone of Habermas' critical theory" (Eastland, 1994, p. 164).

It is tempting to try to reconcile or compare these differences by refining propositions. However, this would be incompatible with social constructionists' own commitments. How precise shall we try to be in our statement that all statements are inherently imprecise? Fortunately, there are preferable alternatives to semantics as a way of sorting out differences among social constructionists.

A CONCEPTUAL SCHEME: GRAMMARS AND TEMPERAMENTS

A century ago, William James claimed that we are differentiated more by our temperaments—"tender-minded" and "tough-minded"—than by the contents of our convictions. James's point is compatible with Ludwig Wittgenstein's claim that we are often captured by the grammars of the language games in which we live. Wittgenstein (1953) claimed that "our grammar is lacking in" the "sort of perspicuity" which affords "a clear view of the use of our words" (paragraph #22). Philosophical problems occur when we "predicate of the thing what lies in the method of representing it" (paragraph #104). Such philosophical issues are in fact illnesses from which we need to escape: "A *picture* held us captive. And we could not get outside it, for it lay in our language and language seemed to repeat it to us inexorably" (paragraph #115).

Following these suggestions, I proposed a three-dimensional model of grammars (Figure 5.1) as a way of differentiating among theorists' commitments (Pearce, 1993). One dimension distinguishes between theorists who want to be right ("quest for certainty") and those who hope, as Gunn (1992) put it, "to be interested and perhaps even interesting, or at least not boorish" (p. 16) ("exercise of curiosity"). Another dimension differentiates those who believe that our social worlds contain stable forms ("social world as monadic") from those who treat the social world as unfinished, inherently unpredictable, and polysemic ("social world as pluralistic"). The third dimension focuses on the perspective taken. The etymology of "theorist" is "spectator."

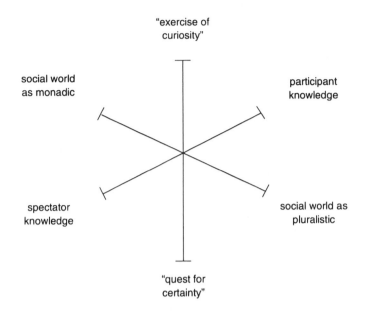

FIGURE 5.1. A scheme for differentiating the temperaments of theorists and the grammars of language games spoken by social constructionists. From Pearce (1993, p. 70). Copyright 1993 by Greenwood Press. Reprinted by permission.

Some theorists think of knowledge as a representation of reality "out there"; call this spectator knowledge. Other people (are they theorists?) think of knowledge as a form of practical wisdom about how to act; call this participant knowledge.

I originally developed this model to differentiate social constructionism from positivism. In this scheme, positivists act within grammars defined by the quest for certainty by theorists functioning as spectators who believe that the social world is monadic. Social constructionists, I claimed, gravitate toward grammars defined by the exercise of curiosity by "practical theorists" functioning as participants in a social world conceptualized as pluralistic. The latter characterization, of course, blurs some real[4] differences among social constructionists. Some constructionists are positioned farther along each dimension than others, and some combine dimensions in ways that differ from others. In the following paragraphs, I use these grammars and temperaments as ways of differentiating among social constructionists.

THE SOCIAL WORLD AS MONADIC
VERSUS PLURALISTIC

What is the nature of the social world, and how can we know it? This question has fretted theorists throughout history, and the social constructionist answer to the first part—that the social world is "made"—creates problems for the second part, for our knowledge of a made social world cannot be "certain."

From "outside," social constructionists sometimes look as if they have no way to stave off rampant relativism. If we make the world, so the perception goes, what is to prevent us from just making up anything that pleases us? This perception is hard to refute because various social constructionists give different answers to the question.

To think that the events and objects of the social world are objective is outside the grammar of social constructionism. However, as one moves toward the pluralistic side of the continuum, social constructionists differ in their opinion about reality. A more subtle distinction identifies those who focus on the products of the process of social construction and those who focus on the process itself. Pearce and Cronen (1980) teased out this distinction by contrasting the phrase "the social construction of *reality*" (as used by Berger & Luckmann, 1966) with their own interest in "*constructing* social realities." Sigman (1992) identified the "critical choice node" separating these various approaches as involving "an ontology of communication":

> One choice is to assume that the significant "stuff" of communication transpires prior to, or at the least, behind the scenes of, the behavior being displayed by the communicating entities. . . . The alternative choice . . . suggests that there is a unique influence that the process of communication itself has in human affairs. . . . This second choice requires theorizing not merely *about* communication, but *from* communication as well. . . . In other words, the process of communication itself . . . is consequential, and it is *the "nature" of that consequentiality* that should (might) be the appropriate focus for a discipline of communication. (p. 351)

Sigman's first option focuses on products of communication; the second, the process.

Like Sigman, Carbaugh and Hastings (1992) described two "feet" on which social approaches stand. One emphasizes what I here call process; it foregrounds "the situated, interactional patterns that creatively evoke, sometimes validate, sometimes negotiate, sometimes embattle, sometimes transform, social selves, relations, and institutions." The other "foot" foregrounds products of this process; it brings into view "the locally distinctive symbols, symbolic forms, and meanings that participants themselves consider significant and important" (p. 157). The latter is the subject matter of ethnographies and can be used, they claimed, in building communication theories. Hymes developed what he sometimes called the ethnography of speaking and sometimes the ethnography of communication (see Leeds-Hurwitz, 1984). Whether this should be considered social constructionism is not clear, but it does represent a nonpositivist approach focusing on the products of the social process.

Lannamann (1991, 1992) developed a "materialist" social constructionism, which includes both process and products, the latter understood as preexisting and reconstructed by the process. In a dialogue with poststructural textual analysis rather than the more common interlocutor, positivism, Lannamann (1992) argued:

> Engaging in interpersonal scholarship necessarily entails writing cultural texts of relationships and directing the performance called relational research. A materialist stance in this textual production calls attention to the ways in which the abstractions constructed and maintained by research practices reenter the cultural dialogue as facts. (p. 146)

By combining a poststructural emphasis on texts with a materialist attention to the "specific manifestations of power and domination," his approach raises new questions "that decenter the individual and call attention to the material practices, not the products of communication" (p. 142). These questions are:

1. Whose history is reflected in the research protocol and in whose terms is the research dialogue cast?
2. In what way does the research process articulate subject positions for all participants in the process?
3. To what extent do the textual practices of our discipline silence the voices of those on the margins and shift attention away from the material practices of interaction?

The "coordinated management of meaning" is an explicitly nonobjectivist, realist position that foregrounds the process of communication. "Persons in conversation are treated as material beings in a real world" (Cronen, in press-a). It holds that the activities performed by persons in conversations are themselves real. Persons are not only cognizing entities, we are embodied; our activities are real. Those who set "stories" or "thinking" outside the material world are still, it seems to us, in the pernicious clutches of Cartesian dualism or perpetuating the prejudice that human actions are somehow less real than, for example, rocks and trees. Why does the classic test of realism always focus on the ostensible reality of the brick in the road? Is the "kick" any less real than the brick? Pearce (1994) characterized the social world as in a state of "continuing creation." The actions that you perform in this moment add to the sum total of human experience; the future of the human race is not fixed, it is still being developed through our actions. . . . When we communicate, we are not just talking *about* the world, we are literally participating in the creation of the social universe" (p. 75).

The social constructionist who has devoted most time to articulating a "realist" position is Harré (1986, 1990). Harré insists that we live within an *umwelt*, or that part of the world that is available to us as a species. For humans, the *umwelt* contains moral and interpretive as well as physical events and objects, and our actions within the *umwelt* are real. They affect as well as are affected by the moral and physical ecologies in which they occur. "Conversation is to be thought of as creating a social world just as causality creates a physical one" (Harré, 1983, p. 65).[5]

Shotter's (1993a) "rhetorical–responsive" approach to social constructionism differentiates itself from Harré's realism (see Shotter, 1993b). Basic to all realisms, Shotter (1993a) argues, is the notion that there is a preestablished order of things in the world that serve as "discoverable, indisputable 'foundations,' or 'standards,' or 'limits' in term of which claims to truth can be judged" (p. 13) However, while denying this version of realism, Shotter (1993a) does not want "to go so far as to say that, so long as one can tell a good story in its support, then just 'anything goes'" (p. 13). Rather, the criterion for distinguishing "between what are 'real' possibilities and what are 'fictitious' possibilities" is grounded within the communities that tell the stories themselves.

Shotter (1990) insists that the social world is inherently unfinished: "In everyday life, words do not in themselves have a meaning, but a *use*, and furthermore, a *use only in a context*; they are best thought of, not as having already determined meanings, but as *means*, as tools, or as instruments for use in the 'making' of meanings" (p. 54). This fluidity and emergent quality of meaning implies that "human activities do not just *appear* vague and indefinite because we are still as yet ignorant of their true underlying nature, but . . . they are *really* vague . . . the fact is, there is no order, no already determined order, just . . . an order of possible orderings which it is up to us to make as we see fit" (p. 56).

These realist versions of social constructionism differ from Gergen's (1992) position, which is specifically mute with respect to reality. Everything, he argues, is a narrative.

> Constructionism makes no denials concerning explosions, poverty, death, or "the world out there" more generally. Neither does it make any affirma-

tions . . . constructionism is ontologically mute. Whatever is, simply is. However, once we attempt to articulate *what* there is we enter the world of discourse. At that moment the process of construction commences, and this effort is inextricably woven into processes of social interchange (including conventions of discourse themselves). . . . There is no means of listing words on one side of the ledger, and "what there is" on the other, and then locating identities that transcend the conventions of a particular community. The adequacy of any word, or arrangement of words, to "capture reality as it is" is a matter of local convention. (p. 171)

Social constructionists agree that there is no preverbal, objective reality that we can know, because our "knowing" is inevitably social, linguistic (in some sense), and constructive. This places us all on the pluralistic end of the monadic–pluralistic continuum, but we hold different opinions about what that means. Gergen seems particularly interested in stressing the discursive nature of the reality we know, separating it from whatever, as he puts it, "simply is." Shotter, Cronen, and I, on the other hand, are primarily interested in foregrounding the actions (conjoint, unfinished) by which we make things real. Lannamann occupies a position between these and the more substantial (pun intended!) theories of Harré, Hymes, and Carbaugh and Hastings.

The three-dimensional model of grammars–temperaments in Figure 5.1 claims that the continua for discriminating differences intersect with each other. This is a stronger claim than, for example, that there are three unrelated continua. I believe that some of the similarities and differences among positions on "realism" may be explained by the grammatical connection to positions on other dimensions. For example, the "reality" of the social world constitutes a very different problem depending on where one's grammar falls on the continuum of spectator versus participant knowledge or on the continuum of whether one seeks certainty or exercises curiosity. Carbaugh and Hasting's (1992) ethnography is clearly closer to spectator knowledge and the quest for certainty than is Pearce and Cronen's (1980) Coordinated Management of Meaning (CMM), and both differ from Gergen's social constructionism.[6]

SPECTATOR KNOWLEDGE
VERSUS PARTICIPANT KNOWLEDGE

The etymology of the word "theory" links it to the concept of a spectator, and the "ocular" metaphor of knowledge has shaped Western intellectual history (Dewey, 1929/1960; Rorty, 1979). Although all social constructivists distance themselves from this concept, we do so in different ways and find ourselves endorsing different alternatives to this traditional view.

Constructivists and Social Constructionists

One way of distinguishing among these intellectual cousins is to separate constructivists from social constructionists. Although it is an oversimplification, it is useful to say that constructivists see communication as a *cognitive* process of *knowing* the world and social constructionists see it as a *social* process of *creating* the world. If neither term is taken as excluding the other, constructivists foreground perception while social constructionists foreground action.

In a conference in Buenos Aires in 1991, Ernst von Glasersfeld and I both asserted that "we construct our social worlds." However, as the ensuing discussion revealed, we meant very different things by this phrase which is common to both of our discourses. A constructivist, von Glasersfeld meant (as I construed him, anyway) that we (each one of us, individually) construct (develop a cognitive image of) our social worlds (i.e., our knowledge of objects based on our sensations). A social constructionist, I meant that we (collectively, as interlocutors with each other) construct (participate in the creation of) our social worlds (i.e., the events and objects in which we find ourselves). Our use of the same words masked some fundamental differences in concepts and practices which locate us differently on the spectator–participant continuum of kinds of knowing.

Constructivism has philosophical roots in Kant and its technical development in cybernetics. "The 'founding fathers' knew very well that their concerns amounted to a new science, and christened it with a new name: *cybernetics*. . . . The avowed intention of the cybernetics movement was to create a *science of mind*" (Varela, 1992, pp. 236, 237). As it developed, this movement cut itself off from its original name, and is now known as second-order cybernetics, cognitive science, artificial intelligence, or radical constructivism.

Gardner (1985) defined "cognitive science" as "a contemporary, empirically based effort to answer long-standing epistemological questions—particularly those concerned with the nature of knowledge, its components, its sources, its development, and its deployment" (p. 6). Cognitive science is characterized, Gardner said, by five features.

1. The belief that mental representations are central, and that these cannot be fully explained by either biological or cultural factors.

2. The faith that the electronic computer is central to any satisfactory understanding of the human mind.
3. The deliberate decision to eliminate factors "whose inclusion . . . would unnecessarily complicate the cognitive–scientific enterprise."
4. A predilection for interdisciplinary studies in the hopes that they will blur boundaries in the emergence of a "single, unified cognitive science."
5. The claim that the issues in Western philosophical tradition comprise the agenda that should be addressed.

According to Gardner, further work in this tradition has challenged each of these assumptions. One revisionist movement was radical constructivism as developed by Heinz von Foerster, Ernst von Glasersfeld, Humberto Maturana, Francisco Varela, Terry Winograd, and Fernando Flores. Von Glasersfeld (1988) offered these as "the two basic principles of radical constructivism":

> (1) Knowledge is not passively received either through the senses or by way of communication, but it is actively built up by the cognizing subject.
>
> (2) The function of cognition is adaptive and serves the subject's organization of the experiential world, not the discovery of an objective ontological reality. (p. 83)

In Hoffman's (1988) terms, "constructivism holds that the structure of our nervous systems dictates that we can never know what is 'really' out there . . . we can only know our own construction of others and the world" (p. 110).

Maturana (Maturana, 1988; Maturana & Varela, 1987) has developed an influential constructivism grounded in the biological character of human beings. Human beings are self-organizing systems, functionally closed to information. Maturana claims that there neither is nor can be any "instructive communication" because information does not "enter" the neural structure of the body. Rather, human beings are perturbed by events in the world, including the actions of other self-organizing systems, in ways that are structurally determined by their own organization. From this perspective, "'information' does not exist. . . . The structure of the system fully determines its interactions by specifying the variety of interactions it can undertake while conserving its organization. The structure of the system *specifies* what it will accept as an interaction and what will be ignored" (Kenny & Gardner, 1988, p. 13).

Maturana (1988) understands conversations as "a flow of co-ordinations of actions and emotions that we observers distinguish as taking place between human beings that interact recurrently in language" (p. 50). We are in multiple conversations simultaneously, living in "braids" of coordinations of coordinations. Communities are seen as "networks of conversations (consensual co-ordinations of actions and emotions that constitute them)" and individuals as "a node in a network of conversations" (Maturana, 1988, p. 53).

Constructivists may be characterized by their interest in the *stories we make up* and then, of course, live within. Their research and theory focus on the determinants of these stories and, in the other face of constructivism, deconstructions of these stories. Social constructionists, on the other hand, are characterized by their interest in the *stories we make real* in our actions.

Despite surface similarities, the philosophical roots of social constructionism differs from constructivism. Its intellectual roots lie in the ecological epistemology of Gregory Bateson, American pragmatism and the philosophical critiques of Ludwig Wittgenstein. In these approaches, the real world of social action, not the cognitive world of knowing, is the realm of interest. Accordingly, the grammars of most social constructionists involve ways to engage with those activities as participants. That is, more than knowing about patterns of human action, social constructionists are interested in knowing how to act so that our actions fit into ongoing, unfinished patterns, contributing to the determination of the meaning of these patterns. We often call this acting into a context, understanding that our actions are part of what makes that context real and gives it its meaning.

Knowing as participation is very different than spectator knowledge, as Dewey (1929/1960) and Rorty (1979) have shown. Specifically, although researchers from this perspective may know a great deal *about* the activity under investigation, this knowledge is important primarily as a means of enabling them to engage with it.

This characteristic often confuses nonconstructionists who read our research. For example, Pearce and Cronen (1980) described an interaction between the pseudonymous "Dave" and "Jan." Our research was designed to learn the grammar of this couple's interaction so that we could engage with them. Our description identified a specific pattern of misunderstanding between them that was an essential part of their grammar of interaction. As we would express it now, our point was that if we want to participate in activities involving Dave and Jan's relationship, our actions have to engage this grammar. Many of our colleagues did not understand this purpose of our study; they persisted in asking (slyly), "Who were they really?" (as if the value of the study derived from the identity of the participants) or (puzzled), "Now, just what general principles were supported by this data?"

The "communication turn" in therapy and consultation developed sophisticated ways of acting into the grammars of families and organizations (McNamee & Gergen, 1992). Based on Bateson's ecological epistemology, the Palo Alto group (associated with the Mental Research Institute) began practicing "brief therapy" in which, among other things, paradoxical injunctions were used to engage the grammar of families and individuals (Watzlawick, Beavin, & Jackson, 1967), and the Milan group (associated with the Milan Institute for the Study of the Family) began practicing "long brief theory" used circular questioning and counterparadoxical injunctions (Palazzoli, Boscolo, Cecchin, & Prata, 1978, 1980). As further developed by the Kensington Consultation Centre (London) and other systemic, social constructionist therapists, consultants, and researchers, these ways of working enable consultants to join the grammars of client systems, make those grammars problematic, and co-construct new stories and ways of acting. What a theorist knows, from this perspective, is how to act into an emerging situation in such a way as to avoid several well-trod paths toward undesirable outcomes and to accomplish his or her purposes. Descriptions of this way of working are provided by Oliver (1992), Ugazio and Ferraro (1992), and Fruggeri (1992).

For and against "Theory"

Another way of differentiating among social constructionisms is their attitude toward theory. Again, there is a glittering array of options. Carbaugh and Hastings (1992) argue that ethnographies can produce theory consistent with the conventional criteria of social science. Harré (1980) believes that the "received view" of theory is misguided. Models, not propositions, constitute theory, and, thus understood, social constructionists can develop theory. Cronen (in press-b) distinguishes between theory from a spectator perspective and practical theory consistent with the grammar of participant knowledge. Social constructionists, he urges, should eschew the former and work hard to develop the latter. Shotter (1993b) differentiates three kinds of knowing: knowing that, knowing how, and knowing from. Theory is a form of "knowing that" and social constructionists should avoid it at all costs. Instead, they should have a "tool kit" of concepts to use.[7]

As far as I know, no social constructionists would want a theory consisting of propositions purporting to describe an objective reality. However, there are many opinions about what should take its place. Some social constructionists repudiate the very idea of a theory; others work hard to identify forms of theory compatible with their intellectual commitments. I believe that the most sophisticated and satisfying work on this topic lies before us.

THE QUEST FOR CERTAINTY VERSUS
THE EXERCISE OF CURIOSITY

In my judgment, this dimension is the most important and least well articulated of the three. David Mortensen and Mary Ann Fitzpatrick (personal communication; 1994) recently pointed out that "certainty" and "curiosity" are not semantic opposites, and that even the quest for certainty is often fueled by curiosity. They are right, of course, but the meaning of the exercise of curiosity itself differs depending on how it is related to other aspects of the theorist's temperament.

As part of a grammar that includes spectator knowledge and a view of the social world as monadic, the exercise of curiosity is best understood as puzzle solving or a strain toward closure; it is a motivation to inquiry which will, at last, produce certainty. On the other hand, as a part of a grammar that includes participant knowledge and a view of the social world as fluid, the exercise of curiosity is best understood as a way of acknowledging the reflexive relationship between the knower and the known, the relationships of mutual contingency between "us" and "them" and between "me" and the events and objects in my social world, and the unfinished nature of the events and objects into which we act.

The exercise of curiosity by social constructionists consists of an affinity for paradox and irony, a certain playfulness about our own actions that take into consideration the fact that we make the world that we describe, and an orientation toward mutuality, co-construction, and systems rather than toward reductionism or objectivism. From the perspective of positivism, these forms of curiosity appear frivolous, incomprehensible, and often perverse; from the social constructionist perspective, they are the minimal expressions of the reflexivity between what we know about the world and our place in it.

Giving a close reading to Descartes's "method" of radical doubt, Bernstein (1983) characterized the "Cartesian anxiety" as the belief that if we have anything less than absolute certainty—knowledge that cannot be doubted—we have nothing worth knowing. That is, there are no useful distinctions among knowledge that is less than completely certain. In Bernstein's account, this "anxiety" leads to the neurotic search for certainty in order that we do not fall into the "abyss" of relativism.

Whatever other neuroses we might exhibit, social constructionists are not afflicted by Cartesian anxiety. We believe that the apparent dichotomy between certainty and relativism is false, depending on certain

assumptions about the world and ourselves in it that social constructionists have, for the most part, set aside. Social constructionists recognize
that whatever our interests, our own language and actions are part of the
process by which we know them, whether as spectator or as participant.
Wittgenstein (1953) said:

> Philosophical problems are, of course, not empirical problems; they are
> solved, rather, by looking into the workings of our language, and that in
> such a way as to make us recognize those workings: *in despite of* an urge to
> misunderstand them. The problems are solved, not by giving new informa
> tion, but by arranging what we have always known. Philosophy is a battle
> against the bewitchment of our intelligence by means of language. (para
> graph #109)

Granted Wittgenstein's analysis of our condition, I note that social
constructionists differ among themselves in the extent to which they take
themselves as susceptible to "bewitchment" and the energy they bring to
the "battle" against it. I believe that "mystery" is a universal component
of human life (Pearce, 1989). Language liberates us from "mere facticity"
by enabling us to create human worlds (not just physical spaces) of
significance. However, an inevitable consequence of this liberation is
being ensnared in just those webs of significance prefigured in the
languages we use. We can remain comfortably enmeshed in those languages, but it is also possible to experience a "second liberation," this
time *from* language. This liberation does not consist of escaping the snares
of language but in understanding—and thus becoming able, albeit briefly
and occasionally, to transcend—them.

Social constructionists who exercise curiosity are familiar with paradoxes and irony. All of us, Rorty said (1989), "carry about a set of words
which [we] employ to justify [our] actions, [our] beliefs, and [our] lives"
(p. 73). These sets of words comprise our "final vocabularies." We may
have any of several relationships to those final vocabularies. An "ironist"
is one who

> 1. Has radical and continuing doubts about the final vocabulary she
> currently uses.
> 2. Realizes that argument phrased in her present vocabulary can
> neither underwrite nor dissolve these doubts.
> 3. Does not think that her vocabulary is closer to reality than others.
> (Rorty, 1989, p. 73)

In a similar fashion, Duncan (1962) said that "irony holds belief, the tragic
moment of truth, open to doubt" (p. 381). Was Campbell (1968) speaking
ironically when he said, "The best things cannot be said; the second best

are misunderstood. After that comes civilized conversation"? (p. 84). Is this a statement of "best things"? Or is it part of "civilized conversation"— and hence at best a third-rate statement?

I suspect that those whose constructionisms are closer to the specta- tor knowledge and monadic universe ends of the continua will not resonate with the style of or opinions expressed in the previous para- graphs. Those who believe that the social world is fluid will resonate with this statement by Bennis (1990):

> The physical world is elegant in design, predictable in action, and fixed in purpose. The social world, the world we have made, is vastly inelegant, unpredictable, and unfixed. Made of ambiguity and ambivalence, contra- diction and conflict, it is a clown in the temple. It can change as you look at it. Sometimes, it changes because you are looking at it. It requires alertness, curiosity, impatience, courage, and skepticism. (p. 48)

Those who do research with a view to participating in the activities that they study find themselves having to include themselves as part of the process that they are describing. Jorgenson (1992) describes the reflexivity of doing an interview with this understanding and Bochner and Ellis (Chapter 11, this volume) present a case study that demonstrates reflexivity. Chen and Pearce (Chapter 7, this volume) articulate how "case studies" done from this perspective comprise different communication acts than those which, for example, try to build theory, and thus require different criteria for evaluation.

While I am being a bit playful with disparate sensibilities in this section, I believe that quite different accounts (I am trying to avoid the word "theory") of communication emerge from them. The clearest examples are the two different traditions confused by their similar use of the term "speech act." J. L. Austin and John Searle were concerned to produce a "philosophy of mind" through an analysis of speech acts. It is appropriate—in this tradition—to ask how many speech acts there are and to list the "felicity conditions" for their successful performance. In the tradition stemming from Wittgenstein, the purpose is to learn something about the way speech acts are made and thus to increase our ability to engage in (or avoid) specific language-games. The notion of counting speech acts is—in this tradition—meaningless (Cronen, Pearce, & Xi, 1989/1990; Pearce, 1994, Chap. 3; Sigman, 1992).

The exercise of curiosity has been worked out as a form of practice in systemic consultation and therapy. As the Milan team began their work, they suggested that the therapist/consultant must be neutral with respect to the structure of the family/organization with which they were working. The concept of neutrality became one of the most contested of the terms used by the Milan group and its evolvement has continued. Cecchin (1987, 1992) first suggested the term "curiosity" as a substitute for "neutrality" and then introduced the notion of the irreverent therapist (Cecchin, Lane, & Ray, 1992). The "expert" therapist faces two temptations. On the one hand, people can believe experts too much, and the experts become trapped into repeating in new contexts what they said/did in others; on the other hand, experts can believe in themselves too much, so that they become preoccupied trying to convince doubters or defend the faith of their followers. The solution: principled irreverence.

> You have to know something very well before you are able to be irreverent towards it. You should be conversant with the literature of different therapeutic perspectives and be an "expert" in at least one of them . . . it is the therapist's enthusiasm for a model or a hypothesis that can help him to get close to a family, while simultaneously maintaining a certain level of curiosity and respect. But it is at the moment when the therapist begins to reflect upon the effect of his own attitude and presumptions that he acquires a position that is both ethical and therapeutic. In order to be able to attain this ability for self-reflexivity, we believe that it is necessary to have a certain level of irreverence and a sense of humor, which one acquires by maintaining a continuous conversation with colleagues, people outside the mental health field, students, and patients alike. (Cecchin et al., 1992, pp. 8–9)

What does this irreverence look like in practice? Systemic therapists keep reminding each other not to get "married" to their hypotheses about their clients. Some wags suggested that the "romance" should be interrupted before marriage is even contemplated: Therapists should not "fall in love" with their hypotheses. Extending the line of reasoning, others argue that therapists should not even date their hypotheses. Some say that the reason they have adopted systemic practices is so they can be "promiscuous" with their hypotheses (Peter Lang, personal communication , 1989).

I believe that the exercise of curiosity is a potential source of great confusion among social constructionists because curiosity changes its meaning drastically depending on the rest of the theorist's temperament or grammar. For example, if we are intent on building a theory (in the traditional sense) about the products of the process of social constructionism, irreverence (a fondness for paradox, an affinity for irony, and a certain intellectual promiscuity) by social constructionists is seen as frivolous and counterproductive. On the other hand, if we are interested in engaging with the grammars of the persons/groups that we encounter in a process of co-constructing with them the reality in which we live, this same irreverence is part of the "method" by which we escape the bewitchment of our intelligence by language and by our own beliefs.

The exercise of curiosity is difficult to write about because curiosity cannot be exercised in the abstract and it is incompatible with generalizations. The exercise of curiosity does not lead to empirical generalizations, or—better stated—to the extent that it does lead to empirical generalizations, these are means to the development of what Aristotle called *phronēsis* or practical wisdom in action. Discussions with our "mainstream" colleagues about research methods is difficult because the exercise of curiosity cannot (without an extremely well-developed sense of irony) be described as a series of steps in a methodology textbook or even in a research report. It is better shown than described, and then always in the application of a particular instance of communication.

The exercise of curiosity is a form of skilled behavior that can be evaluated even though it cannot, *a priori*, be fully articulated. It is more akin to the activities of an athlete, dancer, or chef than to the recipe of an unskilled cook or beginner in any of the performing arts. But how does one become a virtuoso? By practice, instruction, critique, and reflection: These are the types of activities that distinguish creativity from random actions; that differentiate the innovations of an expert from the flailings of a neophyte.

There is a substantive irony in that one must learn the forms of any skilled performance before one can be free to improvise. However, we have lived with this irony in many contexts; there is no reason why we cannot understand it in the context of social constructionism. Lang, Little, and Cronen (1990) suggested that "systemic professionals" should differentiate among the "domains" of instruction, explanation, and production as a way of clarifying, to themselves and others, just where they stand in this ironic situation. That is, when "explaining" an activity, one may be happily promiscuous, jumping from one absurd hypothesis to another. However, when "producing" (e.g., a therapeutic intervention), one must commit to a line of (inter)action with the client; to be intellectually promiscuous in this context is to be irresponsible.

CONCLUSION

Social constructionism is the contemporary version of a venerable tradition in Western intellectual history. This tradition has seldom been the dominant one, but it is persistent. In its current form, the differences between it and the dominant paradigm in social science are blurred, in part because the dominant paradigm is calling into question many of its features that most sharply contrast with social constructionism and in part because many social constructionist documents (e.g., Gergen, 1992) take the form of *apologia*, giving "social constructionist answers" to the array of topics that are generated by the grammar of the dominant paradigm.

As the distinctiveness of the social constructionist agenda becomes clearer, we will find ourselves appreciating in a new manner some old teachings. For example, the sophist Gorgias is reputed to have said that 1) nothing exists; 2) if it did, we could not know it; and 3) if we could know it, we could not communicate it. What might we make of such claims?

From a spectator–monadic–certainty perspective, Gorgias's statement is absurd not only because it flies in the face of so many intellectual commitments but because it is a self-referential paradox. If it is true, Gorgias cannot communicate it. But Gorgias was a sophist; a member of a community that delighted in paradoxes. Perhaps he was well aware of the paradoxicality of his statement and did not intend it to be understood literally. After all, as Falletta (1983) said, paradoxes are sometimes "truth standing on its head to attract attention" (p. xvii).

In Gorgias's day, the dominant paradigm worked in this sequence: First ontology (what exists?), then epistemology (how we know what exists?), and only then communication (how we share our knowledge about what exists?). Gorgias's conversation partner, Plato, decided that what exists is eternal, immutable, and objective. That assumption in place, epistemology must account for our ability to know just those sorts of things, and communication, if it is to be ethical, must be based on that kind of knowledge. (Held to this standard, the rhetorics of the sophists seemed intellectually empty and were sharply condemned by Plato.)

However, what happens if we make a different set of assumptions? What if we take our experience as persons in conversation as our starting point? We know that persons in conversations are unfinished, materially located in specific situations, story-telling and story-living entities who both respond to and create the material conditions in which they act, and so on. If this is where we start, epistemology must account for our ability to "know" something as fluid as that, and knowing takes the form of being able to act effectively into such a process rather than standing somewhere (where?) outside it and making statements about it. And if this is what knowledge is, Gorgias is right: Nothing eternal, unchanging and objective exists; if it did . . . and so on. But we *do* communicate, and understanding this process requires a different notion of understanding and knowing than Plato envisioned.

Social constructionists unanimously line up with (at least this rendering of) Gorgias's position. However, as the preceding pages have shown, these are important differences among us. The three "dimensions" of grammar or temperament in Figure 5.1 enable us to articulate some of these differences, but to what end? I do not think social constructionists will ever agree and this consoles me. In fact, I believe that efforts toward consensus, if pursued with very much zeal, are pernicious. My stance here is not one of principled pluralism; rather, it recognizes that social constructionisms are least at home in the abstract world of atemporal, decontextualized propositions and most at home in the always local, historical, specific, unfinished world of actions. Because the social world is fluid and we theorists (if that is the right word) are located in specific places within it, our theories (shudder!) ought to differ in ways that reflect our positioning as well as our temperaments. The proper function of this "sailing guide" is not to eliminate differences but to facilitate the wholesome conversation among us that will refresh and illuminate us.

NOTES

1. An earlier version of this chapter was published as "A Campers' Guide to Constructionisms" in *Human Systems* (1992, *3*, 139–162). Although the general purpose of both contributions is similar, the "Sailing Guide" includes much more attention to recent developments in the discipline of communication, in which social constructionism has suddenly become an important keyword. In both versions, I have struggled to maintain a distinction between my role as a central figure in one of the earliest versions of a social constructionist theory of communication (CMM) and my role as, for these purposes, the self-appointed "guide" to a variety of social constructionisms (of which CMM is one). In the "Campers' Guide," I erred in the direction of effacing my own voice-as-theorist; in this version I try to include both voices, running the risk of appearing at times to be self-serving. I beg the reader's tolerant understanding of the difficulty of including one's own voice in a ventriloquist's performance.

2. Not only are there *many* such approaches, but the approaches are varied beyond hope of compatible reconciliation. See Dervin, Grossberg, O'Keefe, and Wartella (1989) and Pearce (1991.).

3. "Success" brings its own problems, of course. The range of things currently brought under the umbrella of social constructionism has made some of us grumble. There are even suggestions that we need to invent new terms that will more precisely identify various "cousins." To date, this anticipated phase of neologism making has not occurred, and I have not tried to do it here. However, stay tuned.

4. My use of "real" in this context is deliberately playful, given the fact that social constructionists disagree about the appropriate use of this term. The issue hinges on whether we social constructionists should/must abandon this and other terms as part of our emancipation from the language games of objectivism–positivism. My feeling is that we should become *sufficiently* emancipated from these discourses so that we can develop our own language, which will include unapologetic redefinitions of familiar terms. From

the perspective of objectivism, I am clearly *not* a realist, but why should I be limited or governed by the objectivist perspective? Social constructionists are rendered mute (or reduced to stammering) when we try to express *our* perspective within the discourses of objectivism–positivism. As a result, we should distinguish between our *apologias*, in which we address those in the "old paradigms," from the work we do in our "own" language.

I believe that our emancipation from objectivism–positivism would be facilitated by developing a dictionary that contrasts social constructionist usages of terms with the meanings these terms have in other language games. For example, much confusion has occurred by incorporating into social constructionist discourse (even as a "rejected" concept) the objectionist concept of reality as preverbal objects independent of human cognition. Of this notion of reality, as Gergen (1992) and Wittgenstein (in the *Tractatus*) rightly noted, we must be mute. However, for social constructionists, reality is those *activities* in which we "call" things; in which we "construct" the events and objects of our social world. Placing these activities as the "real," a kind of "gestalt shift" in perception occurs in which the objectivist notion of real is irrelevant and, back to the specific reference, to say that there are real differences among social constructionist is to report that the language games that they play have different grammars and that they engage in different activities.

5. Harré's position on realism is subtly argued, has evolved over time (Harré, 1986, 1990), and is still a topic of considerable controversy (see Shotter, 1993b). I have only indexed his work here; I do not know how to do justice to it without changing the whole nature of this chapter.

6. If anyone wants to move from a sailing guide to a full-fledged navigational chart, one procedure would be to locate each social constructionism on all three dimensions, articulating the way the grammar of that approach is structured by the interactions of all three positions. Those of us who have worked in this area know that there are some impossible combinations, and have felt the force of incompatible grammatical forms. In fact, I suspect that the way paradigm change occurs is that someone moves along one continuum, creating strains within the grammar; when these strains become intolerable, the researcher/theorist makes a sudden move along the other dimensions, appearing to have made a discontinuous change and luxuriating in his or her newfound ability to act within a consistent grammar.

I believe that there are some confusions among social constructionists caused by incompatible elements within their grammars that can be explained by locating them along these continua. For example, Cronen and I were trained as social scientists. We quickly moved into "interpretive social science" in that actors' meanings were (obviously) important to us, as were coordinated activities. Our writings during the "first phase of the CMM project" (1975–1980) were confused because we used the language of interpretive social science (e.g., meanings were understood as "in the heads of" our subjects and we viewed ourselves as corrigible observers but not reflexively involved in the cocreation of meaning with our "subjects") to express social constructionist concepts. Only as we continued to refine our thinking did we discover (in conversations with James McCroskey and Charles Berger, among others) that we *could not* say what we were doing in the language of (the dominant paradigm of) social science, and (in conversation with Rom Harré, John Shotter, Kenneth Gergen, and Peter Lang, among others) that we had to "retroactively adopt" a new set of intellectual "ancestors." For us, our new ancestors (with the full sense of the oxymoron) were the American Pragmatists, Wittgenstein, and second-order cybernetics, added to our old ancestors of Bateson and systems theory–cybernetics. Others have gone through similar processes. For example, Lannamann has adapted some aspects of critical theory and Shotter braids Vygotsky, Vico, and Bakhtin. Stewart (1992) offers Heidegger as a candidate for adoption by social constructionists. I offer these autobiographical and biographical tales to endorse projects of clarifying the grammars of social constructionism.

7. The positions taken by social constructionists with regard to "theory"—or, more generally, the form in which "knowledge" should be cast—are not well developed. I expect some interesting discussions of this topic in the next decade, complicated by our differing positions on whether our knowledge is a form of doing or of saying (the spectator–participant continuum) and on whether our purpose is to achieve, as Descartes would have it, clear and distinct ideas or to be, as Gunn (1992) suggested, "interested and perhaps even interesting" (p. 16).

REFERENCES

Bennis, W. (1990). *Why leaders can't lead: The unconscious conspiracy continues.* San Francisco: Jossey-Bass.

Berger. P. L., & Luckmann, T. (1966). *The social construction of reality.* Garden City, NY: Doubleday.

Bernstein, R. J. (1983). *Beyond objectivism and relativism: Science, hermeneutics and praxis.* Philadelphia: University of Pennsylvania Press.

Bernstein, R. J. (1992). *The new constellation: The ethical–political horizons of modernity/postmodernity.* Cambridge, MA: MIT Press.

Boscolo, L., Cecchin, G., Hoffman, L., & Penn, P. (1987). *Milan systemic family therapy.* New York: Basic Books.

Campbell, J. (1968). *The masks of God: Creative mythology.* New York: Viking.

Carbaugh, D., & Hastings, S. O. (1992). A role for communication theory in ethnography and cultural analysis. *Communication Theory, 2,* 156–165.

Cecchin, G. (1987). Hypothesizing, circularity, and neutrality revisited: An invitation to curiosity. *Family Process, 26,* 405–413.

Cecchin, G. (1992). Constructing therapeutic possibilities. In S. McNamee & K. J. Gergen (Eds.), *Therapy as social construction* (pp. 86–95). London: Sage.

Cecchin, G., Lane, G., & Ray, W. A. (1992.) *Irreverence: A strategy for therapists' survival.* London: Karnac.

Cronen, V. E. (in press-a). The consequentiality of communication and the recapturing of experience. In S. J. Sigman (Ed.), *The consequentiality of communication*. Hillsdale, NJ: Erlbaum.

Cronen, V. E. (in press-b). Coordinated management of meaning: Theory for the complexities and contradictions of everyday life. (In J. Siegfried (Ed.), *The status of common sense in psychology*. Norwood, NJ: Ablex.

Cronen, V. E., Pearce, W. B., & Tomm, K. (1985). A dialectical view of personal change. In K. J. Gergen & K. Davis (Eds.), *The social construction of the person* (pp. 203–224). New York: Springer-Verlag.

Cronen, V. E., Pearce, W. B., & Xi, C. (1989/1990). The meaning of "meaning" in CMM analyses of communication: A comparison of theories. *Research on Language and Social Interaction, 25,* 37–66.

Dervin, B., Grossberg, L., O'Keefe, B. J., & Wartella, E. (Eds.). (1989). *Rethinking communication* (2 vols.). Newbury Park, CA: Sage.

Dewey, J. (1960). *The quest for certainty*. New York: G.P. Putnam's Sons. (Original work published 1929)

Duncan, H. D. (1962). *Communication and social order*. New York: Oxford University Press.

Eastland, L. S. (1994). Habermas, emancipation, and relationship change: An exploration of recovery processes as a model for social transformation. *Journal of Applied Communication Research, 22,* 162–176.

Falletta, N. (1983). *The paradoxicon*. Garden City, NJ: Doubleday.

Fruggeri, L. (1992). Therapeutic process as the social construction of change. In S. McNamee & K. J. Gergen (Eds.), *Therapy as social construction* (pp. 40–53). London: Sage.

Gardner, H. (1985). *The mind's new science: A history of the cognitive revolution*. New York: Basic Books.

Gergen, K. J. (1992). Social construction in question. *Human Systems, 3,* 163–182.

Gergen, K. J. (1994). *Toward transformation in social knowledge* (2nd ed.). Thousand Oaks, CA: Sage.

Gunn, G. (1992). *Thinking across the American grain: Ideology, intellect and the new pragmatism*. Chicago: University of Chicago Press.

Harré, R. (1980). *Social being*. Totowa, NJ: Littlefield & Adams.

Harré, R. (1984). *Personal being: 'A theory for individual psychology*. Oxford: Basil Blackwell.

Harré, R. (1986). *Varieties of realism*. Oxford: Basil Blackwell.

Harré, R. (1989). Language–games and the texts of identity. In J. Shotter & K. J. Gergen (Eds.), *Texts of identity* (pp. 20–35). London: Sage.

Harré, R. (1990). Exploring the human *umwelt*. In R. Bhaskar (Ed.), *Harré and his critics: Essays in honour of Rom Harré with his commentary on them*. Oxford: Blackwell.

Harré, R., & Secord, P. (1972). *The explanation of social behavior*. Totowa, NJ: Littlefield & Adams.

Hoffman, L. (1988). A constructivist position for family therapy. *Irish Journal of Psychology, 9,* 110–129.

Jorgenson, J. (1992). Communication, rapport, and the interview. *Communication Theory, 2,* 148–155.

Kenny, V., & Gardner, G. (1988). Constructions of self-organizing systems. *Irish Journal of Psychology, 9,* 1–24.

Lang, P., Little, M., & Cronen V. E. (1990). The systemic professional: Domain of action and the question of neutrality. *Human Systems, 1,* 39–56.

Lannamann, J. W. (1991). Interpersonal communication research as ideological practice. *Communication Theory, 1,* 179–203.

Lannamann, J. W. (1992). Deconstructing the person and changing the subject of interpersonal studies. *Communication Theory, 2,* 139–147.

Leeds-Hurwitz, W. (1984). On the relationship of the "ethnography of speaking" to the "ethnography of communication." *Papers in Linguistics, 17,* 7–32.

Leeds-Hurwitz, W. (1992). Forum introduction: Social approaches to interpersonal communication. *Communication Theory, 2,* 131–139.

Maturana, H. R. (1988). Reality: The search for objectivity or the quest for a compelling argument. *Irish Journal of Psychology, 9,* 25–82.

Maturana, H. R., & Varela, F. (1987). *The tree of knowledge: The biological roots of human understanding.* Boston: New Science Library.

McNamee, S., & Gergen, K. J. (1992). *Therapy as a social construction.* London: Sage.

Oliver, C. (1992). A focus on moral story-making in therapy using co-ordinated management of meaning theory (CMM). *Human Systems, 2,* 217–232.

Palazzoli, M. S., Boscolo, L., Cecchin, G., & Prata, J. (1978). *Paradox and counterparadox.* New York: Jason Aronson.

Palazzoli, M. S., Boscolo, L., Cecchin, G., & Prata, J. (1980). Hypothesizing—circularity—neutrality: Three guidelines for the conductor of the session. *Family Process, 19,* 3–12.

Pearce, W. B. (1989). *Communication and the human condition.* Carbondale: University of Southern Illinois Press.

Pearce, W. B. (1991). On comparing theories: Treating theories as commensurate or incommensurate. *Communication Theory, 1,* 159–164.

Pearce, W. B. (1993). Achieving dialogue with "the other" in the postmodern world. In P. Gaunt (Ed.), *Beyond agendas: New directions in communication research* (pp. 59–74). Westport, CT: Greenwood Press.

Pearce, W. B. (1994). *Interpersonal communication: Creating social worlds.* New York: HarperCollins.

Pearce, W. B., & Cronen, V. E. (1980). *Communication action and meaning: The creation of social realities.* New York: Praeger.

Pearce, W. B., & Foss, K. (1990). The historical context of communication as a science. In G. L. Dahnke & G. W. Clatterbuck (Eds.), *Human communication: Theory and research* (pp. 1–20). Belmont, CA: Wadsworth.

Powers, J. H. (1994). *Public speaking: The lively art.* New York: HarperCollins.

Rorty, R. (1979). *Philosophy and the mirror of nature.* Princeton, NJ: Princeton University Press.

Rorty, R. (1989). *Contingency, irony, and solidarity.* New York: Cambridge University Press.

Shotter, J. (1989). Social accountability and the social construction of "you." In J. Shotter & K. J. Gergen (Eds.), *Texts of identity* (pp. 133–151). London: Sage,

Shotter, J. (1990). *Knowing of the third kind.* Utrecht, The Netherlands: ISOR/University of Utrecht.

Shotter, J. (1993a). *Conversational realities: Constructing life through language.* London: Sage.

Shotter, J. (1993b). *Cultural politics of everyday life: Social constructionism, rhetoric, and knowing of the third kind.* Toronto: Toronto University Press.

Shotter, J., & Gergen, K. J. (1989). Preface and introduction. In J. Shotter & K. J. Gergen (Eds.), *Texts of identity* (pp. ix–xi). London: Sage.

Shotter, J., & Gergen, K. J. (1994). Social construction: Knowledge, self, others, and continuing the conversation. In S. A. Deetz (Ed.), *Communication yearbook/17* (pp. 3–33). Thousand Oaks, CA: Sage.

Sigman, S. J. (1992). Do social approaches to interpersonal communication constitute a contribution to communication theory? *Communication Theory, 2,* 347–356.

Stewart, J. (1992). Philosophical dimensions of social approaches to interpersonal communication. *Communication Theory, 2,* 337–346.

Ugazio, V., & Ferrario, M. (1992). Falsifying experiences. *Human Systems, 2,* 233–253.

Varela, F. (1992). Whence perceptual meaning? A cartography of current ideas. In F. Varela & J. P. Dupey (Eds.), *Understanding origins: Contemporary views on the origins of life, mind and society* (pp. 235–264). Boston: Kluwer.

von Glasersfeld, E. (1988). The reluctance to change a way of thinking. *Irish Journal of Psychology, 9,* 83–90.

Watzlawick, P., Beavin, J., & Jackson, D. D. (1967). *Pragmatics of human communication.* New York: W. W. Norton.

Wittgenstein, L. (1953). *Philosophical investigations* (G. E. M. Anscombe, Trans.). Oxford: Basil Blackwell.

CHAPTER 6

The Politics of Voice in Interpersonal Communication Research

JOHN W. LANNAMANN

> The hard sciences are successful because they deal with the soft problems; the soft sciences are struggling because they deal with the hard problems.
> —VON FOERSTER (1984, p. 206)

One of the hard problems for communication researchers is that the noun "communication" is not noun-like. For the three and a half decades since Berlo (1960) popularized the notion that communication involves a "continuous change in time" (p. 23), interpersonal communication researchers have struggled with the implications of studying what Bateson (1991) playfully refers to as "no thing" (p. 237).

Part of the difficulty of studying social processes is that our language beckons us away from the radically open, unfinished tendencies of everyday conversation. Whorf (1956) points out that the logical grammar of our language mandates a distinction between the classes of products and processes. He writes, "Our language gives us a bipolar division of nature" but nature "is not thus polarized" (p. 215). The result of this linguistic division is a constructed world of things and actions with no easy way to talk about the continuous activity of social construction. We can point to people and symbols or we can invent objects such as attitudes, cognitive schemata, and other clever devices, but at best these are only the dirty dishes left after the party. Whatever it is that we describe using the term "communication," it is always over or changed before the label is applied, unless the research itself is recognized as an important form of communicative activity (McNamee, 1988).

Whether we choose to accept Whorf's proposed distinction as "absolute" or to modify it as Reddy (1979) does when he writes that "the stories English speakers tell about communication are largely determined by semantic structures of the language itself" (p. 285), it is clear that communication scholarship is at least partially written by the logical grammar of our language before we even sit down to write.

In this chapter, I identify the tendency to feature the individual in modern communication research as a response to our linguistic constraints and the sociohistorical context of the social sciences. I then discuss the consequences of this version of individualism for the field of interpersonal communication and suggest directions for an alternative, socially oriented, dialogic version of communication inquiry.

CONTAINING LINGUISTIC INDIVIDUALISM

In my interpersonal communication courses I often ask students to devise a list with two columns. At the top of the left column are the words "I am" and on the top of the right column are the words "We are." I then ask students to list as many responses to each of these statements as come to mind. Students consistently fill the left column but have difficulty coming up with terms for the column on the right. There are a few terms that consistently cross over between columns, for example, "I am lazy–we are lazy," but the use of these terms only makes sense in the plural case when the word "both" is implied, suggesting that the term really describes two individuals rather than the single relationship. Relational terms such as "in rapport" (Jorgenson, 1992) or "in love" are scarce.

Part of the difficulty the students encounter as they try to come up with relational terms is that the logical grammar appropriate for individual terms cannot be generalized to a relational way of speaking. The linguistic practices that sustain individualism involve more than a vocabulary; the competent use of individualist terms entails the production of particular grammatical constructions and metaphors. Reddy's (1979) critique of the "conduit" metaphor is a useful illustration of this point. He calls attention to common examples such as "Try to get your thoughts *across* better" and "You still haven't *given* me any *idea* of what you mean" to demonstrate his claim that the logical grammar of English incorporates a conduit based understanding of communication. Meaning is inserted into words and then transferred. The journey ends with another container, the individual, the container of the self (Cushman, 1990; Sampson, 1977, 1981). Thus, the conduit metaphor invites an understanding of the person as the owner and master of personal attributes such as leadership, aggressiveness, or self-esteem.

The logical grammar of the conduit metaphor requires that personal attributes be located *in* individuals. In this way of speaking, the social processes generating the self and its proposed internal states are not given voice. It is not surprising, then, that the students in my classes have difficulty coming up with relational terms. The difficulty the students encounter when they try to list relational terms is that the grammar of the container metaphor fails. Participants in a conversation cannot claim that rapport is *in* them. Instead, they must locate themselves in the relationship. *They* are *in* rapport. Here the metaphor of the person as container must yield to the metaphor of the relational process as container. In fact, it is more useful to drop the container metaphor entirely and replace it with a conversational metaphor in which contemporaneous action is the principal theme. Time and sequence, not just space, are important dimensions for understanding conversational process.

The difficulty that makes the soft sciences hard is that once the focus of attention shifts from individual products to social processes, we confront the limits of our language practices and forms of life. For example, it is easier to use the concept of individual intentionality than that of joint contingencies when describing conversational processes because we have at our disposal a rich collection of terms to describe individual intentions but very few terms to describe the coproduced drift of conversation. In discussing this problem, Gergen (1985) suggests that in the language of person description, the outcome of action is generally reinstated as the aim of the action. The complex, temporally sequenced nature of action is abbreviated by identifying the " 'aim,' 'attempt,' 'tendency,' 'disposition,' or 'intention' of the person" (Gergen, 1985, p. 119). In this way, individual intentionality is substituted for a cumbersome description of a continually changing interaction. Shotter (1987) refers to a similar problem in his discussion of William James's "psychologist's fallacy," the temptation to describe an unfolding, incomplete, and uncertain social process in terms that are sensible only when the completed activity is known. With a large stock of analytical terms to describe individuals and few terms to describe joint action, it is not surprising that much of interpersonal communication theory is limited to the investigation of individual rather than social and interactional variables. The concept of a self-contained individual (Sampson, 1977) offers the field a seductive unit of observation and offers to rescue the field from the uncertainty and open-endedness of social process. Unfortunately, the concept also diverts attention away from communication.

So far, my discussion of the language-based difficulties of studying interpersonal communication has remained at the level of the text or the discursive practice. As such, my account is both sympathetic to a post-structuralist reading of our field and, at the same time, subject to a materialist critique. A poststructuralist account of interaction emphasizes the discursive and constructed nature of interpersonal relationships, yet to accept that it is all discourse—all stories, surfaces, and sliding signifiers—raises questions about agency, responsibility, and politics. If it is all talk, who is talking and in what conditions? This question invites the recognition that talk is a material practice; its instantiation is part of a specific historic moment and it is constrained by the possibilities of that moment.

SOME HISTORICAL ROOTS OF INDIVIDUALISM

The abundance of individualist terms and the relative scarcity of relational terms are the linguistic hangovers of a historical process that positioned the concept of individualism as the centerpiece of social, economic, and political structures. A number of writers, including Geertz (1983), Habermas (1975), Bellah, Madsen, Sullivan, Swidler, and Tipton (1985), and Sampson (1989a, 1989b) have suggested that the current emphasis on the individual is a fairly recent and quite culture-bound phenomenon. Geertz (1983) writes that the "Western conception of the person as a bounded, unique, more or less integrated motivational and cognitive universe . . . is, however incorrigible it may seem to us, a rather peculiar idea within the context of the world's cultures" (p. 59). Habermas (1975) offers a historical overview of the movement toward the concept of the individual by tracing the changing principles of social organization in primitive, traditional, liberal–capitalist, and postcapitalist societies. At the center of each of these formulations is the recognition that the concept of the individuality did not arise because of natural inevitability. In each account, a shift from social identity to individual identity is related to economic changes.

Habermas (1975) reasons that the familial or tribal sense of identity in primitive social formations was weakened by the rise of bureaucratic state authority in traditional society and eventually overcome in a liberal–capitalist society by the model of the profit-oriented entrepreneur. Where kinship or tribal membership once defined persons, in liberal–capitalist structures it is the rational self-interest of autonomous individuals in the marketplace that defines the person. In this system, status, success, and failure are largely determined by the economic pursuits of an individual rather than by tradition or birth.

The emergence of the autonomous individual and the emerging dominance of capitalism were linked phenomena. The liberal–capitalist social form both generates and depends on the model of the individual as an autonomous actor pursuing self-interest by exchanging labor power or capital. Adam Smith (1776/1952) was clear about the primacy of the individual when he wrote that the individual "intends only his own gain, and he is in this, as in other cases, led by an invisible hand to promote an end which was no part of his intention" (p. 194).

The emergence of the individual as the central social unit in liberal capitalism can also be understood in terms of industrial change and modernity. With the appearance of industrial society in the 17th century, production moved from the household, where identity was tied to family, to the factory, where identity was shaped by class position—a relationship between the factory owner and the individual worker (Jhally, 1989). The premodern, preindustrial conception of communal identity was replaced by the notion of identity formed in the marketplace of competing individuals. In the early 20th century, as ownership of capital became concentrated, increases in efficiency led to greater specialization within the labor force. The specialization required on the assembly line further isolated individual workers and contributed to the continued fragmentation of personhood.

In this liberal–individualist version of society, the fundamental social unit is the self-determining individual who pursues goals according to personal choices. The social community plays only a supporting role for the pursuits of sovereign individual. Sampson (1989b) refers to the "self-contained" character of the modernist conception of personhood. He writes: "Individuals were to be set free from all the ties and attachments that formerly defined them. Individuals, understood as self-determining, autonomous sovereigns, authors in charge of their own life's work, became the central actors on the social stage" (p. 915). It is not difficult to see that when the cultural concept of individuality is granted primacy, the concept of social interaction becomes secondary. If individuals pursue goals and shape their destiny, the assumed role of community is a supporting one, not a constitutive one. As Sampson (1989b) points out, in the modernist version of society, community is seen as an instrumentality for self-made individuals who are relatively independent of the society in which they live. In this case, the process of social interaction is conceived of as a simple combination of individual traits; it is summative, but the combination has no emergent systemic properties because personal identity is assumed to be antecedent to the social process. Thus, products rather than processes of interaction are the privileged terms in a communication theory of modernity.

In the modernist epistemology, knowledge about communication is built from data about the mental world of individuals. The unit of observation is the individual who presses levers, marks questionnaires, or responds with fragments of conversation in a variety of settings designed to simulate a communication setting. Because social identity is considered to be a matter of possessing various individual characteristics, these characteristics become the relevant variables for the study of interaction. The social interaction becomes secondary, or in some cases invisible, while the concept of the "self-contained" individual accumulates further cultural authority.

THE LEGACY OF INDIVIDUALISM IN COMMUNICATION RESEARCH

The historical and linguistic urge to study individual characteristics rather than interpersonal relational processes has had a negative impact on the field of communication. Using a discourse of individualism to examine social processes invites incoherence and marginalization.

Incoherence in the Tradition

From the perspective of self-contained individualism, personhood is a matter of private ownership. Attributes, motivations, cognitive schemata, traits, and so on are assumed to be individual possessions rather than elements of discursive, socially constituted identities. When applied to the study of interpersonal relationships, these individualist narratives obscure the material conditions—including the microprocesses of power and domination—in which relationships emerge. Narratives about relationships that ignore these processes offer incoherent accounts of human behavior because possessive individualism cannot be resolved into relationalism. Vološinov (1927/1987), whose materialist critique of subjectivist accounts of consciousness is centered on dialogue, writes that "every utterance is *the product of the interaction between speakers* and the product of the broader context of the whole complex *social situation* in which the utterance emerges" (p. 79). He goes on to write that "nothing verbal in human behavior (inner and outward speech equally) can under any circumstances be reckoned to the account of the individual subject in isolation; the verbal is not his [*sic*] property but the property of his *social group* (his social milieu)" (p. 86). When human behavior is reckoned to the account of isolated attributes, the language of individuality produces contradictions. An example of such a contradiction can be found in traditional accounts of interpersonal relationship development.

Both social penetration (Altman & Taylor, 1973) and step (Knapp, 1978) models of relationship embrace an individualist version of personhood that celebrates individual rationality (Bochner, 1984) and tends to reify an economic metaphor of individual profit. Penetration models separate the person from the social process. During interaction, the person, sometimes modeled as a multilayered onion, is probed by the autonomous other. The traits, personalities, and values discovered through this probing are treated as the private property of self-contained individuals who choose whether or not to disclose these possessions. From the early stages of "initiating" and "experimenting" the unitary individuals move toward "bonding" (Knapp, 1978).

The metaphors used in the penetration model to describe the early stages of change evoke images of objective scientists probing the properties of isolated molecules. The metaphors of later stages suggest that the individual molecules bond to form a composite—a combination of two distinct, autonomous units. Yet, these metaphors present a contradiction. If the primary model of the subject is anchored to the self-contained individual, what does it mean to bond with another? How do two individuals bond to form one relationship? The transformation from individual to relationship remains a theoretical abstraction.

Unlike Knapp's (1978) adaptation of the penetration model, Altman and Taylor's (1973) final stage of penetration does not suggest bonding. Their model maintains the individualist slant and emphasizes only "stable exchange" between individual communicators.

The contradictory aspects of the penetration and stage models are compounded when the larger cultural context is considered. The concept of exchange or integration clashes with the market ideal of individual consumerism. Enveloped in an ideology that values private consumption, couples are surrounded by commercial messages and films that celebrate individuality and self-realization as a goal attainable only through private consumption. Commercial messages imply that private ownership of various products makes us socially desirable, yet, paradoxically, these messages stop short of celebrating social mergers of individuals and collective ownership unless the larger social context helps to define a new market. Even when the apparent focus is on families or communities of friends, the selling point seems to be the promise of enhanced individual identity.

The narratives of commercial culture are consistent with the individualist slant of relationship development models only to a point. The early stages of experimentation and exploration identified in relationship development models fit well with the stories of consumer culture. Commercial culture glorifies a continuous chase; desire cannot give way to satiation. It is the later stages involving joining together that do not coincide with the narratives of consumerism. The abstract stages of "affective exchange" (Altman & Taylor, 1973), "integration," or "bonding" (Knapp, 1978) are subverted by the cultural narratives of consumption. What survives and resonates within these narratives is the concept of personality as a private possession—a thing that needs to be continuously enhanced by the accumulation of consumer goods. In an individualist ideology, the relationship becomes a commodity form.

Marginalization

The legacy of individualism in interpersonal communication research has also weakened the field of interpersonal communication by keeping it from entering discussions in the public sphere. As interpersonal communication researchers embraced attitudes, cognitive process, self-disclosure, and other modernist research topics, they limited their potential contributions to public discussions about communication. Ironically, as interpersonal communication researchers echoed the mainstream traditions in psychology, they disqualified themselves from a legitimate role in the discourse of public policy.

As long as the ideology of individualism remains the basis of common sense in both research and in everyday life, there is little need for a communication discipline. The discourse of individualism gives authority to psychological explanation. Once the psychological language game is chosen, supporting a knowledge claim with references to another discipline counts as weak evidence. To the extent that interpersonal communication research mimics the ideological story lines that constitute our cultural narratives, the field disqualifies itself from entering into a dialogue about social change.

This marginalization of the discipline is evident in the popular press. Topics directly related to interpersonal communication grace the front covers of most popular magazines. Yet, an examination of the sources of the information presented in the stories does not yield a list of references to researchers in the communication discipline. Psychologists and psychiatrists, not communication scholars, serve as the credible sources for articles about interpersonal communication (Lannamann, 1991, 1992). An unintended consequence of using the individualist frame is that the communication field is marginalized. An additional consequence of going swimming in the mainstream discourse of individualism is that the potential of entering into a productive dialogue about social change is swept away.

RECOVERING SOCIAL INTERACTION AS A THEORETICAL TERM

It would be a mistake to claim that historical change follows a neat, linear progression and that individualism is characteristic of a single, bounded time period. However, numerous commentators from a variety of fields have identified a number of trends suggesting that a shift away from the project of modernism is currently under way (K. J. Gergen, 1991; Gitlin, 1989; Jameson, 1984; Lyotard, 1984). Although the emerging social form is not singular, the term "postmodernism" has been widely applied to refer to this transition.

If modernism dissolved the unity of social community by championing the individual, postmodernism involves the interaction between the fragments. Gitlin (1989) puts it well: "Modernism tore up unity and postmodernism has been enjoying the shreds" (p. 351). The roots of the postmodern shift are multiple, with parallel movements in architecture, art, literature, and music. The appearance of postmodernism is coincident with certain global economic and technical developments that undermined the sovereignty of the individual (K. J. Gergen, 1991). Sampson (1989b) points to several examples of the shift from the individual to a global era. These include the rise of interlinked transnational corporations that function interdependently with multiple local constituencies, the development of communication technologies that break down informational boundaries, and the growing recognition that individual actions have global environmental consequences.

As a historically situated concept, has individualism outlived its usefulness? Sampson (1989b) argues that it has, that individualism arose in a specific historical context that has now given way to a global, linked world system. The alternative to the individualist model of the person, Sampson argues, is a model that recognizes the constitutive role of social interaction in the construction of personal identity. This theme of social construction is central to the work of a variety of other writers (Cronen, 1994; K. J. Gergen, 1991; Pearce, 1994; Shotter, 1993) who highlight the interactive processes that give rise to social identity. The shift away from individualism is a significant one for communication scholars because it places communicative interaction at the center of investigation rather than treating it is a by-product of the mental states of individuals.

A return to the study of the social requires an exploration of three themes. These include (1) the overlap between the unit of observation and the unit of analysis, (2) the unintentional nature of conjoint action, and (3) the materiality of interaction.

An appropriate unit of observation for the analysis of social interaction is the dialogical process. While this may seem obvious, in practice, interaction researchers often use the self-reports of participants or other forms of individual questionnaires in an attempt to access interactional data. In this instance, although interaction is the assumed focus of attention, the individual—not the interaction—is actually observed. Questionnaires completed by individuals introduce the risk of casting interaction in terms of individual perceptions, and although these perceptions may provide valuable information about personal experiences, they provide little information about *inter*personal interaction. Interactional research requires a large enough frame of observation to include the complex patterned processes through which participants construct their relationship.

A second theme in the recovery of the social is that interaction is shaped by its own unintended outcomes. Because interaction involves the conjoint action of two or more participants, the process is not controlled unilaterally by a single party (Pearce & Cronen, 1980). A conversation that begins with a compliment may end with an exchange of insults much to the dismay of one of the participants. Participants may reflect on a conversation and claim that the outcome was an intentional one, but individual intentionality explains only individual actions. When interactively combined, the intentional behaviors of participants produce outcomes that are nonrandom but not controlled by individual intentions (Pearce & Cronen, 1980). Participants may have an idea about the genre of an interaction, but particular acts are contingent upon the emerging sequence. The shape of interaction is a function of joint action (Shotter, 1980).

A third theme in a social approach is the proposition that interaction is a material practice. The term "material practice" is used here to refer to human action conceived of in terms of its unfolding context, shaped by the unique combination of language, history, choice, and constraint. A materialist approach to the study of interaction supplements assumptions of subjectivity with an analysis of the conditions in which a particular subjectivity emerges. For example, Tannen (1990) suggests that the difficulties men and women have understanding each other is the result of differences in the subjective worlds inhabited by men and women. A materialist approach to this problem would not stop with the identification of the differing subjectivities but would go on to explore the everyday practices that gave rise to these differences. This might include an investigation of unequal access to particular, concrete experiences that form the basis of gendered discourse. When interaction is studied as a result of subjective experience, abstractions are likely to obscure the everyday sources of power and authority. Because interaction never occurs as an abstraction, it is important to attend to the material details of interaction. Material practices both influence and are influenced by the particular sociohistorical contexts in which they occur.

In spite of what Derrida (1976) refers to as the continuous slippage of signifiers, some meanings do survive and are privileged while others are muted. Hall (1985) argues that "without some arbitrary 'fixing' or . . .

'articulation,' there would be no signification or meaning at all" (p. 93). The ideological process of articulation positions subjects in constantly evolving contests of power and authority. To the Derridian claim, "Nothing but the text," the materialist must also add an inquiry concerning the ideologically positioned voices that articulate the text. This invites the recognition that textual practices are always embedded in particular forms of life where social and historical constructions of privilege are made to appear as natural facts.

Instead of focusing on the material practices of subjects *in the moment of telling* their relationship narratives, mainstream communication researchers tend to gather details about conceptual categories abstracted from the specific context and moment when the social interaction occurred. This practice maintains the abstract concept of individually owned personalities by shifting attention away from the dialogical nature of research. A poststructuralist would claim that this dialogue is all researchers have to work with; a materialist would claim that this dialogue is shaped by specific manifestations of power and domination. Combined, the approaches raise new questions that decenter the individual and call attention to the social practices, not the products, of communication.

In the remaining space, I will identify some of these questions and discuss their implications. A starting point for a thoroughly social approach to communication inquiry is to explore the historical and institutional context of the research. *Whose history is reflected in the research protocol and in whose terms is the research dialogue cast?* This question calls attention to the politically reflexive nature of communication research. Participation in communication research, whether as principal researcher or as principled subject, is a form of communication. As such, the research is shaped by its historical context and it inevitably shapes and validates particular identities and histories. In this way it becomes part of the political present. The reflexivity between history and politics is conspicuous in the popular press where the self-help movement in psychology has provided a constant stream of data, resources, and metaphors endorsing the politics of the day. Hidden from view in these articles is the fact that the ideas about the child in us, the codependent, the wild man, and other designer labels are ideas with a history and written by a politically positioned author. The legacy of reductionism and individualism characteristic of modernism affects not only the cultural practices of everyday life but also the cultural practices of writing about everyday life.

During the 1991 Persian Gulf War, commentators were quick to incorporate many of the individualist themes from various self help movements. In a National Public Radio commentary aired during the war, the poet and patriarch of the men's movement, Robert Bly (1990) was invoked in a discussion of post-Gulf War domestic policy. The commentator said:

> Who can possibly have more credibility with an inner-city black, or a rural white, than young men and women who have just returned from the Gulf. We should not glorify war or warriors, but we need authentic heroes. In his new best-seller, *Iron John*, the poet Robert Bly writes about the loss of heroes since mid-century. . . . "We need new heroes," Bly says "so that in admiring their virtues, each of us growing up can become an inner warrior able to stand on our own feet as adults." The warriors coming back from the Gulf can help a lot of young people learn to stand straight, too. (D. Gergen, 1991)

It is no surprise that the uses of disciplinary writing often stray from the uses envisioned by the author. Although scholarly writing and other forms of fiction are always subject to new uses in various political arenas, it is time to offer scholarly writing from an alternative ideological position, one that calls attention to the social roots of power, and one that is not so easily transformed into a further celebration of possessive individualism and violence, its mode of interaction.

Commenting on the connection between the practices of research and the historical background of social inquiry, Parker (1989) calls for a similar transformation of scholarly work. He argues : "It is not enough to present a history of the research topic, but the method used, and the theory chosen, should also be interrogated. Link the method and the theory with cultural changes, and say who would object to it, and why" (p. 155). Communication models, theories, and research methods have historical contexts. Investigating these contexts may generate questions about the taken-for-granted practices that shape interpersonal research.

Leeds-Hurwitz (1990) provides an example of the kind of historical analysis necessary for cultural and institutional critique. In her exploration of the historical development of intercultural communication research, she argues that the field of intercultural communication evolved from developments at the Foreign Service Institute of the U.S. Department of State. There, between 1946 and 1956, the government made an effort to train American diplomats. This focus on training, Leeds-Hurwitz (1990) points out, shaped the emerging field of intercultural communication by placing a premium on skills-oriented training and attenuating theory-oriented research. To meet the pragmatic concerns of seminar participants who wanted concrete information about how to interact with specific cultures, Foreign Service Institute trainers adjusted their macrocultural approaches and provided microcultural analyses of interaction. Leeds-Hurwitz (1990) writes: "These smaller units of a culture, having obvious and immediate impact on interaction between members of different cultures, were very attractive to the foreign service personnel" (p. 268).

It is easy to extend Leeds-Hurwitz's historically based explanation of the skills training emphasis to explain the unexamined ideological practices of researchers in the intercultural field. The smaller units of culture may have met the needs of those at the Foreign Service Institute during the early years of the cold war, but the fact that the Institute model was adopted by intercultural scholars in the communication discipline suggests that a specific ideological frame was also imported into the field. The narrow unit of analysis encouraged by the governmental context conveniently shifted attention from issues of cultural domination and other macrosocial or political issues that might problematize U.S. hegemony and the ideological practices that contribute to it. Instead, variables addressing proxemics, kinesics, and other microlevel processes became the building blocks of intercultural research. As a result, the field of intercultural communication has had much to say about individual blocks but little to say about power structures. For example, studies of cross-cultural communication apprehensiveness (Watson, Monroe, & Atterstrom, 1989) or studies that assess differences in uncertainty reduction processes between cultures (Gudykunst & Nishida, 1986) translate North American cultural forms for use in new cultural contexts, but the direction of this translation (usually from west to east or from north to south) suggests a form of cultural imperialism. In the narrow focus of these comparative studies, the effects of cultural hegemony are invisible. The building-block approach exports the ideology in which the blocks were shaped and imports further confirmation of their ideological "naturalness." It is ironic but not unexpected that the critical cultural studies perspective (Hall, 1980; Hebdige, 1979; Willis, 1977) found a home not in the established intercultural communication wing of the discipline but rather in the mass communication area where issues of ideological critique were less neglected.

A similar examination of the historical roots of the interpersonal relationship literature would provide important clues about whose history and whose terms are inscribed in the social scientific findings of the last several decades. Historical accounts of related issues in interpersonal communication (Pearce, 1985; Rawlins, 1985, Wilder-Mott, 1981) contribute useful information about choices researchers have made. An intriguing task is to identify the institutional constraints that shaped these choices. For example, did the military context of early cybernetic research condition the discourse inherited by interpersonal scholars? Terms such as "deviation amplification" and "calibration" are rarely examined for excess ideological baggage when imported for use in the study of human relationships.

From the confluence of poststructuralist and materialist analyses emerges a second question, one that concerns the tension between representation and performance. *In what ways does the research process articulate subject positions for all participants in the process?*

In the *German Ideology*, Marx and Engels (1947/1965) caution against the ruling illusions made possible by generating an "abstraction from fact" and then proclaiming that "the fact is based on the abstraction" (p. 530). Although the distinction between facts and abstractions is blurred from a social constructionist perspective, each has political consequences and thus warrants a careful consideration of who is subjected in the research process. The ruling illusions that Marx and Engels warn about are made possible by a representational orientation to communication. Communication, from this perspective, works by pointing out features in the world. Research in this tradition involves the careful mapping of various abstractions. The researcher is not considered responsible for how a subject ends up in the descriptive process because the research is assumed to represent a preexisting social order.

In contrast to the representational approach, a performance-oriented approach to research begins with the recognition that given the hermeneutic nature of interpersonal research, all findings are performances, not representations, in an ongoing conversation between the researcher and the subject of the research. It is through the performance of the research that participants are implicated in various webs of significance and domination. Conquergood (1991), whose poststructuralist approach to ethnography calls attention to the intersection of research and cultural politics, writes:

> Performance-centered research takes as both its subject matter and method the experiencing body situated in time, place, and history. Whereas the Cartesian split devalued bodily experience, the performance paradigm restores the body as both a source of knowing and a site of ideological inscription and struggle. The performance paradigm insists on face-to-face encounters instead of formal abstractions. (p. 16)

Conceived of as a cultural performance, research on interpersonal relationships requires an awareness of how researchers participate in the enactment of cultural narratives concerning coming together and apart. The enacted narratives are not politically neutral, however. The researcher, buttressed by the trappings of institutional authority, has the privilege of casting and directing the performance. The questions asked and the populations selected help shape the cultural performances and ought to be critiqued just as decisions about scripting and casting are judged by film reviewers. Viewed as a script, a research protocol casts its subjects in particular roles. What, for example, is the effect of using questionnaires developed for heterosexual, college-age couples in a study of a diverse population? Even if applied to a population of college sophomores, how does the protocol participate in the cultural oppression of gays and lesbians? That our journals are filled with the relationship narratives of a fairly narrow spectrum of white, middle-class individuals suggests that it is time to rethink the way the performance called relationship research produces and legitimates knowledge.

The textual practices that we recognize as signs of professional competence distance and, in many cases, silence the people we study. Commenting on a similar problem in social psychology, Shotter (1990) writes:

> No matter how benevolent as a professional psychologist one may be towards those one studies, no matter how concerned with "their" liberation, with "their" betterment, with preventing "their" victimisation, etc., the fact is that "their" lives are not made sense of in "their" terms . . . their claims cannot pass the appropriate institutional tests. (p. 168)

A third question, then, is: *To what extent do the textual practices of our discipline silence the voices of those on the margins and shift attention away from the material practices of interaction?*

In many studies of interpersonal relationships the experience–near terms (Geertz, 1983) of everyday language are displaced with the experience–distant terms of the professional lexicon. Arguments become "symmetrical escalations," sneers become "metacommunication," and loose discussions are recast in terms of "interaction goals." Although it is tempting to treat these technical terms as distortions of the "essences" of experience, as poststructuralists like to point out, every decoding is just another encoding and therefore no signifier is necessarily closer to the "real" thing. As moves in a language game, technical terms become tools for doing certain kinds of things. The use of technical terms transforms experience into a less immediate context. While such a transformation opens new discursive possibilities for the researcher, it also eclipses the dialogical nature of the relational narratives.

Interviews, markings on questionnaires, and recorded transcripts are elements of a larger interactive sequence involving the researcher. The recursive relation between research participants is often presented as a unilateral one. Yet, as Rosenthal (1966) has demonstrated, social research involves the construction of meaning on both sides of the imaginary line separating subject and object. This suggests that interpersonal communication research requires a dialogical model of understanding. Bakhtin (1986) writes that "a meaning only reveals its depths once it has encountered and come into contact with another, foreign meaning: they engage in kind of a dialogue, which surmounts the closedness and one-sidedness of these particular meanings, the cultures" (p. 7). Rorty's (1980) metaphor is apt; instead serving as a mirror that reflects the essences of nature, research is more like a conversation. This metaphor is particularly relevant to interpersonal communication inquiry. The research conversation is a dialogue between communicators—the researcher and the subject(s).

In his criticism of mental testing, Gergen (1985) points out that the language used in social psychology to describe conduct "does not specifically refer to the spatiotemporal activities themselves but to people's underlying motives, intentions, meanings and the like" (p. 123). He observes that it is not that the respondent placed a check mark in the "agree" column that attracts rigorous scrutiny. Rather, it is the assumed mental state underlying the conduct that is of central concern to researchers. Gergen (1985) comments that the actual behavior of checking "agree" might have been "carried out rapidly or slowly, in pencil or with quill, with a sigh or a shrug—the spatiotemporal character of the act is virtually of no consequence" (p. 124) because attention is focused on the abstract concept of mental state. When the concrete practices of the participants in the research setting become incidental, the politics of the research are obscured by abstract generalizations.

CONCLUSIONS

As authors of texts, we share the same cultural resources as those we write about. We share the limits of what can be said gracefully. The history and ideology that shape our professional writing also shape our daily lives. I have argued that these conditions have generated an individualist orientation to communication that undermines the potential of the field. Yet, the condition of sharing these cultural resources could not be better for a dialogical understanding of communication. Unlike those in the "hard" sciences, those in the "soft" sciences can at least talk about their hard problems with the subjects of their study. A social approach to communication is a constant reminder that our understanding is based on conversations with others. Instead of suppressing the other, it is time to celebrate the other (Sampson, 1993). The performance called interpersonal scholarship involves the researcher in a supporting role. A social approach to communication research is a dialogical process.

Participation in the dialogue of research requires a social rather than individual unit of observation–relation, a sensitivity to the exquisite possibilities of joint action, and a recognition of the material constraints of situated practices. A social approach to communication does not stop with the publication of research findings. It continues by calling attention to (and being responsible for) how the research findings re-enter the cultural dialogue as facts.

REFERENCES

Altman, I., & Taylor, D. (1973). *Social penetration: The development of interpersonal relationships.* New York: Holt, Rinehart & Winston.

Bakhtin, M. M. (1986). *Speech genres and other late essays* (C. Emerson & M. Holquist, Eds.; V. W. McGee, Trans.). Austin: University of Texas Press.

Bateson, G. (1991). Men are grass: Metaphor and the world of mental process. In R. E. Donaldson (Ed.), *Sacred unity: Further steps to an ecology of mind* (pp. 235-242). New York: HarperCollins.

Bellah, R. N., Madsen, R., Sullivan, W. M., Swidler, A., & Tipton, S. M. (1985). *Habits of the heart: Individualism and commitment in American life.* Berkeley: University of California Press.

Berlo, D. K. (1960). *The process of communication: An introduction to theory and practice.* New York: Holt, Rinehart & Winston.

Bly, R. (1990). *Iron John: A book about men.* New York: Addison-Wesley.

Bochner, A. (1984). The functions of human communication in interpersonal bonding. In C. Arnold & J. W. Bowers (Eds.), *The handbook of rhetoric and communication theory* (pp. 544-621). Newton, MA: Allyn & Bacon.

Conquergood, D. (1991). Rethinking ethnography: Towards a critical cultural politics. *Communication Monographs, 58,* 179-194.

Cronen, V. E. (1994). Coordinated management of meaning: Practical theory for the complexities and contradictions of everyday life. In J. Siegfried (Ed.), *The status of common sense in psychology* (pp. 183-201). Norwood, NJ: Ablex.

Cushman, P. (1990). Why the self is empty: Toward a historically situated psychology. *American Psychologist, 45,* 599-611.

Derrida, J. (1976). *Of grammatology* (G. C. Spivak, Trans.). Baltimore: Johns Hopkins Press. (Original work published 1974)

Geertz, C. (1983). *Local knowledge: Further essays in interpretive anthropology.* New York: Basic Books.

Gergen, D. (1991, March 11). *All things considered.* [Editorial aired on National Public Radio.]

Gergen, K. J. (1985). Social pragmatics and the origins of psychological discourse. In K. J. Gergen & K. E. Davis (Eds.), *The social construction of the person* (pp. 111-128). New York: Springer-Verlag.

Gergen, K. J. (1991). *The saturated self: Dilemmas of identity in contemporary life.* New York: Basic Books.

Gitlin, T. (1989). Postmodernism: Roots and politics. In I. Angus & S. Jhally (Eds.), *Cultural politics in contemporary America* (pp. 347-360). New York: Routledge, Chapman & Hall.

Gudykunst, W. B., & Nishida, T. (1986). Attributional confidence in low- and high-context cultures. *Human Communication Research, 12,* 525-549.

Habermas, J. (1975). *Legitimation crisis.* Boston: Beacon Press.

Hall, S. (1980). Cultural studies: Two paradigms. *Media, Culture and Society, 2,* 57–72.

Hall, S. (1985). Signification, representation, ideology: Althusser and the post-structuralist debates. *Critical Studies in Mass Communication, 2,* 91–114.

Hebdige, D. (1979). *Subculture: The meaning of style.* London: Methuen.

Jameson, F. (1984). Postmodernism, or the cultural logic of late capitalism. *New Left Review, 146,* 53–92.

Jhally, S. (1989). The political economy of culture. In S. Jhally & I. Angus (Eds.), *Cultural politics in contemporary America* (pp. 65–81). New York: Routledge, Chapman & Hall.

Jorgenson, J. (1992). Communication, rapport, and the interview: A social perspective. *Communication Theory, 2,* 148–156.

Knapp, M. L. (1978). *Social intercourse: From greeting to goodbye.* Boston: Allyn & Bacon.

Lannamann, J. W. (1992). *Discursive constraints and the marginalization of interpersonal communication studies.* Paper presented at the Mainstreams and Margins Conference, University of Massachusetts, Amherst, MA.

Lannamann, J. W. (1991). Interpersonal communication research as ideological practice. *Communication Theory, 1,* 179–203.

Leeds-Hurwitz, W. (1990). Notes in the history of intercultural communication: The Foreign Service Institute and the mandate for intercultural training. *Quarterly Journal of Speech, 76,* 262–281.

Lyotard, J. F. (1984). *The postmodern condition: A report on knowledge* (G. Bennington & B. Massumi, Trans.). Minneapolis: University of Minnesota Press. (Original work published 1979)

Marx, K., & Engels, F. (1965). *The German ideology.* London: Lawrence & Wishart. (Original work published 1947)

McNamee, S. (1988). Accepting research as social intervention: Implications of a systemic epistemology. *Communication Quarterly, 36,* 50–68.

Parker, I. (1989). *The crisis in modern social psychology–And how to end it.* London: Routledge.

Pearce, W. B. (1985). Scientific research methods in communication studies and their implications for theory and research. In T. W. Benson (Ed.), *Speech communication in the 20th century* (pp. 255–281). Carbondale: Southern Illinois University Press.

Pearce, W. B. (1994). *Interpersonal communication: Making social worlds.* New York: HarperCollins.

Pearce, W. B., & Cronen, V. E. (1980). *Communication, action, and meaning.* New York: Praeger.

Rawlins, W. K. (1985). Stalking interpersonal communication effectiveness: Social, individual, or situational integration. In T. Benson (Ed.), *Speech communication in the 20th century* (pp. 109–129). Carbondale: University of Southern Illinois Press.

Reddy, M. J. (1979). The conduit metaphor: A case of frame conflict in our language about language. In A. Ortony (Ed.), *Metaphor and thought* (pp. 284–324). Cambridge: Cambridge University Press.

Rorty, R. (1980). *Philosophy and the mirror of nature.* Oxford: Basil Blackwell.

Rosenthal, R. (1966). *Experimenter effects in behavioral research.* New York: Appleton.

Sampson, E. E. (1977). Psychology and the American ideal. *Journal of Personality and Social Psychology, 35,* 767–782.

Sampson, E. E. (1981). Cognitive psychology as ideology. *American Psychologist, 36,* 730–343.

Sampson, E. E. (1989a). The deconstruction of the self. In J. Shotter & K. Gergen (Eds.), *Texts of identity* (pp. 1–19). London: Sage.

Sampson, E. E. (1989b). The challenge of social change for psychology: Globalization and psychology's theory of the person. *American Psychologist, 44,* 914–921.

Sampson, E. E. (1993). *Celebrating the other: A dialogic account of human nature.* Boulder, CO: Westview Press.

Shotter, J. (1980). Action, joint action, and intentionality. In M. Brenner (Ed.), *The structure of action* (pp. 28–65). Oxford: Basil Blackwell.

Shotter, J. (1987). The social construction of an "us": Problems of accountability and narratology. In R. Burnett, P. McGee, & D. Clarke (Eds.), *Accounting for personal relationships: Social representations of interpersonal links* (pp. 225–247). London: Methuen.

Shotter, J. (1990). Social individuality versus possessive individualism: The sounds of silence. In I. Parker & J. Shotter (Eds.), *Deconstructing social psychology* (pp. 155–169). London, Routledge.

Shotter, J. (1993). *Conversational realities: Constructing life through language.* London: Sage.

Smith, A. (1952). *An inquiry into the nature and causes of the wealth of nations (Great books of the western world* Vol. 39). Chicago: William Benton. (Original work published 1776)

Tannen, D. (1990). *You just don't understand: Women and men in conversation.* New York: Morrow.

Vološinov, V. N. (1976). *Freudianism: A critical sketch.* (N. H. Bruss, Ed.; I. R. Titunik, Trans.). Bloomington: Indiana University Press. (Original work published 1927)

von Foerster, H. (1984). *Observing systems.* Seaside, CA: Intersystems Publications.

Watson, A. K., Monroe, E. E., & Atterstrom, H. (1989). Comparison of communication apprehension across cultures: American and Swedish children. *Communication Quarterly, 37,* 67–76.

Whorf, B. L. (1956). Science and linguistics. In J. B. Carroll (Ed.), *Language, thought, and reality: Selected writing* (pp. 207–219). Cambridge, MA: MIT Press.

Wilder-Mott, C. (1981). Rigor and imagination. In C. Wilder-Mott & J. H. Weakland (Eds.), *Rigor and imagination: Essays from the legacy of Gregory Bateson* (pp. 5–25). New York: Praeger.

Willis, P. (1977). *Learning to labor: How working class kids get working class jobs.* New York: Columbia University Press.

Part IV

Applications

CHAPTER 7

Even if a Thing of Beauty, Can a Case Study Be a Joy Forever?

A Social Constructionist Approach to Theory and Research

VICTORIA CHEN
W. BARNETT PEARCE

The allusion to Keats's poem in our title is intended to highlight the deeply embedded assumption that permanence and generality are criterial attributes of "knowledge." Contemporary "communication scientists" articulate this vision of knowledge as "theory," or "a set of constructs that are linked together by relational statements that are internally consistent with each other" (Chaffee & Berger, 1987, p. 101). Within this definition, "Constructs are concepts that are formed inductively by generalizing from particulars. . . . Constructs are abstractions; they are given meaning through theoretical definitions" (Chaffee & Berger, 1987, p. 101). This prevalent conceptualization of theory in interpersonal communication generates a set of evaluative criteria in which case studies have a limited and insignificant place. Even if performed according to the most rigorous standards of research (i.e., as "a thing of beauty"), case studies produce "findings" that are only local and temporary (and thus *not* "a joy forever").

It has been more than a decade since Gronbeck (1981) pointed out that it is not supposed to be that way. Theoretical and methodological tolerance emerged as lauded virtues from what Wilder-Mott (1981)

135

characterized as the "great 'metatheoretical debate' " (p. 18). The result of this debate was a promising respect for a "pluralism which may allow multiple perspectives to flourish" (Wilder-Mott, 1981, p. 19). Bochner (1985), among others, wrote that "interpersonal communication cannot be sensibly limited to the narrow range of problems and methods that would permit the unrestrained application of a single perspective to all conceivable inquiries" (p. 27). He proposed viewing interpersonal communication "as a subject that can be legitimately approached in several different ways, described in several different vocabularies, and studied with several different purposes in mind" (p. 27).

Despite the seeming celebration of multiplicity in research activities, there is ample evidence that much research in interpersonal communication is still evaluated by criteria based on the assumption that knowledge must be of things objectively derived, permanent, and universal. Consequently, those who conduct case studies often find themselves forced to speak in an inhospitable vocabulary and to demonstrate that their research satisfies criteria incommensurate with their purposes. We believe that there are two reasons for the continued hegemony of this particular notion of knowledge and the criteria for evaluating research that derive from it.

First, the ethic of tolerant pluralism has blurred our attention to the radical differences among intellectual traditions and theoretical orientations. The notion persists that if researchers could get beneath the surface features that differentiate various projects, they would find that all theories are ultimately compatible, and that the same set of criteria could be applied to assess studies done with different methodologies. To the contrary, we believe that some contemporary communication theories as well as cultural discourses created from different traditions are incommensurate (see Pearce, 1991; Chen, 1994). They comprise alternative discursive networks, each of which "privilege certain insights and displace other viewpoints" (Conquergood, 1989, p. 82). In other words, these theories differ about what the central features of a theory are, about the meaning of such features as they have in common, and about the procedures (e.g., "rationality") by which claims can be established or differences adjudicated (see Bernstein, 1983; Kuhn, 1970; Pearce, 1991). If we take the thesis of incommensurability seriously, we must accept the possibility that research "ends" (purposes, goals, intentions) as well as "means" are constructed within paradigms. The difference between at least some of us who conduct case studies and those who do not goes far beyond a preference (e.g., for quantitative or qualitative methods); it consists of a radically different notion of what, why, by whom, and in what context we are engaging in activities we call research.

The second reason for the current "ambiguous" status of case studies, we suspect, is that the criteria by which case studies should be evaluated have not been sufficiently or clearly established. As we show later, a research method is not a clear indicator of a conceptual paradigm, and case studies can certainly be conducted from a variety of theoretical and methodological frameworks. As a result, it is often not clear just what criteria should be applied when rendering a critique or performing a review of case studies. If not the venerable triad of validity, reliability, and generalizability, what criteria should distinguish "good" research?

In this chapter, we provide an explanatory context for case studies conducted specifically within the social constructionist paradigm, which we argue is incommensurate with the communication science paradigm. Our purpose is to address the role of case studies within social constructionism while simultaneously elucidating social constructionism by using case studies as an exemplar of its research activities. We put forth the notion of the case-as-a-thing-itself, arguing that whether it can or cannot be used in other situations, what we are interested in is the study of *a particular case*, not a use of that case as an instance of something else or a means of studying other cases. We also work toward a more rigorous elaboration of our discursive domain from a social constructionist perspective, hoping that such an elaboration will be useful to other social constructionists as part of the process by which criteria for evaluating and critiquing case studies can be established and to those outside the paradigm to better understand our line of work.

AN UNCERTAIN TRUMPET: TWO POSITIONS ABOUT CASE STUDIES

Case studies can be approached from the perspectives of communication science or social constructionism; each sees the role of case studies differently within its agenda.[1] In communication science, case studies play a subordinate role; in social constructionism, performing case studies is the primary form of activity. We argue that at least some case studies are appropriately understood only in the context of an alternative paradigm to the scientific framework and should be evaluated by different criteria.

Case Studies as Subordinate

Communication scientists pride themselves on their ability to "verify" theories rather than engaging in messy and "unsystematic" processes by which theories are "discovered." From this standpoint, case studies are treated as second-class citizens, subordinated, in a larger category of research methods. They may be useful in the initial development of a project, but those who conduct them must content themselves with a minor role in the heroic social drama of science in which chains, not wings, are attached to the imagination.

To subordinate case studies does not necessarily deem them insignificant. Even the most cursory examination of the history of science shows that case studies played an important role in the development of many scientific theories. Dukes (1972) compared classic single case studies to a "single pebble which starts an avalanche" (p. 219). Within the scientific perspective, case studies should thus be appreciated for their ability to provoke theory building in the preliminary stage within the larger and longer context of the development of a scientific project. As Berger and Chaffee (1987) explained: "Communication science seeks to understand the production, processing, and effects of symbol and signal systems by developing testable theories, containing lawful generalizations, that explain phenomena associated with production, processing, and effects" (p. 17).

Underlying this treatment of case studies is the assumption that no case study can be appreciated *for and by itself*. The value of a case study must be judged in terms of its contribution to something else later or larger (e.g., the "real" study that is conducted in a more scientific way). The result is a set of institutional practices that preclude positive evaluation of case studies *per se*.

With this conception of what counts as important communication project, a case study of the speaking style of Dr. Martin Luther King, Jr. (e.g., Keith & Wittenberger-Keith, 1988/1989) would clearly be dismissed as insufficiently scientific, no matter how interesting, enlightening, and provocative it is. Its value, if any, is heuristic. A communication scientist encountering this study in his or her leisure hours might find in it an insight that could be developed into a hypothesis that could be scientifically tested later. As Berger and Chaffee (1987) contended:

> Studying the speaking style of Dr. Martin Luther King, Jr., in an attempt to understand how he was able to become the leader of the civil rights movement is not, in our terms, an activity of communication science. But when the same scholar examines a large number of leaders of social movements in the hope of drawing a generalization about the relationship between communication style and effectiveness, the scholar is acting in the role of scientist. (pp. 17–18)

Social constructionists find such treatment of this or any other case study both insulting and untenable. Consider what would be left out of a more scientific study of the relationship between communication style and effectiveness should the same scholar follow the communication scientist's recipe for producing knowledge. Dr. King was an African American, Baptist minister, with a doctorate from Yale, influenced by Gandhi, from and working in the American South, focusing on the civil rights of the descendants of slaves (whose ancestors had been officially "emancipated" for 100 years but who were "segregated" from the majority culture), whose leadership occurred during the so-called War on Poverty and the beginnings of the war in Vietnam, and who used a particular prosody with a distinctively rich speaking voice. How can we evaluate Dr. King's communication style and effectiveness without understanding these "particulars" unique to the speaker? Does anyone really believe that a better understanding of Dr. King and his speeches is produced by ignoring these factors? Shall we dismiss Dr. King's effective leadership style in our study of communication simply because other speakers of social movements cannot duplicate it?

Similarly, from the standpoint of communication science, the interesting (re)construction of a couple's decision making on abortion (Bochner & Ellis, 1992) would best be seen as anecdotal, instead of as a significant story that enlightens us on real people's lived experience. From our criteria for useful communication research, this case study—despite Sigman's (1992) critique—should not be dismissed simply for a lack of generalizability.

Case Studies as Primary

> It is pictures rather than propositions, metaphors rather than statements, which determine most of our philosophical convictions. (Rorty, 1979, p. 12)

The very notion that there are multiple paradigms commits us to a "contextualist" conception of meaning. The various paradigms of communication theory thus do not sort themselves out on the basis of research methods. For example, Gronbeck (1981) noted that the use of quantitative rather than qualitative methods of data analysis does not sufficiently distinguish practitioners of various paradigms in communication. It is the *meaning* and *purposes* of the research, not necessarily its particular method, and the interpretive and evaluative criteria in which it is constituted that differ among paradigms.[2]

Despite our specific focus in this project, we know well that social constructionism is not the only alternative paradigm to communication science, and that case studies are not the only form of activity in which social constructionists engage. However, we do believe that case studies done within different paradigms consist of distinct discourses, entailing different sets of vocabularies and interpretive and evaluative criteria. In other words, there are reasonable connections among (1) the ends for which one engages in research activities, (2) the assumptions about the nature of what one is researching, and (3) the form of activities that one accepts as research. Social constructionism differs from communication science in its assumptions about the nature of communication, and thus about the form of research and the intended end of that activity (see Cronen, Chen, & Pearce, 1988; Gergen, 1978, 1982; Shotter, 1990).

Aristotle, cited in *Nicomachean Ethics* clearly differentiated between those things that cannot be other than they are and those that can, that is, that are historically contingent. We can aspire to theoretical knowledge about the former, but Rorty (1979) has shown that the assumption that there are lawlike properties of the world generates a "spectator" orientation and research programs that attempt to "represent" the world "accurately." In this perspective, the goal is *theoria* "in which man [*sic*], as a detached spectator, simply investigates and studies things as they are without desiring to change them" (Ostwald, 1962, pp. 315–316), and its method is *epistēmē* or "factual knowledge" in the *contemplation* of reality. However, historically contingent matters change, and they change as a function of the involvement of the "knower." As such, the goal is *praxis* or "practical wisdom or good judgment" in the activities of the "knower" as a *participant* in reality. Praxis requires *phronēsis*, or "wisdom in action, and hence a moral intelligence" (Ostwald, 1962, p. 312).

One of the major discoveries in the 20th century has been how little remains in the category of "things that cannot be other than they are"; that is, of atemporal, abstract, unchanging reality such that we could have a spectator's knowledge of it. Indeed, we find it impossible to imagine that communication should be treated as something to be comprehended in "theory." Social constructionists understand social life—specifically "communication"—through the metaphor of "conversation."[3] This metaphor directs our attention to social life as a nonsummative, interactive, co-created, co-creating, and inherently unfinished process that can only be apprehended by a participant. In other words, "knowledge" of conversation must always come from the relationship between the observer and the observed as part of a reflexive process in our inquiry. As Aristotle would insist, the attempt to inscribe disembodied, ahistorical, lawlike statements on God's Own Chalkboard in the Sky is wrong-headed. If communication is a form of *praxis*, then, as Aristotle noted, knowledge of it is inevitably tied to specific and unique events; it cannot be concerned with universals only. It must also recognize the particulars, for it is practical, and practical wisdom is concerned with action (see McKeon, 1941, pp. 1028–1029).

We understand *phronēsis* as dealing with particular instances in and of themselves, not as instances of a class or "data points" for a generalization. Dewey (1929) worked through the implications of this argument in his attempt to place activity (making and doing), instead of knowledge, at the center of Western philosophy. "Judgment and belief regarding actions to be performed," he wrote, "can never attain more than a precarious probability. . . . Practical activity deals with individualized and unique situations which are never exactly duplicable and about which, accordingly, no complete assurance is possible. All activity . . . involves change" (Dewey, 1929, p. 6).

If communication is understood as historically and situationally contingent, case studies are the central feature of research, not an ancillary or means to something else. Dewey (1929) wrote, "The full and eventual reality of knowledge is carried in the individual case, not in general laws isolated from use in giving an individual case its meaning" (pp. 207–208). Therefore, rather than functioning as a more or less useful basis for generalization, the criterion by which a case study is evaluated is its ability to explicate the richness and particularity of what it describes. More important, our position is that case studies are *not intended* to be (although could be) used as a "sample" of something else; the end of our research is to treat any case study as *the* study in and of itself.

This focus on the particular is deeply antithetical to the communication science paradigm's preference for generality, and it has often engendered the accusation that nothing of (statistical) significance can come from knowing a single case. That judgment is inappropriate, because case studies in the social constructionist paradigm do not produce *epistēmē* and are not intended as a part of *theoria*; they produce *phronēsis* and are very much a part of *praxis*. The report of a case study is, from a social constructionist perspective, itself an activity that may include a report of other activities; it is poorly understood as a transparent representation of a state of affairs.

CRITERIA FOR INTERPRETING AND EVALUATING CASE STUDIES

Thus far we have argued that case studies are seen as marginal within the communication science paradigm, and the thrust of our argument deals with the inappropriateness of applying criteria derived from communication science to case studies conducted from a social constructionist framework. So what can be the "native" criteria by which social constructionist case studies are to be interpreted and evaluated? We suspect that much of the reluctance to embrace or treat case studies as legitimate stems from the belief that they contain no standards for rigor in research and for the evaluation of the "findings" of research. There has been an increasing amount of literature on conducting and evaluating qualitative research in our discipline (e.g., Denzin & Lincoln, 1994; Yin, 1989). Joining others' efforts, we believe that there are standards for discerning the quality of the many "stories" told by researchers, and for assessing the implications of case studies. Figure 7.1 illustrates our attempt to articulate the goals of conducting and criteria for evaluating case studies through a comparison and contrast of the two paradigms.

Reading down the columns in Table 7.1, the final comparison is the role of case studies in the activities of each framework. In the context of

Table 7.1. Comparison and Contrast of Two Paradigms

	Communication science	Social constructionism
Goals	Knowledge (*theoria* and *epistēmē*)	Sophistication Intelligence Practical wisdom Local knowledge (praxis and *phronēsis*)
Interests	Ability to describe, explain, predict, and control	Ability to describe, interpret, translate, illuminate, enlighten, and engage
Mode of operation	Subsuming specific cases under general principles or laws	Depicting the richness and particularities of unique cases; constructing vocabularies in which to compare cases and to engage in them
Criteria for interpreting and evaluating theories	Generality Certainty Necessity Falsifiability	Specificity Contingency Complexity Reflexivity
Criteria for interpreting and evaluating research	Objectivity Reliability Validity Generalizability	Coherence Intelligibility Richness Comprehensiveness Interconnectedness Probability Plausibility Open-endedness
Case studies	Marginal	Central

the other comparisons, it should be clear that the two paradigms occupy different places in our scholarly activities with disparate goals and interests in research.

Goals

Although the goal for communication scientists is as benign as the term "knowledge," a particular notion of knowledge is presumed and privileged. In its paradigmatic form, knowledge often consists of a mathematical equation (or its verbal equivalent) describing a precise and quantifiable relationship among (operationally defined) variables, each of which represents a concept in a theory. Among the usually unnoticed characteristics of this conception of knowledge are that (1) knowledge is impersonal—in fact, its "objectivity" is taken as a virtue; (2) knowledge is ahistorical—in fact, its generality across specific situations is taken as a virtue; and (3) knowledge is immutable, describing relationships that not only are but must be the case.

This notion of knowledge originated with Socrates in his search for acceptable fundamental definitions and has been elaborated in different ways throughout Western intellectual history. However, this is far from the only notion of knowledge. Another useful notion of knowledge involves "construction of a natural world and a social community in which man [sic] can live and enjoy. Knowledge becomes the conspicuous experiences of life endowed consciously and enriched continuously by an individual person's understanding of its importance and meaning" (Cheng, 1987, p. 29). In this view, knowledge should not be seen as isolated and scientifically discovered information independent of individuals' life and social interaction.

From our perspective as social constructionists, the goal of our research is not a search for factual and theoretical information about an event but is a way of understanding or approaching practical wisdom of life's experiences that enables us to engage creatively in the process of communication. Our use of the term "sophistication" is an attempt to describe *phronēsis*, similar to Dewey's (1929) notion of "intelligence," which is always in activities, and Geertz's (1983) "local knowledge."

Dewey (1929) argued that knowledge of the richness and particularities of cases produces "intelligence." For Dewey, intelligence is not abstract knowledge "which grasps the indemonstrable truths about fixed principles" (p. 213) because "knowing is. . .to be a participant in what is finally known" (p. 200). Rather, one acts intelligently "in virtue of his [sic] capacity to estimate the possibilities of a situation" (p. 213).

"Local knowledge" is a technical term among sailors. It refers to what people who have sailed in a particular area know that is not on the charts. There is a general theory of tides, but local knowledge is an awareness of how the current runs through a particular channel and around a particular set of rocks on a falling tide. Geertz (1983) may not indicate the nautical origin of the term, but he used it in a compatible manner when he described the product of ethnographies. What makes any ethnographic description "thick" and worth reading is not the assumption that it mirrors the true reality of the native's ways of life but the intelligent, richly detailed, locally significant, and intricate accounts constructed by the ethnographer for the reader. Geertz argued that any ethnographic description is local in the sense that its validity should be assessed in terms of the specific relationship between the ethnographer and his or her informants within a specific social and cultural context during a particular historical period. Rosaldo (1989) also contended that "the truth of objectivism—absolute, universal, timeless—has lost its monopoly status. It now competes with the truths of case studies that are embedded in local contexts, shaped by local interests, and colored by local perceptions" (p. 21). Further, an interpretation is local, of course, in terms of the specificity and uniqueness of the stories that are being told, interpreted, and reconstructed.

In contrast to knowledge, which is impersonal, universal, and objective, sophistication is personal, situational, cultural, and mutable. Whereas knowledge uses propositions suitable for inscription on chalkboards, sophistication is what makes people capable of assessing and then responding to situations. Such people may or may not be capable of "telling" a neophyte what they know, and their attempts to engage in such "tellings" may produce inconsistent stories, but it is certain that just being told is not sufficient to become sophisticated.

Instead of describing what is common to all (or a specified range of) situations at the willingly paid price of disregarding that which is unique to each, sophistication attends to the details of the specific local situation in which dialogues and activities occur. Sophistication thus entails an ability to assess critically and vary the prediction, to be sensitive to the unique features of each instance, and to be flexible in the application of strategies in research.

Knowledge and sophistication thus present sharply contrasting concepts of goals for performing the scholarly act. How should we choose among them? Given a choice, which would be better to have? Try this thought experiment: In your seaworthy but fragile sailboat, you are entering a harbor on the rocky New England coast for the first time and you have no charts. Whom would you rather have in your crew: a person who knows all the mathematical relationships between the spin of the earth, the movement of the moon, and the rise and fall of the tides or a person who has local knowledge of many harbors?

Interests

The two lists in Table 7.1 are further apart than they appear. Social constructionists consider an explanation that simply subsumes a specific instance under a generalization as a trivialization. We see inadequacy in activities that treat "prediction" and "explanation" (thus defined) as more important than "mere description and interpretation."[4]

We propose an array of terms that may seem more congenial to literature and interpretive anthropology than to communication studies, not because we think communication scholars should emulate what scholars in other disciplines have accomplished but because these terms provide a broader conceptual framework for reassessing our traditional research activities. For social constructionists, description and interpretation are primary, and they are linked with the cluster of terms, such as "translation" and "engagement," that have no counterpart in the other paradigm. If the human sciences are essentially interpretive, as Geertz (1973, 1983), Rabinow and Sullivan (1979), Ricoeur (1971), Taylor (1971), and others insist, the meaning of "description" and "interpretation" differs from what the same terms designate in the communication science paradigm. More than just an alternative research method, interpretation and description "provide a different vocabulary that introduces a certain point of view about human experience and aims to cope with it" (Bochner, 1985, p. 35).

In social constructionist research, the participants' voices are privileged; their publicly performed conversations and activities as well as their own interpretations of their life experiences are taken as the primary data. Geertz (1973) claimed that the ethnographer inscribes social discourse by writing it down and turning the passing event into an account. The relationship between the researcher and those studied is taken as part of the process by which the events being explored are jointly created. The researcher both constructs and is constructed by his or her interactions with the persons in dialogue, and vice versa. This process of inscription is far from neutral and certainly not without consequences for both the writer and those written about.

Geertz (1983) argued that interpretation of different cultural phenomena is possible, and translation is a viable means to accomplish this goal. However, translation is desirable not because it provides a one-to-one comparison or a simple recasting of other's ways of putting things in terms of our own ways of putting them. Rather, translation involves "displaying the logic of their ways of putting them in the locutions of ours; a conception which again brings it rather closer to what a critic does to illumine a poem than what an astronomer does to account for a star" (Geertz, 1983, p. 10).

Interpretation and translation always require a re-creation of lived experiences, and this is the heart of the creative practice in studying communication. If our notion of sophistication precludes the intention and the possibility to mirror the object of our study separate from our act of studying, then a case study functions to illuminate and enlighten the convoluted process of communication and the complex nature of our social worlds. Social constructionists are interested in refining and contributing to what we see as a continuing human conversation. Our theories and research are best understood as "turns" in that conversation, in which we often quote and paraphrase, as well as add elaborations and critiques to what others say and do. To engage in our research is to fully participate in and acknowledge the process of co-construction. We are not interested in a spectator form of knowledge "about" some state of affairs but a "practical wisdom" about how to act into and out of a specific situation.

Mode of Operation

Although social constructionists may agree to distance themselves from *theoria* and particularly the definition of theory offered by communication scientists, they disagree about whether their work is described appropriately as theoretical in any sense. Without engaging the rival positions in this debate, it is clear that social constructionists "operate" by giving close descriptions of particular events and activities, calling into being narratives that interpret them. This process often requires the creation of terms that sensitize the readers of those narratives to what the writer believes is going on in them.

For example, Pearce (1989) offered the terms "coordination," "coherence," and "mystery" as theoretical concepts, the explication of which in any given situation presumably illuminates the process of communication. Perhaps whatever might be called theory from our social constructionist standpoint is more like a set of systematically collected accounts or socially and culturally specific stories. Because the actions of the observer are a part of the observed, social constructionists are also agents of change (Gergen, 1982). To the extent that we are theory builders, researchers are never "spectators" but always implicated in a creative process that simultaneously expresses and constructs events and experiences.[5]

Criteria for Interpreting and Evaluating Theories

Different conceptions of theory and modes of inquiry entail different sets of criteria for what counts as a useful and elegant theory. We do not intend the list to be one-to-one alternatives; the comparison should be made by taking the two sets of vocabulary as a whole. We agree with Geertz (1973) when he said, "I have never been impressed by the argument that, as complete objectivity is impossible in these matters . . . one might as well let one's sentiments run loose" (p. 30). Our goals and interests in social constructionism suggest a very specific kind of rigor in the study of communication.

Human beings are second-order cybernetic systems; we have the unique capacity to reflect upon, monitor, evaluate, and change our social behavior (Bateson, 1972). Moreover, we have the ability to do this symbolically, playing out much of our lives within webs of significance that we have invented. To the extent that these symbolic creations underrepresent the complexity, multidimensionality, and fluidity of human activity, we are bound to misunderstand ourselves in profound and perhaps tragic ways.

The problem with generalizations in traditional scientific theories is that they often go beyond the range of actual concrete experiences and benignly neglect the complex relationships between social actors and the specific context in which activities occur. Among others, Geertz's (1973, 1983) work informed us that persons become human not by learning culture "in general" but by learning *a* particular culture. By the same token, we learn about communication not by studying the covering laws of human behavior but by knowing the specificities, differences, and contingencies of social actions performed in a certain context. In bridging the gap between theory and practice, Wood and Cox (1993) argued for situated knowledge in our theory building. They emphasized the importance of interlinked roles of theory and lived experience and the embodied person engaged in activities. Therefore, acknowledging and celebrating the unique social position that an embodied person occupies in interaction should be a primary consideration for evaluating theories. In a similar vein, Tracy (1993), critiquing research that is equipped with an array of methods to uncover commonalities, said, "But these methods are problematically applicable to understanding differences. I find differences more intriguing" (p. 197). Writer Richard Rodriguez (1982, 1989) also insisted on singularity in understanding cultural experiences: "I abhor the notion of a typical life" (1989, p. 12); he reminded us that "the magnifying power of literature is exactitude. . . . The characters one remembers best are not typical; just the opposite—they are specific, they are unforgettable" (1989, p. 12).

Behind the criteria of theories in communication science is the quest for certainty, and Dewey (1929) cautioned us of "the danger of the glorification of the invariant at the expense of change" because "all practical activity falls within the realm of change" (p. 17). Because experimental knowledge and survey findings take place at a time, in a place, and under specifiable conditions in connection with a definite problem, the search for certainty ultimately becomes "the search for methods of control" (Dewey, 1929, pp. 102–128). Communication is contingent and involves a sequence of events that is not fully predictable. Interaction opens up new possibilities and often generates surprises.

We believe that communication is knowable from the participant's point of view, and one criterial attribute of social theory should be its ability to account for itself, its history, and its place in the larger system of human communication. A good theory from a social constructionist viewpoint therefore should address the multilayered and ever evolving complexity of each instance under investigation while having the power to engage in self-critique. We concur with Gergen's (1982) suggestion that "certainty" be replaced by "reflexivity" in our theory construction, thus transforming the notion of knowledge into something more fluid and useful instead of fixed and true. Communication is inherently reflexive. As McNamee (1988) argued, "To be valuable, a theory should speak to the creation and transformation of contextual patterns" (p. 55).

Criteria for Interpreting and Evaluating Research

In the communication science paradigm, the well-known criteria for interpreting and evaluating research assume that the object of study stands still external to the investigator's perspective. Social constructionists believe that human conversation is in principle unfinished and imperfect, that the researcher stands in a participant's perspective, both changing it and being changed by the conversation as part of the process of inquiry. Good research then consists of engaging with (instead of remaining distant from), and thus affecting, that which is studied. We propose a set of criteria, none of which stands alone, for interpreting and evaluating case studies. All these terms bear consonance with the array of terms suggested for our research interests as previously discussed.

Coherence and intelligibility ask whether the case study makes sense to the reader. "A coherent interpretation . . . is based on materials that are historical, relational, processual, and interactional" (Denzin, 1989, p. 64). A good study must, of course, also be intelligible to the informants whose life experiences are being inscribed. However, as necessary as they are, coherence and intelligibility are certainly insufficient for a "thick" description, for as Geertz (1973) pointed out, "There is nothing so coherent as a paranoid's delusion or a swindler's story" (p. 18). Communication researchers often confront events that seem irrational or nonsensical. The move is to illuminate the context in which the reason or sense can be displayed through translation. A good translation shows patterns of connections and distinctions among all the relevant aspects of the story, recognizing that inconsistency and contradiction are significant forms of relationship.

Richness of a case study involves the polyphonic and polysemous quality of the stories told. "A good interpretation of anything. . .takes us into the heart of that of which it is the interpretation" (Geertz, 1973, p. 18). To illuminate the reader, "An interpretation must bring alive what is being studied" (Denzin, 1989, p. 63). A comprehensive case study certainly does not mean that it identifies all the possible variables pertinent to the case. Rather, it takes the historicity of the case into account, pays attention to the nuances of the observed phenomenon, calls attention to the multiple perspectives of the interpretation, and accounts for the recursive features of the case that the process of communication generates. Various pieces of the stories told in a case study should also be interconnected; however, this does not mean that they should (or can) be totally consistent with one another. One way to strive for comprehensiveness and interconnectedness in a case study is to realize that what we call social facts are historically situated and culturally created (Gergen, 1978). Often communication can be paradoxical, and it is far more significant to discern structural similarities (the patterns that connect) that are developed over time than to argue for the internal consistency across situations.

As our interests in doing case studies are not to predict and control but to enlighten and illuminate while acknowledging the complexity and contingency of communication, a case study should also be judged by how probable and plausible the interpretations are within the context of inquiry. Ricoeur (1971) argued that any given text opens up multiple probabilities of understanding. In the hermeneutic process of evaluating multiple interpretations, we can always discuss the probability of each reading of the text, how likely or plausible a certain interpretation is when judged by the reader and compared with competing interpretations. If social knowledge is indeed historically created, one way to assess the quality of a case study is to see whether the interpretations are historically and situationally conscious.

Finally, open-endedness is an essential criterion for a case study. The pragmatist tradition sees meaning as a social product that is always unfinished and incomplete. Even the most carefully conducted case study that satisfies all (and more than) the above criteria still does not have the "final say" of what the event means. Rather, it provokes readers to think beyond what the text provides and invites them to offer a different interpretation. Geertz (1973) believed that ethnographic assertion is "essentially contestable," and that "cultural analysis is intrinsically incomplete. And worse than that, the more deeply it goes the less complete it is" (p. 29). Similarly, Rosaldo (1989) argued that "all interpretations are provisional; they are made by positioned subjects who are prepared to know certain things and not others" (p. 8). Denzin (1989) also claimed that all interpretations are unfinished, provisional, and incomplete; to think otherwise is to "foreclose one's interpretations before one begins" (p. 65). Therefore, to enact the metaphor of conversation, a case study should generate a forum for continuing conversation and open up possibilities for further dialogues.

CONCLUSION

In this chapter we argue that the case itself in a case study is best seen as the "figure," not just as an "instance" of something else. That is, the particularities of the case are the constitutive substance of what is being studied, not distractions, variables to be controlled, or examples to be subsumed under a generalization. In the context of communication science, case studies have a potentially important but inherently limited function. The subordination of case studies to other preferred modes of research, we believe, derives from an insufficient emancipation from a failed attempt to emulate an inaccurately perceived model of a so-called higher-status discipline (19th-century physics). The failure to reproduce what is perceived to be the model of natural science is particularly distressing because it brings a pernicious sense of self-loathing. When findings do not fit well into the established framework of science, researchers lament and blame it on their lack of theoretical or methodological sophistication.

As scholars and researchers in interpersonal communication, we are often made to apologize for doing that which we do best: the illumination of specific communication practices in specific social relationships. The appeal of doing case studies within social constructionism derives from the resonance among its goals, interests, criteria, and that which our case studies reveal about the nature of communication per se. Conducting case studies also suggests an other-oriented (instead of a researcher-centered) approach to study communication. Although the researcher may eventually authorize the final presentation of the study, the authority of the discourse no longer rests fully in the researcher's hand. The process of reconstructing the informant's own stories and narratives is a dialogical one, and this fits well with our metaphor of conversation in studying communication.

Works such as this typically end with the observation that "more research needs be done." To vary that a bit, we conclude that more case studies aiming for the criteria discussed earlier need to be done and need to be welcomed and evaluated more favorably in interpersonal communication. They constitute the heart of what we as a discipline should be doing, not a preliminary or a fringe. Kuhn (1970) claimed that "history suggests that the road to a firm research consensus is extraordinarily arduous" (p. 15). Noting Kuhn's point on the difficulty of paradigm shift, we offer this chapter in the spirit of providing alternatives instead of seeking consensus in our research activities. Table 7.1 was constructed with an open-ended quality; we welcome further dialogues to refine the sophistication of doing case studies within social constructionism. As Wood and Cox (1993) suggested, "Research is inevitably a conversation between parties" (p. 282). Doing case studies within social constructionism is our scholarly commitment to a particular style of intellectual pursuit. We take Geertz's (1973) position to heart when he said, "Interpretive anthropology is a science whose progress is marked less by a perfection of consensus than by a refinement of debate. What gets better is the precision with which we vex each other" (p. 29).

If Geertz is right, the most beautiful case studies are those that enrich our conversation the most. They embody eternal joy, and yet rather than a timeless "joy forever," they are enjoyed because they enable the conversation to move beyond them.

ACKNOWLEDGMENT

The authors wish to thank Larry Frey for his helpful comments on the manuscript.

NOTES

1. We understand that case studies can certainly be conducted within theoretical frameworks (e.g., "naturalistic paradigm") other than the two we discuss here. The development of social constructionism has often included a conscious differentiation of itself from "scientific" approaches to the study of social phenomena in general, and of communication in particular. Many stress that social constructionism is not so much a new set of answers to the same questions posed by the "dominant paradigm" in social science but constitutes a full-blown paradigm shift in which what was previously seen as

central questions are now seen as relatively unimportant or wrong-headed, and new questions are posed.

2. As social constructionists, we do not treat "meaning" and "purposes" as intrapsychic cognitive states. To do so creates the "problem" of how the "external" object (the case study) is affected by the "internal" subject. In our view, this problem is a conundrum successfully avoided by locating meaning and purposes within the real, social world of communicative actions (see Cronen, Pearce, & Xi, 1989/1990). Erlandson, Harris, Skipper, and Allen (1993) also stated that "the operational difference between the two types of research (positivistic and naturalistic) are not so well defined by their different methodologies as by the reasons for which methods are selected and by how the data obtained from them are intended to be used" (p. 35).

3. The argument we are making about communication as one of those things that can be other than it is leads to a variety of metaphors in addition to "conversation." These metaphors include Bateson's (1972, 1979) multilayered contextualized patterns, Geertz's (1973, 1983) symbols and texts, Goffman's (1959) and Conquergood's (1986, 1989) performance, Mead's (1938) symbolic interaction, Dewey's (1922, 1929) activity, Rorty's (1979) edification, Wittgenstein's (1953) meaning in use, and Kingston's (1977) "talk story." These metaphors share our assumption that communication is fluid and that the activities of practicing, interpreting, performing, experiencing, storytelling—and conducting case studies—provide the multidirectional potential for the continued unfolding of the conversation.

4. We separate "description" from "interpretation" simply for the purpose of explication. These two terms are, of course, inseparable. Communication is inherently interpretive; any attempt to describe involves interpretation.

5. We are aware of the brevity of our discussion in this section. Because this is a conceptual piece, we do not see the need to elaborate on the specific procedure for conducting case studies here.

REFERENCES

Bateson, G. (1972). *Steps to an ecology of mind.* New York: Ballantine.

Bateson, G. (1979). *Mind and nature: A necessary unity.* New York: Dutton.

Berger, C. R., & Chaffee, S. H. (1987). The study of communication as science. In C. R. Berger & S. H. Chaffee (Eds.), *Handbook of communication science* (pp. 15–19). Newbury Park, CA: Sage.

Bernstein, R. J. (1983). *Beyond objectivism and relativism.* Philadelphia: University of Pennsylvania Press.

Bochner, A. P. (1985). Perspectives on inquiry: Representation, conversation, and reflection. In M. L. Knapp & G. R. Miller (Eds.), *Handbook of interpersonal communication* (pp. 27–58). Beverly Hills, CA: Sage.

Bochner, A. P., & Ellis, C. (1992). Personal narrative as a social approach to interpersonal communication. *Communication Theory, 2,* 165–172.

Chaffee, S. H., & Berger, C. R. (1987). What communication scientists do. In C. R. Berger & S. H. Chaffee (Eds.), *Handbook of communication science* (pp. 99–122). Newbury Park, CA: Sage.

Chen, V. (1994). (De)hyphenated identity: The double voice in *The woman warrior*. In A. González, M. Houston, & V. Chen (Eds.), *Our voices: Essays in culture, ethnicity, and communication* (pp. 3–11). Los Angeles: Roxbury.

Cheng, C. Y. (1987). Chinese philosophy and contemporary human communication theory. In D. L. Kincaid (Ed.), *Communication theory: Eastern and western perspectives* (pp. 23–43). San Diego: Academic Press.

Conquergood, D. (1986). *Between experience and expression: The performed myth.* Paper presented at the annual conference of Speech Communication Association, Chicago.

Conquergood, D. (1989). Poetics, play, process, and power: The performative turn in anthropology. *Text and Performance Quarterly, 1,* 82–88.

Cronen, V. E., Chen, V., & Pearce, W. B. (1988). Coordinated management of meaning: A critical theory. In Y. Y. Kim & W. B. Gudykunst (Eds.), *International and intercultural communication annual,* (Vol. 12, pp. 66–98). Newbury Park, CA: Sage.

Cronen, V. E., Pearce, W. B., & Xi, C. (1989/1990). The meaning of 'meaning' in the CMM analysis of communication: A comparison of two traditions. *Research on Language and Social Interaction, 23,* 1–40.

Denzin, N. K. (1989). *Interpretive interactionism.* Newbury Park, CA: Sage.

Denzin, N. K., & Lincoln, Y. S. (1994). *Handbook of qualitative research.* Newbury Park, CA: Sage.

Dewey, J. (1922). *Human nature and conduct.* New York: Holt.

Dewey, J. (1929). *The quest for certainty: A study of the relation of knowledge and action.* New York: Minton, Balch.

Dukes, W. F. (1972). N=1. In R. E. Kirk (Ed.), *Statistical issues: A reader for the behavioral sciences* (pp. 217–223). Monterey, CA: Brooks/Cole.

Erlandson, D. A., Harris, E. L., Skipper, B. L., & Allen, S. D. (1993). *Doing naturalistic inquiry: A guide to methods.* Newbury Park, CA: Sage.

Geertz, C. (1973). *The interpretation of cultures.* New York: Basic Books.

Geertz, C. (1983). *Local knowledge.* New York: Basic Books.

Gergen, K. J. (1978). Toward generative theory. *Journal of Personality and Social Psychology, 36,* 1344–1360.

Gergen, K. J. (1982). *Toward transformation in social knowledge.* New York: Springer-Verlag.

Goffman, E. (1959). *The presentation of self in everyday life.* Garden City, NY: Doubleday/Anchor.

Gronbeck, B. E. (1981). Qualitative communication theory and rhetorical studies in the 1980s. *Central States Speech Journal, 32,* 243–253.

Keith, W. M., & Wittenberger-Keith, K. (1988/1989). The conversational call: An analysis of conversational aspects of public oratory. *Research on Language and Social Interaction, 22,* 115–156.

Kingston, M. H. (1977). *The woman warrior: Memoirs of a girlhood among ghosts.* New York: Vintage Books.

Kuhn, T. (1970). *The structure of scientific revolutions* (2nd ed.). Chicago: University of Chicago Press.

McKeon, R. (Ed.). (1941). *The basic works of Aristotle*. New York: Random House.

McNamee, S. (1988). Accepting research as social intervention: Implications of a systemic epistemology. *Communication Quarterly, 36,* 50–68.

Mead, G. H. (1938). *The philosophy of the act*. Chicago: University of Chicago Press.

Ostwald, M. (Trans.). (1962). *Nicomachean ethics*. Indianapolis: Bobbs-Merrill.

Pearce, W. B. (1989). *Communication and the human condition*. Carbondale: Southern Illinois University Press.

Pearce, W. B. (1991). On comparing theories: Treating theories as commensurate or incommensurate. *Communication Theory, 1,* 159–164.

Rabinow, P., & Sullivan, W. M. (Eds.).(1979). *Interpretive social science*. Berkeley: University of California Press.

Ricoeur, P. (1971). The model of the text. *Social Research, 38,* 529–555.

Rodriguez, R. (1982). *Hunger of memory: The education of Richard Rodriguez*. New York: Bantam.

Rodriguez, R. (1989). An American writer. In W. Sollors (Ed.), *The invention of ethnicity* (pp. 3–13). New York: Oxford University Press.

Rorty, R. (1979). *Philosophy and the mirror of nature*. Princeton, NJ: Princeton University Press.

Rosaldo, R. (1989). *Culture and truth: The remaking of social analysis*. Boston: Beacon Press.

Shotter, J. (1990). *Knowing of the third kind: Selected writings on psychology, rhetoric, and the culture of everyday social life*. Utrecht, The Netherlands: University of Utrecht.

Sigman, S. J. (1992). Do social approaches to interpersonal communication constitute a contribution to communication theory? *Communication Theory, 2,* 347–356.

Taylor, C. (1971). Interpretation and the sciences of man. *Review of Metaphysics, 25,* 3–34, 45–51.

Tracy, K. (1993). It's an interesting article! *Research on Language and Social Interaction, 26,* 195–201.

Wilder-Mott, C. (1981). Rigor and imagination. In C. Wilder-Mott & J. H. Weakland (Eds.), *Rigor & imagination: Essays from the legacy of Gregory Bateson* (pp. 5–42). New York: Praeger.

Wittgenstein, L. (1953). *Philosophical investigations* (G. Anscombe, Trans.). New York: Macmillan.

Wood, J. T., & Cox, R. (1993). Rethinking critical voice: Materiality and situated knowledges. *Western Journal of Communication, 57,* 278–287.

Yin, R. K. (1989). *Case study research: Design and methods* (rev. ed.). Newbury Park, CA: Sage.

CHAPTER 8

Re-relationalizing Rapport in Interpersonal Settings

JANE JORGENSON

I n everyday language, there are few terms that are truly relational in the sense of capturing that which is shared or jointly experienced in interpersonal relationships. "Rapport" is one of them. It is a term that resists precise definition. Its dictionary equivalents are "communication, harmonious relationship, or connection" (*Concise Oxford Dictionary*, 1987). To speak of "being in rapport with" or "having rapport with" another person is to express a basic insight about the nature of the relationship, to offer a "double description" in which multiple points of view are present.

My personal associations with the word "rapport" are complex. As a student of communication I am intrigued by the richness of its relational implications and yet doubtful of settling on a mode of investigation of rapport that would fully allow for its emergent, systemic nature. As a teacher working in the context of distance education, teaching televised courses via satellite, I have practical and strategic questions concerning the importance of teacher–student rapport in learning, and of the possibilities for achieving rapport in the absence of face-to-face interaction.

I also recognize another set of associations around rapport as "that mysterious necessity of fieldwork" (Geertz, 1973, p. 416). To the extent that my own research has relied on various forms of interviewing, I have always understood rapport as something that facilitates the data-gathering process. In interviews, which constitute a basic tool of data collection in communication research, the establishment of rapport is conceived as an aid in the elicitation of candid and full disclosures of information from the research participants. This is the core of my concern—our research-related uses of the term and their stress on its "instrumental" potentialities at the expense of its interpersonal and relational implications. The concept of rapport embodies precisely the sort of opposition denoted by Geertz's (1976) experience–near/experience–far axis. "Love" is an example of an experience–near term, according to Geertz, "one which an individual—a patient, a subject . . . an informant—might himself naturally and effortlessly use to define what he sees. . . ." Experience–distant concepts, such as social stratification or object cathexis, are those that a specialist employs "to forward his scientific, philosophical or practical aims" (p. 223). In this sense, the term "rapport" poses a special problem as an experience–near concept whose terms of definition move between "near" and "distant" poles—between the forms of understanding at play among people in everyday conversation and those constructed by researchers.

As a focal construct in communication research, rapport seems to suggest possibilities for understanding interpersonal communication process in a noninstrumental way, and yet with regard to our own professional practices, we regard rapport as *a means to* the acquisition of data on interpersonal relationships. This chapter explores some of these tensions and circularities by bringing together several perspectives on rapport that constitute its family of uses. These include, first, theoretical conceptualizations concerning the nature of rapport. As they embody particular interactional metaphors, theoretical perspectives indicate some of the contours of a "social" approach to interpersonal communication. I also include some versions of rapport that appear to operate in applied settings and, in particular, to guide practitioners in the fields of psychotherapy and communication research, and, finally, some reflections based on my own research experiences. In showing how our specialized uses have served to "de-relationalize" an essentially relational term, my intent is to reconsider interview methodology from a social constructionist perspective (Gergen, 1985; Steier, 1991) and to outline a reformulation of the particular activities that constitute the research process.

UNDERSTANDING THE "NATURE" OF RAPPORT

Ordinary usage suggests that not all relationships are candidates for rapport insofar as it is often tied to particular kinds of social partnerships. A teacher, for example, is said to have "good rapport" with her students or an employer with her employees. Yet we would probably be surprised to hear the term used to describe a husband–wife relationship, where the mutual understanding implied by rapport is redundant with the intimacy that the marital relationship presupposes. Furthermore, in ordinary talk about professional partnerships, it is common to speak of building or establishing rapport, in effect, to treat rapport as a valued potentiality of those very relationships in which its achievement is assumed to be somehow problematic.

Theorists and researchers appear to have drawn on at least some of these everyday nuances in constructing questions about the nature of rapport. They have tended to view professional relationships as promising sites for the study of rapport phenomena—relationships of doctors and their patients (Harrigan & Rosenthal, 1986), academic advisers and advisees (Fiksdal, 1988), teachers and students (Bernieri, 1988), and therapists and clients (Charny, 1966). Each of these is characterized by an asymmetry of role—by differences between the participants in status, in expertise, and in the capacity to provide support. In selecting these relationships as the relevant contexts, re-searchers have undertaken the search for communicative "forms," especially nonverbal behaviors, associated with the "experience" of rapport.

An example of recent theorizing on the nature of rapport by Tickle-Degnan and Rosenthal (1987, 1990) illustrates some of the dilemmas inherent in trying to conceptualize human relationships in social and relational terms. Their work is notable in its effort to sustain a relationship-level, rather than an individual-level, focus, to "preserve the essence of the nature of rapport" and yet make it accessible to operationalization. They propose a tripartite structure of rapport as "coordination," "mutual attentiveness," and "positivity" (Tickle-Deg-nan & Rosenthal, 1990), terms designating both the experiential aspects of rapport and their correlated behavioral expressions. The authors further hypothesize differences in the relative weightings of these components at different points in the development of a relationship. In initial encounters, for example, participants would judge rapport chiefly by levels of positivity and warmth; the progression toward greater familiarity would entail changing expectations such that part-ners would pay relatively more attention to the degree of coordination as their perceptions of the other stabilize. The basis of coordination is "the ability to adopt the other's perspective," which increases as famili-arity develops (Tickle-Degnan & Rosenthal, 1990, p. 288).

Several models of human interaction are prominent in this concep-tualization, including the concept of interactional synchrony to denote the mutual behavioral responsiveness of social partners (the orchestra metaphor is also alluded to by the authors as a model of coordination).

Another organizing image is that of relationship "trajectory," which builds on social penetration models of relationship development (Altman & Taylor, 1973). The choice of these models and their linkage by Tickle-Degnan and Rosenthal is, however, at odds with their larger goal of achieving a "relationship" level of description. Interactional synchrony and the orchestra metaphor connote the rhythmic integration of social partners as each behaves in accordance with the behavior of the other (see Leeds-Hurwitz, 1989, for a summary). Yet in the research context Tickle-Degnan and Rosenthal have constructed of relationship growth and progressive familiarity, the achievement of rapport gets reduced to an individualistic explanation—to the capacities of the partners to adopt the other's perspective. At the same time, important connotations of the orchestra metaphor are obscured, particularly those pointing to the emergent character of meaning in human interaction. The meaning of a musical piece results from the playing of the "entire orchestra," rather than one instrumental part (Leeds-Hurwitz, 1989). The trajectory model invites an explanation of communication process cast in terms of individual functioning, so that the systemic character of rapport (implied in the musical metaphor) is lost.

In contrast to the focus on individual "identity" characteristics that marks many psychological approaches, a social approach involves the thick description of specific relational contexts, including participants' understandings of those contexts. A sensitivity to the creation of contexts led Erickson and Schultz (1982) over a decade ago to conceptualize rapport as a social accomplishment. Their work on academic counseling interviews builds on the convergent metaphors of "ecology" and "improvisation," images that enlarge the meaning of social in several ways. For Erickson and Schultz, rapport is understood to be a valued element in academic counseling interviews, where the participants—counselor and student—make communicative choices *jointly* so as to define an interactional ecosystem. The ways of speaking and listening of one member make impressions on the other whose reactions reflexively influence the first. Each is seen as an *environment*, not a stimulus, for the other. The musical analogy of improvisation here highlights the process by which participants or "players" choose from among communicative options conventionally agreed upon, yet whose range changes from moment to moment. Erickson and Schultz (1982) point to the ways in which the counselor and student establish the grounds for rapport by invoking their comemberships or shared social statuses. These may be obvious normative statuses, such as gender and race, or particularistic ones, such as participation in the same high school sport. It is the revelation of these shared social attributes that provides the participants with many optional ways of "getting the business done" (p. 37).

RAPPORT IN PROFESSIONAL SETTINGS

A social approach to rapport necessitates some exploration of interpretive frameworks through which participants experience and assess rapport in particular relationships. Professional helping relationships are a good place to begin, for psychotherapists, doctors, and other professionals understand and value rapport, based on their particular views of "appropriate" professional stance and assumptions about the goals of the helping relationship. Clients, too, may understand the helping relationship in a variety of ways—as advice giving, teaching, or simply "listening," and their understandings create expectations that condition the assessment of rapport.

The term "rapport" has a long history in psychotherapy. Early in this century, Freud (1914/1948) referred to "suggestible rapport on the part of the patient" (p. 293) as an essential precursor to the achievement of therapeutic transference. Since that time, success in therapy has been seen by both therapists and clients as linked to the qualities of the therapeutic relationship, to levels of trust, understanding, mutual liking, and respect. In psychotherapy, there are, of course, a wide range of therapeutic stances. Humanistic psychologists, for example, see rapport between therapist and client as largely *self*-validating. The point of therapy is the establishment of an empathic understanding of the client's internal frame of reference and "flow of experiencings" (Rogers, 1980, p. 142). In other approaches rapport is treated more instrumentally, signifying the degree of emotional contact between therapist and client, which, in turn, serves as a kind of "thermometer" registering the success of therapeutic interventions. Clients' self-disclosures of feelings are the signs of deepening rapport, and thus confirm to the therapist the appropriateness of his communication (Malon, 1979).

In the field of family therapy, an explicitly systemic language has evolved to describe the development of the therapeutic relationship, including terms such as, "coupling," "forming a treatment alliance," and most notably in this literature, "joining." Although these terms do not connote the same relational richness as rapport building, they present an interesting parallel, for the intention of systems practitioners was to capture in this language a new model of relational life, conceptualizing problems in terms of interactional patterns rather than individual pathologies (Yerby, 1992). The word "joining" in this context, derives from Ashby's (1960) cybernetic model in which parts of a complex system are linked together ("joined") in an interdependent way, or in which two systems are linked (Ashby, 1960; see also Hoffman, 1981).

What is paradoxical in the family therapy literature is the extent to which joining is presented as an individual, rather than a social, accomplishment, the result of the therapist's interpersonal skills. In order to join with the family, the therapist uses himself mimetically, adopting the family's affect, and adjusting to its unique style. Specific joining operations include code switching, appropriating the client's word choices, and generally "speaking the client's language" (Tyler & Tyler, 1990; see also Minuchin, 1974; O'Hanlon & Wilk, 1987). Such techniques are consistent with generalized strategies for displaying "positive politeness" in everyday interaction through the establishment of common ground (Brown & Levinson, 1978). However, their presentation as prescriptions for successful joining overlooks the fact that the client family is apt to deal with the unfamiliar therapeutic situation (and the therapist/stranger) with its own rapport building work. Joining, coupling, and rapport building all connote an interactional process, and yet the family itself is not portrayed in this work as a participant.

Therapists have also employed the term "resistance" as a complementary notion to indicate the failure of rapport or joining. The term "resistant patient" was traditionally used to describe an individual who responded uncooperatively to therapeutic interventions; family therapists continued to apply the term "resistance" in talking about family systems that appeared to resist "environmental inputs" (including therapeutic interventions) as a result of their essential homeostatic constitution (Dell, 1982). Such uses of these concepts have been at the core of a dispute within the field. Family therapist Paul Dell argued against the epistemological errors of such an orientation, noting that resistance is best understood in terms of the mutual adaptation (or relationship) between family and environment rather than as a property of the family or the patient. And so, we might add, is joining a joint accomplishment between the therapist and the patient.

Joining is presumed to be a delicate and uncertain process in part because traditional therapies are based on the idea of a separation or "boundary" between therapist and client. The therapist is considered an expert who is expected to be personally uninvolved with the client—in the analytical tradition, a "blank screen," onto which the client transfers past relationships and needs (Parvin & Biaggio, 1991). In the psychoanalytical tradition, the therapeutic relationship is by definition a relationship in which corrective feedback characteristic of ordinary two-person communication is withheld (Ruesch, 1972). Family systems practitioners caution the therapist against becoming "inducted" into the family pathology. Even in less directive therapies it is considered a breach of ethics for therapists to have outside contacts with their clients, and learning facts about the therapist's life can be considered a damaging boundary failure (Ryder & Bartle, 1991). The therapist's difficult communicative task, then, is to maintain a sense of boundary in order to prevent certain forms of intimacy while building a sense of trust in order to facilitate self-disclosure.

Alternative paradigms in psychotherapy have recently emerged in which the focus shifts from families as cybernetic systems to families as social or meaning-creating systems, and in which family problems are recast as "stories that people have agreed to tell themselves" (Hoffman, 1990, p. 3). The clinical implications of social constructionism are far-reaching, and are explored in a collection of essays brought together by McNamee and Gergen (1992). With regard to definitions of the therapeutic relationship, social constructionism proposes a very different mode of engagement between the therapist and client. The therapist no longer assumes a hierarchically superior stance but instead comes into the family from a position of "not knowing" and endeavors in the therapy conversation to develop with the family a mutual understanding of the problem (Hoffman, 1990). Social constructionism draws attention to the recursive nature of the therapist's efforts to understand the client, and to the process by which knowledge about the client is communicatively constructed in their interaction. These shifts in the stance of the therapist are paralleled in the research domain. For those who utilize face-to-face interviews as a research modality, social constructionism implies corresponding changes in how interviewers situate themselves in relation to respondents.

RAPPORT IN THE INTERVIEW SETTING

There are, of course, differences between the therapeutic interview and the research interview as social episodes. Psychotherapy is likely to imply a more sustained relationship than a research interview. It is also typically initiated by the client, who expects to derive direct benefit; in research, on the other hand, the interviewer seeks out the respondent. At the same time, there are marked similarities in the professional stances of therapist and researcher. As traditionally conceived, the observations of both therapist and interviewer are understood to be independent of the phenomena they observe rather than interdependent and collaborative (Yerby, 1992; see also Steier, 1991). Like the customary prescriptions for effective therapy, discussions of effective interviewing in methodology texts have tended to emphasize the interviewer's techniques of behavior management as a means of maintaining control of the interaction.

Interviewing, of course, takes many forms in interpersonal communication research, ranging from questionnaires or surveys to more open-ended, "epistemic" or knowledge-seeking interviews (Werner & Schoepfle, 1987) in which protocols are relatively fluid and respondents are permitted to talk at length on each topic. ("Formal" and "informal" interviewing are other terms that coincide with this distinction.) However, these two types of interviews are variations on a basic form of conversational interaction guided by a tacit rule in which one party asks questions and the other answers them. In terms of its implicit cultural meanings, the research interview, like the counselor–student or doctor–patient relationship, is an instance of social asymmetry. Insofar as the very act of "asking questions" obligates a response from one's partner (Goody, 1978), the research interview embodies a particular relationship definition in the sense that the interviewer assumes the right to require a response from her subject. Still, as Cicourel (1964) notes, interviewees exercise "power" over interviewers as well in the sense that they may show their disinterest or reluctance to sustain the interaction. The entry stage of participant observation has been modeled as a kind of social exchange or "negotiated reciprocity" (Jorgensen, 1989; Patton, 1990). Native participants find reasons to cooperate with the research, either because of useful feedback from the researcher or the pleasure of the interaction or from some other feeling that their cooperation is worthwhile.

An implicit theme in "classical" guides to structured and survey interviews (Babbie, 1979; Cannell & Kahn, 1968), as well as recent qualitative and ethnographic approaches (Lofland & Lofland, 1984; Patton, 1990; Spradley, 1979; Werner & Schoepfle, 1987), is that the establishment of rapport in the interview setting is achieved through the interviewer's skillful management of the research encounter. As Brenner (1985) has noted, the definition of the interviewee role in methodological guides tends to be vague, requiring merely that the respondent provide "adequate answers" according to the researcher's standards of relevance and completeness. Galtung (1967) describes the ideal survey respondent as "well socialized and disciplined, used to examinations, to listening, to answering honestly and clearly" (p. 157).

It is the interviewer's responsibility, on the other hand, to create a friendly, relaxed atmosphere and put the respondent at ease. This involves a wide range of behaviors and activities on her part; how, for example, she introduces herself and her study to prospective participants, how she formulates her questions (in the case of open-ended interviews) and paces them so as to establish a conversation rhythm, how she expresses her gratitude and indicates that the purposes of the interview are being fulfilled. These and many other behaviors are seen as crucial in achieving the cooperation of research participants. Much of the interviewer's interactive work involves skilled self-presentation. The interviewer who is "supportive, cordial, interested, nonargumentative, courteous, understanding, even sympathetic" is apt to elicit the fullest information (Lofland & Lofland, 1984, p. 38). In her efforts to present such an idealized "self," the interviewer draws on many of the same "positive politeness" strategies familiar in everyday conversation, such as small talk, jokes, and expressions of interest and approval.

By building rapport with the respondent, the interviewer is seen as accomplishing interrelated goals, one of which is motivational. The growth of rapport helps to sustain the respondent's willing participation in the research project (and to this end, the interviewer must make clear the importance of the information obtained from the participant.) A second goal of rapport building is to overcome informants' anxiety, what psychologists have referred to as evaluation apprehension, by demonstrating the nonthreatening nature of the research situation. The atmosphere must be one in which the respondent feels "fully understood, and in which it is safe to communicate without fear of being judged, criticized, or subsequently identified and disadvantaged" (Cannell & Kahn, 1968, p. 581). The long-standing practices of telling respondents that there are no right or wrong answers and pledging to protect their confidentiality, although not directly rapport-related, are intended to overcome this initial reluctance.

Another, largely tacit part of the rationale for building rapport in interviews seems to relate to goals of research reliability. The interviewer who practices the recommended strategies of impression management is likely to present a more uniform "self" from one interview to the next and thus reduce the possibility of interviewer bias. From a traditional research perspective, the cultivation of interview rapport facilitates the flow of data from the respondent and, in effect, supports the standardization and generalizability of results. In monitoring the flow of data, the interviewer assesses the effectiveness of rapport building in terms of criteria external to the relationship. Far from being interpersonal and intersubjective, rapport becomes specifiable according to what it produces for one of the participants—here, the interviewer.

In these standard accounts, the interviewer's goal of achieving a supportive and accepting climate is balanced against the need for scientific objectivity and detachment. Interpersonal rapport in the interview, we are warned, is not the same as friendship or intimacy; the interviewer is neither "judge" nor "therapist" (Patton, 1990, p. 354). According to conventional wisdom, too much intimacy is said to compromise the comparability of interview data across multiple respondents. Thus, as the feminist critic Oakley (1981) notes, the strategies for avoidance are explicit: "Never provide the interviewee with any formal indication of the interviewer's beliefs and values. If the informant poses a question . . . parry it" (p. 35). The dangers of emotional involvement have been succinctly captured in the concept of "overrapport." This term refers to a persistent trap, particularly in fieldwork situations of prolonged contact between the observer and observed, in which closeness and friendship inhibit the observer's ability to question the basic attitudes of the group under study (Miller, 1952). Anthropologists express a similar idea when they speak of the dangers of "going native."

A RESEARCH CONTEXT

Several years ago, I conducted open-ended interviews with married couples who had recently become parents (Jorgenson, 1989; 1991). The project was intended as an exploration of families' conceptions of family. The interviews included separate phases with each spouse, followed by a longer joint interview. At the time, I was aware of variation in the level of rapport from interview to interview, gauged according to the flow of the conversation and depth of the disclosures; in those interviews of greatest rapport, I felt the mood was simply friendlier, the conversation more reciprocal and open to digression. I remember one such instance in which, following a lively, and lengthy interview, a couple invited me to stay for a late supper and insisted I call my husband to join us (in the end he did, and we all shared a pleasant evening).

Looking back on the instances of good rapport, I still find it difficult to identify specific factors to account for the differences. In general, the elements that seemed to contribute to the growth of rapport were the discovery of shared social identities, but it was difficult to explain or predict which of these would come into play in a given encounter. Gender was one obviously relevant category; I found that interviewing the wives on the definition of family felt less awkward than asking their husbands the same questions. I have written elsewhere about the effects of my pregnancy on the research process (Jorgenson, 1991). As I became more visibly pregnant over the course of the study, participants were more likely to comment (e.g., "When is your baby due?") and thus create new avenues of discussion around topics such as childbirth and hospitals. (In some cases the conversational genre then shifted from interviewing to advice giving.)

I believe another, more subtle frame in *some* cases, was a shared understanding of the research context itself, in terms of a familiarity with the implicit rules of the interview. Willingness (or reluctance) to play "by the rules" was usually indicated during the first few minutes of the interview in response to my initial questions. I began the interview by asking husband and wife, individually, to list on a piece of paper those individuals they thought of as family, and then, afterwards, to explain to me any reasons they had for making the particular lists they did. My rationale was to use these ambiguous yet structured questions as points of departure for a conversation about the kinds of criteria by which the concept of family is constructed. Typically, informants answered my opening questions by asking their own questions of clarification, as in the following excerpt:

Informant: When you think about "family," who do you consider as part of your family?

Respondent: Just as far as like, my mother and dad?

Informant: Well, whatever "family" means to you. . . . It could be. . . .

Respondent: (*Writing*) It could go on endlessly, but. . . .

Such exchanges were usually brief; once respondents realized that the question was *meant* to be ambiguous, they tended to settle down to the listing task.

By beginning the interview in this way, I was, in fact, violating a recommended practice in open-ended interviewing of asking descriptive questions early on and moving to more complex and evaluative questions once rapport has been established (Whyte, 1984). I recognize now that the ambiguity in these "commonsense" questions, in some cases, worked against the establishment of rapport. The situation was broadly analogous to Platt's (1981) experiences interviewing sociologists about their own research projects. Her questions appeared odd and incongruous because respondents knew she knew many of the things she was asking about. In my own case, my questions were heard by some respondents as a kind of projective psychological technique. One woman, a psychiatric nurse, complained that the form of questioning made her feel she was under going evaluation, although she said that she knew that "you have to do this, to get your study" (Jorgenson, 1991). I sense, looking back on these interviews, that I would have been better served by adopting Whyte's (1984) recommended practice of moving from the specific and "descriptive" to the broad and "evaluative." Yet the range of different types of research relationships that I experienced in the course of this single project also suggests that the recommended strategies, though they may facilitate the growth of rapport, cannot ensure it; we cannot specify how we will be seen (or heard) by our coparticipants.

RE-RELATIONALIZING RAPPORT: IMPLICATIONS

As researchers, we have tended to forget that interviews themselves are social situations that embody basic communicative processes. Like other communicative events, interviews embed multiple orders of information: report and command (Bateson, 1968). As interviewees make sense of and respond to an interviewer's questions, they are simultaneously engaged in coming to know who the interviewer is. The ideal of the neutral, detached interviewer that we find embedded in standard accounts of interviewing has undergone revision in recent critical studies of the interview that redefine the research process as a collaborative rather than an elicitative enterprise. The research subjects now become coparticipants, and their interpretations of the research situation and of the researcher's conclusions are given a voice in the presentation of findings.

Scholars in diverse fields are finding common ground in the idea that any analysis of research interviews needs to take better account of respondents' social and personal contexts of meaning, including the interpretive frames they apply to the interview situation itself (see especially Briggs, 1986; Mishler, 1986; Oakley, 1981; Potter & Wetherell, 1987; Stephen, 1981). Rather than seeking to minimize the personal involvement of the interview, they argue for greater responsiveness to respondent reactions to the interview situation. How respondents construct the interviewer as a social type profoundly influences the form of their responses—whether they see her as a detached scientist, as a knowledgeable expert with valuable resources, as a critic, or as a comember of a particular social category (such as "mothers of 2-year-old children") will shape their interpretation of her questions, and consequently, their responses (see, e.g., Jorgenson, 1991; Wax, 1983). For the analyst whose task is making sense of their responses, some awareness of those constructions is crucial. Unfortunately, these sorts of insights are difficult to achieve either in the course of a proper interview or later, upon reflection, as long as the "ideal" interviewer is conceived as a depersonalized participant in the research process. In seeking rapport, the researcher engages in a process of "empathic dialogue" with the research participant (Stephen, 1981), attempting to establish accurately the meaning the subject creates "for understanding and coping with the research situation itself" (p. 43). Social psychologists Potter and Wetherell (1987) address this issue head on by suggesting that the research interview needs to become a more "interventionist and confrontative arena" (p. 164) in the sense that it generate a fuller range of respondents' interpretive contexts. In such an approach the reactions of interviewers and respondents to one another as social actors move to center stage in the analysis.

If we move to a more relational understanding of rapport as arising in cointerpretive processes, what, then are the implications for rethinking how we conduct ourselves in interviews, how we interpet our interactions with respondents, and how we write our reports? However we researchers define it, "effective interviewing" will always depend on our facilitative work, our strategic excercise of social skills; sensing the other's experience in Rogerian terms, and communicating those sensings to the other, constitutes necessary, though not sufficient, conditions for the accomplishment of rapport. We can try to establish the grounds for rapport by assuming a more open and acknowledging stance in the interview, but we cannot guarantee the outcome of our strategies. Rapport is elusive because it arises in the situation created between researcher and collaborators.

What researchers can do in reformulating rapport from a social perspective is to change the priorities given to interview *content* compared to those of interview *process* (Briggs, 1986). We can begin to reprioritize those elements by listening more carefully to apparent divergences and contradictions in respondents' accounts and by hearing those topic shifts and apparent irrelevancies as possible transformations on the stated topics rather than as peripheral to the research goals (Jorgenson, 1991). The resolution of divergences into "relevant" content depends on our recognizing that the respondent's construction of the interviewer as a conversational "you" may change from moment to moment in the interview, from knowledgeable expert to critic, from critic to fan; "what matters to us at any one moment is our social identity, i.e. how we are 'placed' in relation to those around us. . ." (Shotter, 1990, p. 16), and it is those (often unpredictable) shifts in identity construction that, in turn, guide subjects' formulations of responses to our questions. Our analysis of respondents' accounts and our preparation of reports for the research community must recognize how our findings are shaped by these cointerpretive activities, even though such recognitions may entail a reformulation of questions or a reworking of original hypotheses.

What we also do in reformulating rapport is to orient our efforts toward more particularistic descriptions of how social contexts are communicatively constructed. In viewing rapport instrumentally as a starting point in the pursuit of interview data, we have tended to value standardizing and aggregating, seeing the individual as the unit of analysis. Re-relationalizing rapport invites a fundamental change—from standardizing to particularizing, with the relationship in context as the focus.

REFERENCES

Altman, I., & Taylor, D. A. (1973). *Social penetration: The development of interpersonal relationships.* New York: Holt, Rinehart & Winston.

Ashby, R. (1960). *Design for a brain.* London: Chapman & Hall.

Babbie, E. (1979). *The practice of social research* (2nd ed.). Belmont, CA: Wadsworth.

Bateson, G. (1968). Information and codification: A philosophical approach. In J. Ruesch & G. Bateson, *Communication: The social matrix of psychiatry*. New York: W. W. Norton.

Bernieri, F. (1988). Coordinated movement and rapport in teacher–student interactions. *Journal of Nonverbal Behavior, 12,* 120–138.

Brenner, M. (1985). Survey interviewing. In M. Brenner, J. Brown & D. Canter (Eds.), *The research interview: Uses and approaches*. New York: Academic Press.

Briggs, C. L. (1986). *Learning how to ask: A sociolinguistic appraisal of the interview in social science research*. Cambridge: Cambridge University Press.

Brown, D. & Levinson, S. (1978). Universals in language use: Politeness phenomena. In E. Goody (Ed.), *Questions and politeness: Strategies in social interaction*. Cambridge: Cambridge University Press.

Cannell, C., & Kahn, R. (1968). Interviewing. In G. Lindzey & E. Aronson (Eds.), *The handbook of social psychology* (2nd ed.). Reading, MA: Addison-Wesley.

Charny, E. J. (1966). Psychosomatic manifestations of rapport in psychotherapy. *Psychosomatic Medicine, 28,* 305–315.

Cicourel, A. (1964). *Method and measurement in sociology*. New York: Free Press.

Concise Oxford dictionary. (1987). Oxford: Oxford University Press.

Dell, P. (1982). Beyond homeostasis: Toward a concept of coherence. *Family Process, 21,* 21–42.

Erickson, F., & Schultz, J. (1982). *The counselor as gatekeeper: Social interaction in interviews*. New York: Academic Press.

Fiksdal, S. (1988). Verbal and nonverbal strategies of rapport in cross-cultural interviews. *Linguistics and Education, 1,* 3–17.

Freud, S. (1948). On the history of the psychoanalytic movement. In E. Jones (Ed.), *Sigmund Freud: Collected papers* (Vol. 1). London: Hogarth Press. (Original work published 1914)

Galtung, J. (1967). *Theory and methods of social research*. Oslo: University of Oslo Press.

Geertz, C. (1973). Notes on a Balinese cockfight. In *The interpretation of cultures*. New York: Basic Books.

Geertz, C. (1976). "From the natives" point of view: On the nature of anthropological understanding. In K. Basso & H. Selby (Eds.), *Meaning in anthropology*. Albuquerque: University of New Mexico Press.

Gergen, K. J. (1985). The social constructionist movement in modern psychology. *American Psychologist, 40,* 266–275.

Goody, E. N. (1978). Towards a theory of questions. In E. Goody (Ed.), *Questions and politeness: Strategies in social interaction*. Cambridge: Cambridge University Press.

Harrigan, J. A., & Rosenthal, R. (1986). Nonverbal aspects of empathy and rapport in physician–patient interaction. In P. D. Blanck, R. Buck, & R. Rosenthal (Eds.), *Nonverbal communication in the clinical context*. University Park: Pennsylvania State University.

Hoffman, L. (1981). *Foundations of family therapy*. New York: Basic Books.

Hoffman, L. (1990). Constructing realities: An art of lenses. *Family Process, 29,* 1–12.

Jorgensen, D. (1989). *Participant observation: A methodology for human studies.* Newbury Park, CA: Sage.

Jorgenson, J. (1989). Where is the "family" in family communication research: Exploring families' self-definitions. *Journal of Applied Communication Research, 17,* 27–41.

Jorgenson, J. (1991). Co-constructing the interviewer/co-constructing the family. In F. Steier (Ed.), *Research and reflexivity.* London: Sage.

Leeds-Hurwitz, W. (1989). *Communication in everyday life: A social interpretation.* Norwood, NJ: Ablex.

Lofland, J., & Lofland, L. (1984). *Analyzing social settings.* Belmont, CA: Wadsworth.

Malon, D. (1979). *Individual psychotherapy and the science of psychodynamics.* London: Butterworths.

McNamee, S., & Gergen, K. J. (1992). *Therapy as social construction.* London: Sage.

Miller, S. M. (1952). The participant observer and "over-rapport." *American Sociological Review, 17,* 97–99.

Minuchin, S. (1974). *Families and family therapy.* Cambridge, MA: Harvard University Press.

Mishler, E. (1986). *Research interviewing: Context and narrative.* Cambridge, MA: Harvard University Press.

Oakley, A. (1981). Interviewing women: A contradiction in terms. In H. Roberts (Ed.), *Doing feminist research.* London: Routledge & Kegan Paul.

O'Hanlon, B., & Wilk, J. (1987). *Shifting contexts: The generation of effective psychotherapy.* New York: Guilford Press.

Parvin, R., & Biaggio, M. K. (1991). Paradoxes in the practice of feminist therapy. *Women and Therapy, 11,* 3–12.

Patton, M. (1990). *Qualitative evaluation and research methods* (2nd ed.). Newbury Park, CA: Sage.

Platt, J. (1981). On interviewing one's peers. *British Journal of Sociology, 32,* 75–91.

Potter, J., & Wetherell, M. (1987). *Discourse and social psychology.* London: Sage.

Rogers, C. (1980). *A way of being.* Boston: Houghton-Mifflin.

Ruesch, J. (1972). Transference reformulated. In J. Ruesch (Ed.), *Semiotic approaches to human relations.* The Hague: Mouton.

Ryder, R., & Bartle, S. (1991). Boundaries as distance regulators in personal relationships. *Family Process, 40,* 393–406.

Shotter, J. (1990). "Getting in touch": The metamethodology of a postmodern science of mental life. *The Humanistic Psychologist, 18,* 7–22.

Spradley, J. (1979). *The ethnographic interview.* New York: Holt, Rinehart & Winston.

Steier, F. (Ed.). (1991). *Research and reflexivity.* London: Sage.

Stephen, T. (1981). Toward a phenomenological methodology for the study of symbolic communication. In S. Deetz (Ed.), *Phenomenology in rhetoric and communication.* Washington, DC: Center for Advanced Research in Phenomenology & University Press of America.

Tickle-Degnan, L., & Rosenthal, R. (1987). Group rapport and nonverbal behavior. In C. Hendrick (Ed.), *Review of personality and social psychology: Vol. 9. Group processes and intergroup relations*. Newbury Park, CA: Sage.

Tickle-Degnan, L., & Rosenthal, R. (1990). The nature of rapport and its nonverbal correlates. *Psychological Inquiry, 1*, 285–293.

Tyler, M., & Tyler, S. (1990). The sorcerer's apprentice: The discourse of training in family therapy. In B. Keeney, B. Nolan, & W. Madsen (Eds.), *The systemic therapist* (Vol. 1). St. Paul, MN: Systemic Therapy Press.

Wax, R. (1983). The ambiguities of fieldwork. In R. Emerson (Ed.), *Contemporary field research*. Prospect Heights, IL: Waveland Press.

Werner, O. & Schoepfle, G. (1987). *Systematic fieldwork* (Vol. 1). Newbury Park, CA: Sage.

Whyte, W. F. (1984). *Learning from the field*. Beverly Hills, CA: Sage.

Yerby, J. (1992). *Family systems theory reconsidered: Integrating social construction theory and dialectical process into a systems perspective of family communication*. Paper presented at the annual meeting of the Speech Communication Association, Chicago.

CHAPTER 9

A Role for Communication Theory in Ethnographic Studies of Interpersonal Communication

DONAL CARBAUGH
SALLY O. HASTINGS

During the past decade, students of interpersonal communication have heard calls from several prominent courtyards urging investigators to enter socially situated scenes and, once there, to explore the "natural" communication of social life. Constructivists have invited us to explore "interpretive processes" of individuals within "sociocultural communities" through a "reflective empiricism," with special attention to "free response data" (Delia, O'Keefe, & O'Keefe, 1982). Similarly, after exposing the hidden workings of an ideology in some research, Parks (1982) proposed a closer examination of real-world practices, urging us "off the couch and into the world" (p. 79). More recently, Duck (1991) reexamined many concerns in research about relationships, finding a new focus on the "realization" of "symbolic union," "universes," and "meanings" refreshing. Yet, how does one conduct basic research about interpersonal practices in a way that brings into view their communicative forms, functions, and meanings? Our claim is that a version of ethnography and cultural analysis provides one such social approach to interpersonal communication, with our main goal being to reflect on the role of communication theory within this investigative process. We hope, like Berger (1991), to make "theory development . . . an integral part of the training of all communication researchers" (p. 102). To begin, we sketch some social and cultural bases of our approach.

To use the term "social" to characterize a general approach to interpersonal communication is to say something about that approach that is distinctive to it. Some prominent connotations of social include "seeing" and "hearing" communication as a situated accomplishment (Stewart & Philipsen, 1985), as a reflexive process (Pearce, 1989; Pearce & Cronen, 1980), as interactive even in its various monological forms (Sanders, 1987), and as constructing conceptions of the self or person, relations with one another, social structures, and institutions (Carbaugh, 1988b; Leeds-Hurwitz, 1989; Sigman, 1987). Conceiving of communication as such is to stand one foot firmly on a social foundation, to see (hear and feel) on this base the social life in communication, the situated, interactional patterns that creatively evoke, sometimes validate, sometimes negotiate, sometimes embattle, and sometimes transform social selves, relations, and institutions.

But we have left one foot dangling. An "adequately ambulatory" theory of communication—if it is to penetrate the meanings of selves in societies—would stand firmly also on a "cultural" foundation (see Hymes, 1990, p. 420). Brought into view, on this base, would be the locally distinctive symbols, symbolic forms, and meanings that participants themselves consider significant and important (Carbaugh, 1988b, 1991). What do they presume as they interact? And, when asked, how do they render their social lives? How do they construe the world during their many situated, reflexive interactional social performances? In short, how, if at all, is their interpersonal communication culturally coded through their own system of symbols, symbolic forms, and meanings?[1]

With one's social and cultural footing established, one can be responsive to these kinds of questions and calls and thus create interpersonal communication theory accordingly. So positioned, a few have developed an ethnographic approach to communication, as well as produced methodological proposals, programmatic statements, and reviews that suggest a central place for communication theory (e.g., Philipsen, 1989; Stewart & Philipsen, 1985). Further, the role of communication theory is evident in several fieldwork reports (see, e.g., Bauman & Sherzer, 1974; Carbaugh, 1990a; Gumperz & Hymes, 1972). But to our knowledge, none of these essays has explicated in detail the various phases of communication theorizing within ethnographic studies, although the general role of theorizing is mentioned and its various phases are evident in many ethnographic studies.

Our aim is to contribute to an understanding of ethnography as a way of theorizing interpersonal communication. We first briefly discuss ethnography as a cyclical research process and then present four distinct phases of theorizing within this process. We cite fieldwork-based studies that demonstrate our points throughout. Our specific objectives are to show how an ethnographic approach includes interpersonal communication theory in its research design and to show how such theory can be developed in an ethnographically informed, culturally sensitive way. We do not claim to be offering a wholly new way of doing ethnography, only to be formulating a cyclical research design and phases of theorizing that we find endemic in the process. Making this explicit may, we hope, help other practitioners and consumers of this kind of interpersonal communication research.

ETHNOGRAPHY AS A CYCLICAL INVESTIGATIVE PROCESS

The sociocultural model that we adopt suggests designing and reading ethnography as a theoretically focused, descriptive, culturally interpretive, and comparative mode of research (Carbaugh, 1991; Philipsen, 1977, 1989). However, designing and conducting research to meet these requirements is difficult. How can one describe the various tasks that go into ethnographic research, and why characterize them as cyclical?

One description of the investigative process draws attention to three of its general phases—prefieldwork, fieldwork, and postfieldwork—each with attendant tasks. Prefieldwork activities typically involve three kinds of interrelated reading, each motivated by a specific purpose: (1) readings about ethnographic theory and method that orient investigators to a way of conceptualizing communication as partly constitutive of sociocultural life; (2) readings about particular intellectual problems that the ethnographer finds interesting, and explication of these problems as theoretical, communication problems, such as face work, symbolizing personhood, emotion expression, terms for talk, relational development, speech acts, turn taking, narrative, address terms, and so on; and (3) readings about diverse local patterns of communication including, if possible, those about a field site or community of an anticipated study. This is hardly an exhaustive list, but we find it representative of tasks that are prominently conducted prior to entering the field. Note also how such tasks position the ethnographer, respectively, within a general approach, with particular intellectual problems and interests, as well as with knowledge of particular, culturally situated communicative practices. This equips ethnographic investigators with a general orientation that suggests some kinds of questions about communication and communicative phenomena and, eventually, leads each investigator—with his or her own interests—to some field sites rather than to others.

Fieldwork typically involves "living in a field," seeing, hearing, breathing, and feeling what goes on there. Ethnographic methodology derives from this *in situ* experience and typically involves distinct tasks such as generating data (through interviews, observations, document collection, surveys, etc.), recording data (through audio and video recordings, transcribing, and other field notation systems), analyzing data (through various quantitative and qualitative procedures), and continuing the reading program mentioned earlier. Work in the field thus is experiential and exploratory, though it is also purposive in that it gets done by using, in an open, reflective, and heuristic way, the orientation(s) developed prior to entering the field that is formulated during prefieldwork studies.

Postfieldwork activity typically continues with the analyses begun in the field (sometimes leading back to the field—in both senses, geographic and intellectual—in order to generate better perspective and new data), and with the always audience-driven phases of intensive writing (usually begun in the field).

Note how the above description draws attention to distinct stages within ethnographic research that reflect, following Philipsen (1977), a "weak commitment" to a linear ethnographic process (p. 42). But also note, within each general stage in the process, the ethnographer cycles through distinct activities, just as each such stage, once moved through, becomes a potential point of return. Conceptualizing ethnographic research this way suggests both a linear sequence of activities through which ethnography gets done as well as a cyclical dynamic among these activities. We hope to provide, as does Philipsen (1977), "a middle way between rigid linearity and deliberate non-linearity" (p. 45). But what is the role of theorizing within this process? What are the ways in which communication theory provides a foundation for, and is thus woven into this process?

FOUR PHASES OF THEORIZING INTERPERSONAL COMMUNICATION WITHIN ETHNOGRAPHY

What we describe here are four distinctive but interrelated phases (or moments) of theorizing that are incorporated in the above description of the ethnographic research cycle.[2] We pull them out and sketch them here in order to amplify our point about phases of theorizing communication within ethnography. At the outset, we wish to emphasize that each phase of theorizing we discuss, like each stage above, provides a context for, and is itself contextualized by, the others, though we present them here in their logical, chronological sequence.[3]

A first phase of theorizing involves the ethnographer in developing a basic orientation to communication. What assumptions ground our view of communication? Through what conceptual lens will we hear or look at communication (rather than, say, personality, society, culture)? What general conceptual framework enables us to study and theorize about communication practices (rather than, say, psychological states, sociological structures, or anthropological institutions)? Note, then, that communication is treated both as basic data and as a primary theoretic concern.

Most typically, ethnographies of communication have drawn upon and subsequently developed the *assumptive base* laid by Hymes (1962); that is, that communication is systematic, social, and culturally distinct. Hymes's (1972) subsequent *conceptual system* has suggested various social units for analysis and observation (speech communities, communicative situations, events, acts, styles, and general ways of speaking) as well as a schematic vocabulary for doing such analysis, the SPEAKING mnemonic (*Situation*: setting and scene; *Participants*: personalities, roles, relations; *Ends*: goals and outcomes; *Acts*: message content, form, sequences, dimensions, and types of illocutionary force; *Key*: tone or mode; *Instrumentality*: channel or media; *Norms*: of and for interaction and interpretation; *Genre*: native, formal). Based on such a view, and through this system, communication is conceptualized (heard and felt) and explicated as a sociocultural system. More than 250 ethnographic reports have been published that have adopted and developed this general theoretical orientation (Philipsen & Carbaugh, 1986). The basic goals of these studies have been, to paraphrase Hymes (1972), to particularize from this general theoretical orientation (i.e., to understand communication, through fieldwork studies, as constitutive of particular sociocultural lives), as well as to generalize from these particular cases (i.e., to discover, if possible, general dynamics and dimensions of communication). For example, in a much celebrated book, Moerman (1988) integrated ethnography and conversation analysis into an orientation that sought, for example, both how cultural agents were communicatively constructed in Thai culture and how this symbolic activity occurred within an apparently universal conversational structure of person reference. Moerman's study demonstrates how the analysis of conversations can help ethnographers identify interactional mechanisms that may be powerful sites of cultural information, just as ethnography can help conversation analysts identify the cultural uses and interpretations of such mechanisms.

The goal of theorizing in this phase is to conceptualize communication broadly by keeping in view basic communicative units (e.g., speech acts, styles, and situations) as well as the multiple dimensions of several components (e.g., scenes, classes of participants, and channels). Communication is conceptualized basically and rigorously, then, as a complex of units and components that constitute—or construct—sociocultural life.

From this conceptual starting point, we do not usually focus initially on one single dimension of a single unit (e.g., uncertainty reduction in initial encounters). Why? Because the theory commits us first to asking whether such a thing as "reducing uncertainty" is salient and then, if so, to investigating multiple social "units" where it is so (e.g., in particular events and situations). The theory suggests further that if such a dimension is operating, it is doing so in culturally distinctive ways (e.g., according to local norms of interpretation) and is analyzable through the multiple components that comprise these units and ways (e.g., sequences, participants, goals, and norms). In this sense, we use the theory to conceptualize communication phenomena as a complex of units and components that are operating, in the first case, in culturally distinctive ways.

A second phase of theorizing involves explicating specific kinds (or classes) of communication activities, practices, or dimensions that we are interested in investigating. Theoretical attention moves here from the more comprehensive conceptualization of communication in the first phase to more specific theories of communication activities or phenomena that we "find" in the literature. For example, theories of communication forms, such as address forms, sensitize investigators to variability in a form (from title plus last name to nicknames) and its subsequent associated meanings (from power to solidarity to intimacy). Or, by explicating a communication theory of identity, investigators can conceptualize the dimensions and processes that are involved (Carbaugh, 1995). Searle's (1976/1990a) speech act theory suggests a system of 12 possible dimensions that underlie basic types of illocutionary actions. Other examples could include dimensions of any communicative activities such as theories of politeness and implicature or theories of specific communicative phenomena such as narrative, terms for talk, symbolizing persons, emotion expression, turn taking, metaphor (and other tropes), communicative silence, jokes, ritual, myth, conversational repair, agonistic expression, unwanted repetitive patterns, reciprocated diatribe, relational dialectics, and so on. The listing is an effort to indicate the variety of specific dimensions and phenomena that have been and could be further theorized about, each suggesting distinct intellectual problems worthy of further theorizing.

A particular ethnographer might find one such activity of sufficient interest to develop a deep understanding of it and then choose a field site where such an activity is prominent, and thus ideally suited for such a study, as did Lutz (1988), whose fascination with emotion expression led her to the Ifaluk, who have an elaborate vocabulary for such expression. Others, such as Rosaldo (1980, 1982/1990), may move between activities, theorizing each and integrating several, as she did with speech acts, emotion expression, and the symbolic construction of personhood. Whatever the specific theoretical focus may be, it is noteworthy that various theories of communication activities have been developed and should be studied prior to—or at least in conjunction with—intensive fieldwork, in order to be positioned better (i.e., theoretically equipped) to conduct fieldwork. The goal of theorizing in this phase is the explication of a conceptual framework that addresses specific communication theoretical problems, activities, practices, or phenomena such as those mentioned above.

Note that thus far the ethnographer has theorized about communication in two distinct, yet interrelated phases. Each has involved a kind of theorizing that is, in a sense, acontextual and acultural. That is, each kind of theorizing, whether of a basic orientation to communication or about specific communication activities, is of a general, syntactic type, rather than of a specific sociocultural domain (Cushman & Pearce, 1977). The intent is to develop a conceptual system that informs us generally how to "look" into communication (the basic orientation) and sensitizes us to specific practices that we might possibly see (the activity theories). Such a system helps us discover how people in various places construct their world communicatively. It works then as a discovery procedure for specific cultural analyses of communication. It works also, and subsequently, as a basis for comparative and cross-cultural analyses.

So far, then, we have two phases of theorizing that suggest (1) a way to "hear" communication as a construction of sociocultural life, and (2) some communication activities that we might possibly "see" (feel, hear). But we have left open, or unspecified, exactly what we will in fact see (hear and feel) in any particular place. We do not yet know how communication itself (e.g., address terms or speech acts) is culturally configured, or what actual practices obtain in particular fields. We do not yet know whether our general theorizing is adequate (descriptively or explanatorily) to our selected case or place. To know, we must, as Parks (1982) put it, get "off the couch and into the field" and thus enter another phase of theorizing (p. 79).

A third phase of theorizing is perhaps the most celebrated of ethnography, the theory of the case, the formulation of the general ways in which communication is patterned within a socioculturally situated community, field, or domain. Theorizing in this third phase involves formulating a contextually bound, culturally sensitive description and interpretation of communication as it is created and interpreted by a people. We listen to a local world and formulate how specific communicative practices are used, and interpreted, there. The descriptions involve detailed accounts of communication practices as they actually occur in actual social contexts. The interpretations of the practices explore the symbols, symbolic forms, and meanings that participants deem significant and important in those communicative practices (Carbaugh, 1991). Consider, for example, Basso's (1970/1990) study of silence among the Western Apache. He described how silence was used as a communicative strategy by various participants including children, parents, coworkers, young sweethearts, friends and family of mourners, recipients of profanity, and those visiting the sick. Further, he interpreted how it was used, and culturally meaningful, in at least six Western Apache scenes: "meeting strangers," "courting," "children coming home from school," "getting cussed out," "being with people who are sad," and "being with those for whom they sing." By holding the communicative act of silence constant, and exploring associations among participants and cultural scenes, Basso ruled out various components as explanations and eventually was able to formulate specifically the inchoate Apache theory of communicative silence: (1) Silence is used and interpreted as a communicative act; (2) silence is typically directed at a focal participant; and (3) when used, silence is associated with relationships among focal participants that are uncertain, ambiguous, or unpredictable. What Basso provides is a local theory of a communicative activity in a sociocultural context. His ethnographic account replies critically to typical Anglicized stereotypes of "Indians" as "silent and stoic." (He goes on also to suggest that his account has some cross-cultural support and might perhaps be universal.) Similarly, Philipsen (1975/1990) found in a community he called Teamsterville, on the basis of several problematic episodes, that among males, silence was associated with asymmetrical role relationships, whereas speaking was associated with symmetrical role relationships.

These two cases—of silence and of gender role enactment—help make several points. Theorizing communication, in an ethnographic vein, is (1) to theorize in a basic way about a sociocultural accomplishment and (2) to theorize about specific socioculturally situated activities, such as silence or male speaking. Further, it is (3) to theorize about communication activities that occur in specific communities, such as "giving up on words" in Apache culture, or "speaking like a man" in Teamsterville. Theorizing a case is thus not to theorize simply about a context or community but to theorize about communication and communicative activities that constitute a context or community (or, as stated throughout this chapter and this volume, it is to theorize communication as a contingent construction of context or community).

Theorizing about communication within a context in this way is to demonstrate the particular yield of a more general conceptual system, such as the basic theoretical orientation, or the theories of specific communication practices discussed above. Theorizing using an explicit conceptual orientation lays a basis for further comparative study and cross-cultural generalizations, such as the one about silence suggested earlier and presented later by Braithwaite (1990). The latter points are important to repeat because many ethnographic reports indicate their general orientation and theory through brief notes or patterns of citation, creating perhaps the impression that they are of lesser importance than the local pattern (and in some ways they are). What is often elaborated in the field report, therefore, is the theory of communication as it is lived in a field, the socioculturally situated theory, more than the general theoretical orientation or specific activity theory grounding the ethnographic report. This literary dynamic is an important one for interpersonal communication researchers to recognize (see, e.g., Van Maanen, 1988). The goal of theorizing in this third phase, then, is the explication of the nature and uses of—or the beliefs and values associated with—communication, or some feature of communication, in its sociocultural context.

A final phase of theorizing involves a direct evaluation of the general theory (of the communication activity or general orientation) from the vantage point of our situated case or cases. Based on what we have found in the field, the actual situated practice(s), we examine our general way of looking: Is the general lens (or hearing aid?) observationally adequate? Does it warrant some revising, developing, or discarding? For example, Rosaldo (1982/1990) undertook an ethnographic study (the basic orientation) of speech acts (the activity theorized about) among the Ilongot. She found (the situated field theory) that Ilongot speech acts such as directives (commands and requests) vary by two cultural continua. One has to do with communicative urgency or the desired speed of a response. The other has to do with lines of social rank, especially age and gender. Rosaldo argued further, developing these cultural continua, that they construct a relational identity of social bonds and interactive meanings. On the basis of this cultural patterning of speech acts, Rosaldo then reflected on speech act theory itself (evaluation of theory), calling into question the priority that Searle has given to dimensions of illocutionary force such as "expressed psychological state and point or purpose" (see Searle 1976/1990a, 1990b). These dimensions seem to resonate nicely with Western notions of persons as individuals but risk a misreading of Ilongot speech acts—if applied uncritically. Rosaldo questioned further the wisdom of emphasizing speech acts, outside larger interactional sequences, reflecting the commitment to the system of components discussed in phase 1 above. She thus sounds cautionary notes, on the basis of field research, about the weighting of dimensions within speech act theory and its relationship to a larger taxonomy of communication practices (see Hymes, 1990; Searle, 1976/1990a, 1990b). By reflecting on the conceptual framework used to conduct the ethnography (the basic/activity theory), and critically assessing its use (through situated theory), the framework itself is refined, developed, and/or validated, even, though rarely, discarded. The goal of theorizing in this fourth moment is the critical appraisal, and continual development of communication theory.

To summarize, then, we have discussed an ethnographic approach to interpersonal communication as a cyclical research process that involves four phases of theorizing. The phases can be summarized with the mnemonic BASE as follows:

> *Phase 1. B*asic orientation: assumptions, basic units, and components of communication as constructing sociocultural life.
> *Phase 2. A*ctivity theory: specific theory of communication activities, practices, or dimensions of practice.
> *Phase 3. S*ituated theory: theory of a socioculturally situated communication practice.
> *Phase 4. E*valuation and/or evolution of theory: Evaluating the relationship between the situated theory and the basic orientation–activity theory and modifying the theory when necessary.

Again, we emphasize that the sequence here is not a simple, though it is a weak, linear one. Ethnographic research design and rules of logic suggest that one follows the sequence from 1 to 2 (with *B* and *A* being formulated prior to fieldwork) through 3 and 4 (with *S* and *E* being formulated during or after at least some fieldwork). The dynamics of phase 3 (*S*) often lead back to 1 and 2 (*BA*), and so on. This is the nature of the cyclical process and phases of theorizing within it.

A recent set of studies might serve as a sustained illustration of our general points. These ongoing studies are exploring a politically charged land-use controversy in an economically deprived region of western Massachusetts (Carbaugh, 1992, 1995). The basic orientation for the general studies is ethnographic (*B*), exploring as they do situated communicative practices and the ways these variously organize a speech community. Conceptualizing communication as a socially situated scene of activities, and as creatively evoking locally potent meaning systems, has helped us to understand, in particular, the various identities, political agendas, and often conflicting social relations that are being constructed in these communication practices. By exploring particular ways communication is being used by these participants, we have begun to understand how locally potent genres of communication target specific and conflicting objectives. The speech community is organizing itself, then, with regard to this issue, around a "complex" of objectives, with competing factions and contentious relations being constructed through the communication process.

The studies are focusing specifically on particular communicative activities (A). One has to do with a decision-making process in the form of a social drama. That is, the communication practices are cycling through various phases, including violations, faction–formations, and redressive actions, resulting in further violations but also establishing some possible integrative ground (Carbaugh, in press-a). The other focal activity central in the larger drama is "the verbal depiction of nature." The ways this land is being symbolically constructed, and what these suggest as ways of living with it, are being explored, as are the ways different depictions are being used dialogically to construct conflicting interests, identities, and proposals (Carbaugh, 1995).

The dialogical drama that is constructing this land-use controversy is very much a wrestling over natural (and symbolic) resources and material conditions. For one segment of the community, the depictions in the drama consist through themes of political impotence and economic deprivation. With this depiction, participants argue that the land should be developed for economic (e.g., jobs) and political gain. For others, the land is depicted through themes of natural ecology and historical ancestry, and should be preserved for the "common" (i.e., pan-local) good (S). The dialogical coding of these interests through the various phases of the public drama has been ongoing now for about 6 years, with all parties seeking to construct—with the government's help—an integrative discourse in which the conflicting interests could coexist. The general orientation and specific focus of the study have thus produced an ethnographic reading of the controversy by organizing its communication as social dramatic and depictive. That the studies have provided a productive reading of the controversy was evident when one key participant said of an early report: "That [the ethnographic report] makes a lot of sense of a very complicated situation."[4] The report thus entered productively into the very process it sought to understand.

A phase of theorizing attendant to the above involved the explicit and more abstract formulation of a communication theory of a particular verbal form, the verbal depiction of nature (Carbaugh, 1992). The project as a whole, by reflecting primarily on enactments of "environmentalists" and "developers," and their competing interests, also contributed to a formulation of a communication theory of identity (Carbaugh, 1995). More fundamentally, the project contributed to the extension of a basic philosophy of communication that could integrate natural (i.e., physical) and social worlds, partly through reflections upon the body as a site of communication and culture (Carbaugh, in press-c). The project thus demonstrates ways ethnography can contribute to the continuing evolution of communication theory (E), both in its formulation of theories of specific communicative activities and in its creative reflections on its basic philosophy.

The above illustration of communication theorizing within ethnographic and cultural studies of communication hopefully demonstrates several important qualities of this kind of ethnographic research. For example, several recent commentators have discussed ethnography as consisting of oppositional ethnographic camps, sometimes using the terms "consensus" and "conflict" to characterize these "differences" (see, e.g., Fiske, 1991, p. 331; Lannamann, 1994, p. 137). Such characterization brings to mind the well-worn battles fought in the 1950s and 1960s in sociology between the "functionalists" and the "conflict" theorists. In any event, the approach to ethnographic inquiry being advanced in this chapter hopefully illustrates how our version of ethnography does not dwell in only one of these "camps" but traverses a larger terrain, thereby exploring a complex range of communicative activities including those that construct various social processes such as conflict (e.g., Carbaugh, 1992, in press-a), competing classes of people such as workers (e.g., Baxter, 1993; Carbaugh, 1988a), paradoxical dynamics within cultural systems (e.g., Carbaugh, 1988a), and incommensurate cultural communication systems (e.g., Philipsen, 1986). This kind of ethnography seeks to know communication in all its social forms and meanings, spanning consensus and conflict. Further, we agree with Soltis (1984) that it is time we see ourselves as "members of an *associated community* and not merely as an aggregate of individuals or as warring camps, or as a pluralistic field of multiple unconnected research paradigms without common interests" (p. 9). [5]

The idea of community, then, evident in these ethnographic studies is not merely a reaffirmation of simple consensus but erects a complex notion of community that spans consensus and conflict. The studies as a whole explore, as Giles Gunn (1992) puts it, "communities whose forms of consensus are not [necessarily] convergent so much as [they are] contingent, provisional, changing, disruptive, and perilous" (p. 5). As Hymes (1972) summarized it, a speech community provides ways of organizing variety and diversity. Such a notion of community—and theories built with it—presumes the ethnographer is engaged *in situ* with a social group in a way that can (and does) potentially contribute to it. For example, the study of workers in the troubled, class-structured television station became, as one worker put it at the time of that study, a "hot item around here," meaning that it enabled workers to reflect on their work ways and made it easier for them to build better working conditions for themselves. These ethnographic studies show how the kinds of theorizing discussed here—especially the formulation of situated theories of communication—are engaged with the community or people of concern, can (and does) help people reflect on (and perhaps change) the worlds they routinely construct.

By explicitly conceptualizing phases of theorizing in ethnographic research, not only can we contribute to the sometimes more foreign worlds we study, but we can also help move the academic world along. Explicating our basic orientations, formulating our specific theories of the communication activities we find ourselves studying, analyzing the various ways these are constructed and meaningful among various peoples, and doing this in an open-minded, fluid yet systematic way will help us come to know communities of people and the worlds of communication they jointly weave. Although the nature of this kind of communication theorizing is only sketched and illustrated here (but see Carbaugh, in press-b), we hope it suggests some of the rich potential in studying interpersonal communication processes through ethnographic and cultural analyses.

Following the spirit of reflexiveness in recent interpersonal and ethnographic writings, we would hope our chapter illustrates the general process of theorizing we seek to describe: with our *B*asic orientation to communication being erected firmly on social and cultural footing, the primary *A*ctivity of concern being the theorizing of interpersonal communication within ethnography, the *S*ituated case studies we have cited being particular demonstrations of the theorizing process, and with the *E*volution of theory including—we hope—a more reflective role for communication theory within ethnography and cultural studies. We hope further this chapter contributes to the community of ethnographers who explore communication in—and as—a sociocultural practice. As we write this, we are mindful that the community of concern in this particular chapter, unlike most field-based products of ethnography, is primarily the academic tribe, treating some of its practices, by some of its practitioners, as material for analysis and subsequent reflection.[6]

Kenneth Pike (1967) suggested that theorizing occurs between moments etic (initial, tentative, yet general units) and emic (distinctive and local). He wrote of the two under a section heading, "Caution—Not a Dichotomy," saying, "etic and emic data do not constitute a rigid dichotomy of bits of data, but often represent the same data from two points of view" (p. 41). Hymes (1990) has noted similarly, the etic-1, emic, and etic-2 moments of theorizing in ethnography (p. 421; see also Carbaugh, 1990a, pp. 291–302). We hope the above comments help readers to a similar conclusion about an ethnographic approach to interpersonal communication, as a process that includes at its *BASE*, communication theory, a communication theory that moves cyclically through phases that are of general interest to students of interpersonal communication and ethnography (*BAE*) and those that are sensitive to cultural particulars (*S*).

NOTES

1. The distinction introduced here between social and cultural dimensions of communication research is discussed in more detail elsewhere (e.g., Carbaugh, in press-b).
2. Our view of the process of theorizing is informed by Oakeshott (1991).
3. For ease of exposition and memory, we present the mnemonic device, *BASE*, which summarizes the four phases: *B*asic theoretical orientation, the communication *A*ctivity—or activities—being theorized about, the *S*ituated theory of a sociocultural case, the *E*valuation and *E*volution of communication theory.
4. The comment was made by the director of the Greylock Project on June 12, 1991, a high-ranking employee of the Commonwealth of Massachusetts's Department of Environmental Management.
5. See Sprague (1992, p. 20), where the idea of community introduced here and developed later is also discussed.
6. The exercise in the essay demonstrates one of several kinds of critical analyses possible in ethnographic studies, with this one kind being a brand of "academic criticism" (see Carbaugh, 1990b).

REFERENCES

Basso, K. (1990). "To give up on words": Silence in Western Apache culture. In D. Carbaugh (Ed.), *Cultural communication and intercultural contact* (pp. 303–320). Hillsdale, NJ: Erlbaum. (Original work published 1970)

Bauman, R., & Sherzer, J. (Eds.). (1974). *Explorations in the ethnography of speaking.* London: Cambridge University Press.

Baxter, L. (1993). "Talking things through" and "putting it in writing": Two codes of communication in an academic institution. *Journal of Applied Communication Research, 21*, 313–326.

Berger, C. R. (1991). Communication theories and other curios. *Communication Monographs, 58*, 101–113.

Braithwaite, C. (1990). Communicative silence: A cross-cultural study of Basso's hypothesis. In D. Carbaugh (Ed.), *Cultural communication and intercultural contact* (pp. 321–327). Hillsdale, NJ: Erlbaum.

Carbaugh, D. (1988a). Cultural terms and tensions in the speech at a television station. *Western Journal of Speech Communication, 52*, 216–237.

Carbaugh, D. (1988b). *Talking American: Cultural discourses on Donahue.* Norwood, NJ: Ablex.

Carbaugh, D. (Ed.). (1990a). *Cultural communication and intercultural contact.* Hillsdale, NJ: Erlbaum.

Carbaugh, D. (1990b). The critical voice in ethnography of communication research. *Research on Language and Social Interaction, 23*, 262–282.

Carbaugh, D. (1991). Communication and cultural interpretation. *Quarterly Journal of Speech, 77*, 336–342.

Carbaugh, D. (1992). "The mountain" and "the project": Dueling depictions of a natural environment. In J. Cantrill & C. Oravec (Eds.), *Proceedings of the conference on the discourses of environmental advocacy* (pp. 360–376). Salt Lake City: University of Utah Humanities Center.

Carbaugh, D. (1994). Personhood, positioning, and cultural pragmatics: An American code of dignity in cross-cultural perspective. In S. Deetz (Ed.), *Communication yearbook* (Vol. 16, pp. 159–186). Newbury Park, CA: Sage.

Carbaugh, D. (1995). *Situating selves: The communication of social identity in American scenes.* Albany: State University of New York Press.

Carbaugh, D. (in press-a). Decision-making as social drama: Constructing identities and a natural environment. In R. Harré & P. Stearns (Eds.), *Rethinking psychology 3: Practising psychology.* Newbury Park, CA: Sage.

Carbaugh, D. (in press-b). The ethnography of communication. In B. Kovacic & D. Cushman (Eds.), *Watershed theories of human communication.* Albany: State University of New York Press.

Carbaugh, D. (in press-c). Naturalizing communication and culture. In J. Cantrill & C. Oravec (Eds.), *Environmental discourse.* Lexington: University of Kentucky Press.

Cushman, D., & Pearce, W. B. (1977). Generality and necessity in three types of theory about human communication, with special attention to rules theory. *Human Communication Research, 3,* 344–353.

Delia, J. G., O'Keefe, B. J., & O'Keefe, D. (1982). The constructivist approach to communication. In F. Dance (Ed.), *Human communication theory* (pp. 147–191). New York: Harper & Row.

Duck, S. (1991). *New lamps for old: A new theory of relationships and a fresh look at some old research.* Paper presented at the Third Conference of the International Network on Personal Relationships, Normal, IL.

Fiske, J. (1991). Writing ethnographies: Contribution to a dialogue. *Quarterly Journal of Speech, 77,* 330–335.

Gumperz, J. J., & Hymes, D. (Eds.). (1972). *Directions in sociolinguistics: The ethnography of communication.* New York: Holt, Rinehart & Winston.

Gunn, G. (1992). *Thinking across the American grain: Ideology, intellect, and the new pragmatism.* Chicago: University of Chicago Press.

Hymes, D. (1962). The ethnography of speaking. In T. Gladwin & W. Sturtevant (Eds.), *Anthropology and human behavior* (pp. 13–53). Washington, DC: Anthropological Society of Washington.

Hymes, D. (1972). Models of the interaction of language and social life. In J. J. Gumperz & D. Hymes (Eds.), *Directions in sociolinguistics: The ethnography of communication* (pp. 35–71). New York: Holt, Rinehart & Winston.

Hymes, D. (1990). Epilogue to "The things we do with words." In D. Carbaugh (Ed.), *Cultural communication and intercultural contact* (pp. 419–429). Hillsdale, NJ: Erlbaum.

Lannamann, J. W. (1994). The problem with disempowering ideology. In S. Deetz (Ed.), *Communication yearbook* (Vol. 16, pp. 136–147). Newbury Park, CA: Sage.

Leeds-Hurwitz, W. (1989). *Communication in everyday life: A social interpretation.* Norwood, NJ: Ablex.

Lutz, C. (1988). *Unnatural emotions.* Chicago: University of Chicago Press.

Moerman, M. (1988). *Talking culture: Ethnography and conversation analysis.* Philadelphia: University of Pennsylvania Press.

Oakeshott, M. (1991). *On human conduct.* Oxford: Clarendon Press.

Parks, M. (1982). Ideology in interpersonal communication: Off the couch and into the world. In M. Burgoon (Ed.), *Communication yearbook* (Vol. 5, pp. 79–108). New Brunswick, NJ: Transaction.

Pearce, W. B. (1989). *Communication and the human condition.* Carbondale: Southern Illinois University Press.

Pearce, W. B., & Cronen, V. (1980). *Communication, action, and meaning: The creation of social realities.* New York: Praeger.

Philipsen, G. (1977). Linearity of research design in ethnographic studies of speaking. *Communication Quarterly, 25,* 42–50.

Philipsen, G. (1986). Mayor Daley's council speech: A cultural analysis. *Quarterly Journal of Speech, 72,* 247–260.

Philipsen, G. (1989). An ethnographic approach to communication studies. In B. Dervin, L. Grossberg, B.J. O'Keefe, & E. Wartella (Eds.), *Rethinking communication: Vol. 2. Paradigm exemplars* (pp. 258–268). Newbury Park, CA: Sage.

Philipsen, G. (1990). Speaking "like a man" in Teamsterville: Culture patterns of role enactment in an urban neighborhood. In D. Carbaugh (Ed.), *Cultural communication and intercultural contact* (pp. 11–20). Hillsdale, NJ: Erlbaum. (Original work published 1975)

Philipsen, G., & Carbaugh, D. (1986). A bibliography of fieldwork in the ethnography of communication. *Language in Society, 15,* 387–398.

Pike, K. (1967). *Language in relation to a unified theory of the structure of human behavior* (2nd rev. ed.). The Hague: Mouton.

Rosaldo, M. (1980). *Knowledge and passion: Ilongot notions of self and social life.* Cambridge, MA: Harvard University Press.

Rosaldo, M. (1990). The things we do with words: Ilongot speech acts and speech act theory in philosophy. In D. Carbaugh (Ed.), *Cultural communication and intercultural contact* (pp. 373–407). Hillsdale, NJ: Erlbaum. (Original work published 1982)

Sanders, R. E. (1987). *Cognitive foundations of calculated speech.* Albany: State University of New York Press.

Searle, J. (1990a). A classification of illocutionary acts. In D. Carbaugh (Ed.), *Cultural communication and intercultural contact* (pp. 349–372). Hillsdale, NJ: Erlbaum. (Original work published 1976)

Searle, J. (1990b). Epilogue to the taxonomy of illocutionary acts. In D. Carbaugh (Ed.), *Cultural communication and intercultural contact* (pp. 409–417). Hillsdale, NJ: Erlbaum.

Sigman, S. J. (1987). *A perspective on social communication.* Lexington, MA: Lexington Books.

Soltis, J. (1984, December). On the nature of educational research. *Educational Researcher*, pp. 5–10.

Sprague, J. (1992). Expanding the research agenda for instructional communication: Raising some unasked questions. *Communication Education, 41,* 1–25.

Stewart, J., & Philipsen, G. (1985). Communication as situated accomplishment: The cases of hermeneutics and ethnography. In B. Dervin (Ed.), *Progress in communication sciences* (pp. 177–218). Norwood, NJ: Ablex.

Van Maanen, J. (1988). *Tales of the field.* Chicago: University of Chicago Press.

CHAPTER 10

Order and Continuity in Human Relationships
A Social Communication Approach to Defining "Relationship"

STUART J. SIGMAN

T his chapter summarizes, develops, and extends a number of conceptual issues I have been exploring for the past 12 years under the rubric social communication theory (Sigman, 1987; see also Birdwhistell, 1970; Fogle, 1992; Leeds-Hurwitz, 1989). Social communication theory represents an informed alternative to psychological theorizing about communication processes—informed in the sense that it is acknowledged to be deliberate and an alternative in the sense of "incommensurable" (cf. Garfinkel & Wieder, 1992; Pearce, 1989) with more traditional communication theories. It emphasizes study of both the sociocultural communities which form the bases of behavior (cf. Hymes, 1974), and the multiparticipant, interactive character of communication. The chapter presents a conceptual framework for the study of "interpersonal relationships" that is consistent with social communication theory.

To begin, I offer a description of selected tenets of the theory. Two primary ones for a serious discussion of "relationship" as an analytical concept are the following (see Sigman, 1992a, for a more extensive listing of principles):

1. Communication is the study of the characteristics and consequences of messages, not the characteristics of people.

2. People and their relationships are constituted and engendered by messages.

The first principle argues that, as an academic discipline, Communication must take the nature of "meaning," "message," and/or "information" as its analytical starting point. This suggests that social structure, personality, cognition, and culture are not the phenomena to be studied by Communication scholars. Rather, the basic unit of communication analysis is meaning, what Bateson (1972) describes as a "difference which makes a difference" (p. 453), and the root problematic of a Communication discipline concerns *how* it is that meaning comes to be.

This starting point for communication analysis recognizes the autonomy of the communication system, that is, its nonreducibility to the actions of a single individual and especially to an individual's cognitive or affective states. Meaning is a feature of conjoint action (i.e., the action of multiple participants), is subject to community-specific grammatical constraints and affordances, yet is produced in and during moments of situated behaving (see Cronen, 1995; Sigman, 1995; for discussion of rule-based vs. communication-as-action theories of meaning). Adapting Matoesian's (1993) view of conversation, it can be stated that the "endogenous organization of [communication] activities replaces meaning as reference and/or subjective experience, an analytic maneuver strongly influenced by and reminiscent of the later Wittgenstein" (p. 47). Referential and subjective approaches to meaning are replaced by a communicational view, which sees meaning located in people's publicly displayed and coordinated behavior with each other.

The second principle derives inexorably from the first; it explicitly rejects an "essentialist" position regarding personhood, that is, that a person comprises self-contained features such as personality, and reverses the traditional association said to hold between people (communicators) and communication. The latter deems communication to be the output of an already existing and free-standing person. From the social communication view, in contrast, human beings are independent of neither the behavioral resources (communication channels and grammars) made available to them by their communities nor the interactive, meaning-generating processes that make use of these resources. Indeed, persons are themselves organized clusters of meaning, continuously produced in and through a community's behavioral processes. As Pittenger, Hockett, and Danehy (1960) offer: "It is treacherously misleading to think of language and other communication systems as cloaks donned by the ego when it ventures into the interpersonal world: rather, we think of ego (or 'mind') as arising from the internalization of interpersonal communication processes" (p. 223). In this view, persons are the products, not producers, of communication.

One significant contribution of social communication theory derives from its dual concern for the historically given behavioral resources that permit meaning to emerge in interaction and for the actual moment-by-moment processes that produce meaning (see Leeds-Hurwitz & Sigman, with Sullivan, 1995). Indeed, classical social communication theory, while recognizing that persons and their identities are interactively constructed, places the sociocultural repertoire (with all its constraints, prohibitions, and entailments), which establishes the categories toward which these interactive or constructive processes are oriented, at the center of its analyses. I have previously stated this position thus: "An individual member of society is . . . a *moment* in that society, a moment that has a recognizable (patterned) location in the group's process and structure" (Sigman, 1987, p. 101). This does not deny the possible role of biology, individual psychology, or cognitive functioning in the lives of people, but it nevertheless highlights the role of communication and a transsituational sociocultural repertoire in constituting and sustaining personhood.[2]

A definition of "relationship" consistent with the above social communication framework would propose it as a category of meaning (derived from the sociocultural heritage) requiring patterned behavioral construction (communication) on the part of community members. This category of meaning identifies people (i.e., it defines identities for them), the associations between and among the defined people, and the rights and responsibilities of these people across space and time. A relationship is thus not an entity from which communication emanates but a location in the ongoing behavioral stream (cf. Birdwhistell, 1970).

With persons derived from communication, rather than the initiators or sources of communication (see Sigman, 1987; Thomas, 1980), it is then also the case that the relationships shared by persons are to be viewed as themselves created, constituted, and sustained (or dissolved) by communication. Again, this does not deny the role of affect or intrapersonal psychology in the lives of people, but it nevertheless places in the forefront of our consideration relationships as ongoing behavioral processes shaped by community expectations and conduct rather than as fixed entities or states (cf. Hopper & Drummond, 1991, for a review of "message-extrinsic" and "message-intrinsic" studies of relationships). Relationships and relationship labels are short-hand descriptions for particular, community-specific patterns of behavior; they are not independent of behavior or the communication process more generally. A dual communicational approach views relationships as derived from transcendent grammars and situated communication activities; that is, the negotiation of relationships takes place within a framework of cultural and social constraints about persons, power, and relationships (Fitch & Sanders, 1994).

It is important to recognize that, with identities and relationships viewed as categories of meaning or difference (de Saussure, 1966), there is no clear one-to-one correspondence between biophysiological entities and the socioculturally significant entities that are said to enter into and form relationships. In other words, the temptation to see each living body as the potential anchor ("end," according to Goffman, 1972) for one or more relationships with others must be avoided and must not enter into any *a priori* theorizing about the nature of relationships. Rather, questions about the constitution and membership of relationships must wait until some emic, community-based understanding of who may enter into sanctioned associations with others is generated. For example, in certain traditional Chinese families, when a young lady dies before marriage, her family may try to arrange a betrothal with a local male (Yang, 1945). The survivors act to turn the deceased female into a bride by leaving her picture, a silk scarf she may have worn, or some other artifact near a roadside shrine. In this fashion, they act as good relations who are concerned with the marital welfare of female family members. The young man who happens upon the artifacts, and who subsequently agrees to an "arranged" marriage, is eventually allowed to marry another woman but must also remain respectful of the first wife, for example, by commemorating the anniversary of her death. (See also Kligman, 1988, for a comparable illustration.)

The Chinese example points to a further aspect of relationships, specifically their multiparticipant organization. Birdwhistell (1970, 1977) is credited with suggesting that the dyad is an unstable arrangement for social groups. In part, because communities benefit from and hold a stake in particular relationships, their members may play a role not only in establishing categories of relationships but in becoming involved actively in relationship construction and maintenance (cf. Slater, 1963). There is thus an organization to the "partials" contributed by different persons to the overall integrity of each relationship. For example, marital pairs are sustained by the husband and wife, as well as by friends, family members, representatives of religious and governmental institutions, and so on.

In brief, then, a relationship can be thought of as a "communicative achievement" (Rawlins & Holl, 1987; see also Hopper & Drummond, 1991). A relationship represents a particular category of meaning, distinguishable from other such categories within some target community, and is behaviorally or processually constituted by the conduct of multiple members of the community.

A caveat is warranted at this juncture, however. The previous discussion is not intended to equate relationships with (face-to-face) interaction. Social communication theory rejects the view that "talk," "conversation," and/or "discourse" represents the building blocks of relationships (see Owen, 1987, for a critical review of this literature). Although it is true that talk, conversation, and discourse—when viewed as behavioral genres—are partially the media through which relationships are formed and maintained (or transformed and terminated), it is also the case that the behavioral units and their structural arrangements that engender face-to-face interaction are not the same as those that engender relationships. Different "orders" or organizing logics are proposed by social communication theory for interaction and relationship (Sigman, 1987, 1991). In other words, different rule systems are involved in the construction of the two.

Human communication can be seen to comprise three nonhierarchically related domains: the semiotic, interaction, and social orders. Each order consists of rule sets for particular aspects of behavior: "The interaction order provides a structure for face-to-face discourse; the social order for the social division of labor and responsibility; and the semiotic order, the grammar of particular channels of communication—indeed . . . what constitutes a channel for a particular community . . . " (Sigman, 1987, p. 61). From this perspective, the components of interaction and their arrangements are incapable of building up to a relationship between two or more people.

A clear illustration of the difference between face-to-face interaction (the interaction order) and relationships (the social order) can be found through an exploration of the concept of continuity (Sigman, 1991). Face-to-face interaction moments comprise relatively apparent initiation and termination points (colloquially referred to as greeting and leave-taking behaviors, respectively) (cf. Kendon & Ferber, 1973) and markers for the integrity of each moment (especially the topic-related and proxemic behaviors, which sustain attentiveness to the interaction and one's fellow interactants) (cf. Goffman, 1972; Kendon, 1977, 1978). Social relationships have different initiation and termination points: the beginning of a new conversation may not represent the beginning of a new relationship. Similarly, saying good-bye to a relationship comember (e.g., one's colleagues at the end of the workday) does not terminate that relationship but curiously may require the initiation of an encounter (e.g., a good-bye sequence at the coat rack or elevator) in order to be accomplished. In other words, the segmentations of interaction episodes and social relationships are not parallel or contiguous.

Moreover, social relationships make use of different behaviors from face-to-face interaction for marking their ongoing integrity; topic sequencing and proxemic face formation do not keep a relationship going, for they do not yield the strategic moments or definitions that sustain or transform the relationship. As Owen (1987) suggests, there is a distinction between "conversational influence attempts" and "relational influence attempts." The difference between interaction and relationship can therefore be summarized with the observation that relationships generally continue beyond, and are not bound by, any one interaction moment, and that the two orders are internally constituted by contrasting behavioral contributions.

Everyday members of a community may be aware of this distinction. I recently overheard two men in a pickup truck disparage an interracial pair who were crossing the street in front of us by saying to each other: "I don't mind if they go out to lunch and talk with each other, but I don't wanna see them getting married." I don't know whether the African American male and the Caucasian female were indeed a couple; to me they looked like two office workers who were returning from lunch together. That notwithstanding, the key issue is that the commentators clearly oriented to a distinction between types of associations that the two individuals could have: they could be seen in each other's presence (indeed doing certain things, such as interacting) but were not allowed a long-term affiliation with each other.

As a result of viewing this and similar incidents, I have been moved to the position that, as human beings symbolically (communicationally) connected to others, we engage in two types of relationships with people (cf. Goffman, 1983). The first type of relationship is the one social scientists traditionally study: the interpersonal or societal relationships we have with another (e.g., friend, colleague, and spouse). The second type derives from a person's face-to-face interactional dealings with others, the aforementioned interaction order. Speaker–hearer, questioner–answerer, lecturer–audience, and so on, are relationships of the second type. For ease of distinguishing the two types, I refer to the first as a *social relationship*, and the second an *interactional relationship*.[3]

The two relationship types organize the categories of meaning to which rights and responsibilities are attached by their respective communities. As suggested above, the particular rights and responsibilities contrast. These rights and responsibilities can be thought of as the dimensions of meaning defining particular relationships. Six semantic features of relationships are as follows[4]:

1. *Projected time duration.* Relationships are defined by the amount of time the comembers are expected to commit to it and each other, and

by the patterning of expected activity within the proposed temporal framework. Although certainly subject to negotiation and alteration, husband–wife relationships are usually thought of as permanent, enduring until "death do us part." Extramarital relationships, however, such as affairs and one-night stands, are assumed to be of relatively brief duration—indeed, as pointed out by Sigman (1991), the fatal error in the movie *Fatal Attraction* was that the woman engaged in the affair did not accept the typical (albeit male-defined) temporal expectations. But both these social relationships last longer than many casual face-to-face encounters (e.g., a quick greetings-and-good-bye sequence on the street) and moreover extend across more than one interactional episode (although in the case of *Fatal Attraction*, a limited number).

2. *Degree of on-callness.* Social relationships may make use of face-to-face interaction, but the degree to which they are dependent on such copresent events is varied. The Chinese example illustrates that no copresence may be demanded (or possible) for some relationships. Relationships with one's mail carrier only minimally rely on both parties being in each other's interactional presence; in contrast, American husbands and wives are expected to spend periods of copresent time with each other; and, in the case of health care relationships, doctors are expected to be "on call" and accessible for face-to-face dealings with their patients.

3. *Interruptability.* Related to the copresence or on-callness demanded by the relationship is the degree to which interruptions in copresence may alter the relationship definition. Death, taking out the trash, and going to work or school all extract different prices from social relationships. In certain traditions, women are not permitted to remarry after their husbands die; in fact, they are expected to don black mourning attire for the remainder of their (biological) lives and to remain committed to (i.e., be in a relationship with) their deceased spouse. This all contrasts with side engagements and related attentional shifts in conversation, which involve temporary interruptions within an interactional episode but which may leave the original participants still in each other's presence as one momentarily refocuses with another participant (Goffman, 1963; Kendon, 1977).

4. *Exclusivity.* How many relationships like the target one is a person allowed to engage in? Some relationship categories do not permit more than one instantiation at a time (again, husband–wife pairings in nonpolygamous societies), others permit multiples but are nonetheless limited (the number of new annual pledges to a fraternity or sorority), and still others have no apparent numerical restrictions (university alumni). A related component of the exclusivity feature is the degree to which constraints are placed on the number and type of other relationships we

are permitted to have given participation in some target relationship. Interactional engagements are also subject to membership restrictions, but these are more likely to be handled on each local occasion than through some set of transsituational rules.

5. *Nature of on-behalfness.* The interruptability of a relationship and its exclusivity presuppose that relationship members may be allowed to interact and engage in (certain) relationships with members apart from the target relationship. In some of these "external" dealings, the relationship member may be asked to serve as a representative to outsiders on behalf of the relationship comember(s). In what ways are the relationship members empowered to represent the relationship to others or commit the relationship to certain courses of action? This is a question that generally may be asked of social but not interactional relationships.

6. *Stages.* The ongoing communication stream is punctuated into discrete units or episodes of meaning (Birdwhistell, 1970; Watzlawick, 1977). Consistent with this, there is a set of folk beliefs, sociocultural expectations that may or may not be followed, regarding relationship progression. These include ideas concerning the initiation and termination of particular relationships (appropriate contexts, personnel, and behavioral strategies) and the logical progression of stages and the behavior associated with each stage once the relationship has been established. Watzlawick (1977) discusses the complications resulting from the contrasting stages oriented to by American soldiers and British women during World War II. Such developmental stages, which are likely to occur across several encounters and may result in different labels being applied to the relationship at each stage, contrast with the segmentations of an interactional event into activities (greetings, questions and answers, leave taking), which may be labeled only in highly ritualized encounters.

To summarize the discussion to this point, this chapter proposes that, as a Communication concept, relationships are to be seen as patterns of behavioral enactment that are community-specific, and that depend on a logic of development separate from that for face-to-face interaction. Alternatively, the interaction and social orders generate different types of relationships. Further, social communication theory contrasts with both a psychological framework, which places emphasis on individual goals and affect as they are held to determine people's attachments to each other, and a sociological framework, which views relationships as categories or locations within a social structure to which people respond with their actions. Relationships are seen as categories of meaning that establish identities and associations for persons.

Although I have discussed what a relationship is, I have not as yet fully explained the relevance of communication processes to relationships, or the relevance of Communication analysis to relationship analysis. Relationships can indeed be profitably seen as categories of meaning rather than derivatives of, say, social structure or intraindividual affect, but a Communication analysis cannot rest with describing such categories. This assertion derives from my belief that Communication, as an academic discipline, must concentrate on the processual dynamics of meaning construction (see Sigman, 1995). Although placed under the rubric of a meaning-centered approach to communication, what I have described so far has been the "logics" of relationships, that is, the expectations for and products of behavior, the background understandings and rules of relationship categories, and the semantic dimensions that are said to be achieved by adherence to these rules and categories. But if we have learned anything from ethnomethodology (Garfinkel, 1984; Heritage, 1984), it is that people are not rule-bound automatons. They are active, indeed proactive (strategic) behavers. People perform conduct as adjustments to an ongoing behavioral flow, this behavioral flow not being totally predictable prior to its unfolding production (Sigman, 1992b). These adjustments in multiparticipant behavior take account of relationship logics (the *a priori* categories of meanings), but they are not restricted to them. Persons act so that the meaning of their behavior is, in part, derived from the rules, the morally binding logic, but this behavior-as-performed-in-real-time is distinct from any *a priori* set of rules. When a husband acts in a certain way toward his wife, he is doing so not because he *is* the latter's husband, and not simply because there are rules that impose themselves on him, but rather because he is structuring and producing messages whose meanings *at that moment* are interpretable as the behavior of a husband (or, of that "kind" of husband). He is acting to be a husband in this situation, and a particular husband at that. The husband acts "out of" rules-based knowledge and "into" the ongoing behavioral stream contributed to by himself and others (cf. Cronen, 1995).

This issue returns us to the discussion of the first principle with which this chapter began. Specifically, it is suggested that in-the-moment processes of communication are *sui generis*, not fully dependent on *a priori* social and cultural grammars for conduct. There is a "consequential" character to person's conduct such that "communication is not a neutral vehicle by which an external reality is communicated about, and by which factors of psychology, social structure, cultural norms, and the like are transmitted or are influential" (Sigman, 1995, p. 2). In this way, community-specific interactional and social relationships (qua categories of meaning) emerge through such communication practices as *invocation, revision, alignment,* and so forth, which create situated meaning (see Leeds-Hurwitz & Sigman, with Sullivan, 1995). In other words, community-specific categories of meaning are oriented to in actual moments of behaving, but from a Communication analyst's point of view, describing the *a priori* categories and expectations is not equivalent to accounting for the conduct that produces in-the-moment relationships and alliances. Relationships, while they are categories of meaning defined by their communities, are lived as behavioral productions, adjustments in actual conduct that take account not only of the community-prescribed categories but also of the multiparticipant behavior simultaneously being performed.

Admittedly, the question that leads from such a view of communication concerns why it is (and how it is) that people act in consistent ways toward each other over time; that is, that social relationships (as opposed to interactional ones) are not ephemeral. Rather than make appeals to stable personality traits or relationship parameters, psychological or sociological explanations, respectively, I suggest we maintain our focus on meaning and meaning construction and thus continue to offer communicational explanations. In particular, we must study the nature of the meaning relations and the obligations that are placed on persons as a consequence of their behaving. What is the projected "life history" of a particular meaningful act? What entailments in space and time derive from behavior?

When persons behave, they do so not only by orienting to the *a priori* behavioral logics representing who they are (identity) and who they are supposed to be with others (relationship), but also by producing behavior coherent with and predictable from other behavior they have coenacted with those others. In other words, they fit their behavior so as to be semantically aligned with the ongoing stream of behavior; that is, the particular stream of behavior that has actually (rather than ideally) been produced and coproduced. Moreover, their individual and collective behaviors as they are currently produced obligate them to subsequent courses of action. This does not mean that all such commitments are fulfilled, only that each instance of behaving generates some set of obligations for the participants, and that any next occasion of behaving is likely to demand some orientation to prior established commitments. The stability, coherence, and consistency of relationships across time result from actually produced commitments.

This leads to recognition of a curious irony that communicators find themselves confronting and Communication analysts are obliged to study. Communicationally constructed sociocultural categories do not transpire in an ahistorical vacuum; rather, the seeds of any construction can be found in prior sequences of behavior and transcendent grammars, and any construction can further be seen to lay the semantic groundwork for subsequent sequences of behavior. The irony is that the sociocultural world appears stable, almost thing-like—both external to us and externally encumbering—yet it is a world totally dependent on our behavioral contributions, our active constructions (cf. Berger & Luckmann, 1966). Societal institutions are like this, and so are social relationships.

To summarize, relationships from the Communication viewpoint are categories of meaning regarding the associations between and among persons, but they must be studied as behaviorally or processually engendered and sustained categories of meaning rather than as fixed states. They may depend on, but are analytically distinct from, face-to-face interaction (interaction relationships), and they involve an accretion of meanings across space and time. A social communication analysis of relationship thus provides for a three-part investigation: (1) the sociocultural repertoire permitting and constraining behavior and defining each relationship category; (2) the communication activities that accomplish, negotiate, and orient to these resources; and (3) the character, composition, and continuity of the relationships across selected episodes and time frames that are built on these communication activities.

NOTES

1. When capitalized, Communication refers to the discipline that studies the observable process of (lowercase) communication.
2. A distinction is being drawn here between "communication" and "society" not found in my prior writings. Elsewhere, communication was thought to be placed in the service of society and its *a priori* functional "needs" (Sigman, 1987); in the present discussion, communication is seen as the primary social (collective) process, as consequential in its own right, and as the process out of which societies and their needs emerge (Sigman, 1995).
3. Goffman (1983), Sigman (1987), and Sanders (1995) all provide contrasting analyses of how interaction order-based and social order-based relationships are linked to each other.
4. This list is preliminary and not exhaustive; space limitations do not permit consideration of how the two relationship types differ on the matter of each feature. The features are described primarily with regard to social relationships.

REFERENCES

Bateson, G. (1972). *Steps to an ecology of mind.* New York: Ballantine.

Berger, P. L., & Luckmann, T. (1966). *The social construction of reality.* Garden City, NY: Doubleday.

Birdwhistell, R. L. (1970). *Kinesics and context.* Philadelphia: University of Pennsylvania Press.

Birdwhistell, R. L. (1977). Some discussion of ethnography, theory, and method. In J. Brockman (Ed.), *About Bateson* (pp. 103–141). New York: E. P. Dutton.

Cronen, V. E. (1995). Coordinated management of meaning: The consequentiality of communication and the recapturing of experience. In S. J. Sigman (Ed.), *The consequentiality of communication* (pp. 17–65). Hillsdale, NJ: Erlbaum.

Fitch, K. L., & Sanders, R. E. (1994). Culture, communication, and preferences for directness in expression of directives. *Communication Theory, 3,* 219–245.

Fogle, J.-A. L. (1992). *Testing social communication theory through an analysis of participant–respondent data.* Unpublished doctoral dissertation, State University of New York at Buffalo.

Garfinkel, H. (1984). *Studies in ethnomethodology.* Cambridge: Polity Press.

Garfinkel, H., & Wieder, D. L. (1992). Two incommensurable, asymmetrically alternate technologies of social analysis. In G. Watson & R. M. Seiler (Eds.), *Text in context: Contributions to ethnomethodology* (pp. 175–206). Newbury Park, CA: Sage.

Goffman, E. (1963). *Behavior in public places.* New York: Free Press.

Goffman, E. (1972). *Relations in public.* New York: Harper & Row.

Goffman, E. (1983). The interaction order. *American Sociological Review, 48,* 1–17.

Heritage, J. C. (1984). *Garfinkel and ethnomethodology.* Cambridge: Polity Press.

Hopper, R., & Drummond, K. (1991, May). *Accomplishing interpersonal relationships: A message-intrinsic perspective.* Paper presented to the International Communication Association, Chicago.

Hymes, D. (1974). *Foundations in sociolinguistics.* Philadelphia: University of Pennsylvania Press.

Kendon, A. (1977). *Studies in the behavior of social interaction.* Bloomington: Indiana University Press.

Kendon, A. (1978). Differential perception and attentional frame in face-to-face interaction: Two problems for investigation. *Semiotica, 24,* 305–315.

Kendon, A., & Ferber, A. (1973). A description of some human greetings. In R. P. Michael & J. H. Crook (Eds.), *Comparative ecology and behavior of primates* (pp. 591–668). London: Academic Press.

Kligman, G. (1988). *The wedding of the dead: Ritual, poetics, and popular culture.* Berkeley: University of California Press.

Leeds-Hurwitz, W. (1989). *Communication in everyday life.* Norwood, NJ: Ablex.

Leeds-Hurwitz, W., & Sigman, S. J., with Sullivan, S. J. (1995). Social communication theory: Communication structures and performed invocations, a revision of Scheflen's notion of programs. In S. J. Sigman (Ed.), *The consequentiality of communication* (pp. 163–204). Hillsdale, NJ: Erlbaum.

Matoesian, G. M. (1993). *Reproducing rape: Domination through talk in the courtroom.* Chicago: University of Chicago Press.

Owen, W. F. (1987). Mutual interaction of discourse structures and relational pragmatics in conversational influence attempts. *Southern Speech Communication Journal, 52,* 103–127.

Pearce, W. B. (1989). *Communication and the human condition.* Carbondale: Southern Illinois University Press.

Pittenger, R. E., Hockett, C. F., & Danehy, J. J. (1960). *The first five minutes: A sample of microscopic interview analysis.* Ithaca, NY: Paul Martineau.

Rawlins, W. K., & Holl, M. (1987). The communicative achievement of friendship during adolescence: Predicaments of trust and violation. *Western Journal of Speech Communication, 51,* 345–363.

Sanders, R. E. (1995). A neo-rhetorical perspective: The enactment of role-identities as interactive and strategic. In S. J. Sigman (Ed.), *The consequentiality of communication* (pp. 67–120). Hillsdale, NJ: Erlbaum.

Saussure, F. de (1966). *Course in general linguistics.* New York: McGraw-Hill.

Sigman, S. J. (1987). *A perspective on social communication.* Lexington, MA: Lexington Books.

Sigman, S. J. (1991). Handling the discontinuous aspects of continuous social relationships: Toward research on the persistence of social forms. *Communication Theory, 1,* 106–127.

Sigman, S. J. (Ed.). (1992a). *Introduction to human communication: Behavior, codes and social action.* Needham, MA: Ginn Press.

Sigman, S. J. (1992b). Do social approaches to interpersonal communication constitute a contribution to communication theory? *Communication Theory, 2,* 347–356.

Sigman, S. J. (1995). Introduction: Toward study of the consequentiality (not consequences) of communication. In S. J. Sigman (Ed.), *The consequentiality of communication* (pp. 1–14). Hillsdale, NJ: Erlbaum.

Slater, P. E. (1963). On social regression. *American Sociological Review, 28,* 339–364.

Thomas, S. (1980). Some problems of the paradigm in communication theory. *Journal for the Philosophy of the Social Sciences, 10,* 427–444.

Watzlawick, P. (1977). *How real is real?* New York: Vintage Books.

Yang, M. C. (1945). *A Chinese village.* New York: Columbia University Press.

CHAPTER 11

Telling and Living
Narrative Co-construction and the Practices of Interpersonal Relationships

ARTHUR P. BOCHNER
CAROLYN ELLIS

> The storyteller takes what he tells from experience—his
> own or that reported by others. And he in turn makes it
> the experience of those who are listening to his tale.
> —WALTER BENJAMIN (1936-1969)

Traditionally, interpersonal communication as an academic field of study has ignored or scorned the notion that its subject matter includes moral, ideological, or narrative knowledge. As a result, students of interpersonal communication have not developed a deep appreciation for local and particular cases that focus attention on personal, emotional, and contingent lived experiences. In this chapter, we seek to recover lived experience and local narrative as a central part of the study of interpersonal communication. We believe that the study of interpersonal interaction can be revitalized by broadening the range and scope of research to include personal narratives that display how people participate together in the process of making sense of their local circumstances.

Our intent is to produce reflexive texts that show how lived experience, as anthropologist Michael Jackson (1989) suggests, "accommodates our shifting sense of ourselves as subjects and as objects, as acting upon and being acted upon by the world, of living with and without certainty, of belonging and being estranged" (p. 2). This reflexive sense of lived experience is rarely seen or felt in published research on interpersonal communication, which usually excludes the experiences of the observer and privileges order over ambiguity, stability over change, abstraction over detail, control over improvisation, and graphs over stories. For many of us who entered the field of communication in the 1960s, it was the empirical world of our own "lived experiences" that first attracted us to the study of interpersonal communication (Bochner & Kelly, 1974), yet it is the immediate, active, and intense "experiences of living" that, ironically, seem to have been lost as an empirical field of inquiry (Bochner, 1994).

In this chapter, we offer an option to standard research practices in the study of close relationships. The project described below introduces a narrative approach to interpersonal research that wrestles with important issues of reflexivity, intersubjectivity, emotional expression, and joint action. Instead of paying lip service to these issues and then placing them aside in the name of science, we treat them as necessities to which all inquiry on human *inter*action ultimately must be addressed. The stories that are co-constructed by participants in this research show couples engaged in the specific, concrete, and unique details of daily living, coping with the untidy ambiguities, ambivalences, and contradictions of relationship life and trying to make sense of their local situation.

The crisis of representation provoked by postmodernism has made it nearly impossible to ignore the burdens of authorship and contingencies of language shared by all writers, whether scientists, novelists, or journalists (Marcus, 1994). In the social sciences, there are only interpretations: no facts, pure and simple; only stories, messy and complex. Social scientists may try to elevate the tales they spin by calling them theories, but their abstractions are never free of interpretation (Denzin & Lincoln, 1994; Geertz, 1973, 1983). The social world cannot speak for itself. Thus, all attempts to represent reality involve transforming a speechless social world into a discursive world that makes sense. To the extent our descriptions of the world involve translating "*knowing*" into "*telling*," they are narratives (White, 1980), stories that interpret, construct, or persuade.

The story of personal relationships written by social scientists is a causal story, a story that has been told by employing the familiar metaphors of forces, regularities, and attributes, a vocabulary that fits conveniently with the conventional practices of science. An optional story, the one we want to begin to tell here, is an interpretive story that expresses the lived experience of close relationships, a story that conforms not to the practices and methods of science but to the necessities of interpreting and showing the complex contingencies of relationship life in their rich, ironic, and immediate detail (Bochner, 1990). We are not seeking to privilege interpretive over causal stories but rather to encourage an epistemological openness that will acknowledge and legitimate the different purposes to which each story is addressed.

THE CO-CONSTRUCTED NARRATIVE PROJECT: ISSUES AND OBJECTIVES

For the past several years we have been engaged in a program of research that attempts to move the study of interpersonal communication closer to the ways in which long-term relationships are practiced. In our studies we have asked couples to participate in the creative activity of jointly producing stories about their relationships that attach meaning and significance to their lived experiences. Our research is based on the assumption that all couples confront the "sense-making" problem of transforming "real" events into stories. As White (1980) says: "It is because real events do not offer themselves as stories that their narrativization is so difficult" (p. 8). To form a story out of lived events is to give structure and meaning to "real experience" and to center attention on the cleavage between lived experiences and efforts to describe or tell our experiences to others (and ourselves) in language (Barthes, 1977).

Initially, our research was inspired by John Shotter's (1987) observation that researchers need a way of investigating close relationships that is more concerned with conforming to the *practices* of personal relationships than to the practices of science. Shotter (1987) points out that causal (scientific) approaches to the study of relationships between people emphasize products over processes, transforming passionate lived experiences into "cooler" rational choices and blinding researchers to the bona fide interpersonal processes that define and constitute relationships *between* people. In the name of science, personal relationships have been construed as objective entities that can be intentionally produced by deliberate, independent actions of individuals. When individuals (subjects) are asked to account for their behavior within relationships, their responses are normally regarded as the product of a completed (relational) process that can be specified as an objective entity by an individual (subject). Although these research practices make it possible for relationships to be studied as an object of science, they have the effect of ignoring or obscuring the interdependent and coordinated activities that are indispensable to relationship life.

Our "epistemological" goal has been to broaden the range and scope of research on interpersonal communication by moving beyond "objects" to "meanings." Rather than treating communication as an object, or a discipline studying objects, we think it is useful to regard communication as sequences of interaction and the activities of studying them. Our research focuses on the interactional sequences by which interpretations of lived experiences are constructed, coordinated, and solidified into stories. Over the course of a relationship, communication between partners often is focused on making sense of previous encounters, connecting past actions and episodes into a coherent and unified story of the relationship, and attaching meaning and value to what has been done and said. We equate "meaning" or "sense making" with narrativization because, as Stone (1990) suggests, "our meanings are almost always inseparable from stories, in all realms of life" (p. 244). The local narratives that are jointly produced in our research thus display couples in the process of "doing" their relationships, trying to turn fragmented, vague, or disjointed events into more intelligible and coherent accounts—little stories with big meanings.

In contrast to standard research practices that tend to repress the joint, creative, and passionate qualities of interpersonal life (Shotter, 1987), the procedures we have employed are based on several important premises about how relationships are practiced. First, we assume that relationships between people are jointly authored, incomplete, and historically situated. One person cannot intentionally predetermine the outcome of relational processes (Bochner, 1984). In a relationship between people, the part cannot control the whole. As Bateson (1968) suggests, it is more likely the case that "characteristics of ongoing process in this larger entity (the relationship) control both individuals in some degree" (p. 208). Thus, relationships hinge on contingencies of conversation and negotiation, interactional sequences that often produce novel and unexpected outcomes. One of the main activities of relationship life is "ordering" the relationship, assigning significance and meaning to experiences and events that are, in themselves, vague or amorphous. As Brody (1987) says, "The primary human mechanism for attaching meaning to human experiences is to tell stories about them" (p. 5). Within a close relationship, normally this is a joint activity that is continuous and unfinished. There are no "final negotiations" (Ellis, 1995), only stories subject to revision.

Second, we assume that the coproduction of a relationship story is part of, rather than apart from, the relationship. Any account of what was said, done, felt, or meant is, in effect, a momentary ordering of a yet unfinished experience. The account inevitably becomes part of the continuous and ongoing saga of the relationship. One of the most common experiences in relationship life is the "work" of maintaining, modifying, and/or reshaping the significance of past events through conversation (Berger & Luckmann, 1966). Our relationship realities are subjective realities that require some ongoing affirmation by significant others—usually one's partner. Moreover, relationship life is an intersubjective world; we not only live in the same world as our partner but also participate in each other's existence. To a certain extent we must not only understand each other's views of the world but also be able to make them our own. In the course of performing and negotiating our views of the world within a close relationship, we mediate and modify each other's views. Thus, we are linked by an ongoing conversation that forges a mutual identification in the face of sinister threats of competing definitions of reality that may be encountered. This conversational world of relationship thus plays the important role of implicitly reaffirming and ratifying subjective meanings (Berger & Luckmann, 1966).

Specifically, the procedures we follow are designed to encourage relationship partners to enact the interpretive and communicative processes that define them as a couple. We start by asking partners to identify an epiphany in their relationship. Usually we encourage participants to select an emotionally charged event or turning point in their relationship. Following Denzin (1989), we view an epiphany as an event in which individuals are so powerfully absorbed that they are left without an interpretive framework to make sense of their experience immediately. Whereas epiphanies normally are recalled as significant and intense experiences, often they are experienced initially as disconnected and unintelligible, falling outside the normal stream of daily, relational life.

Once partners have agreed on the epiphany that will serve as their story, each independently constructs a detailed chronology of the events that took place, including emotional reactions to events, significant decisions that were made individually or collectively, conversations with each other and with third parties, and coping strategies. We ask them not to share their chronologies with each other. Next, each partner turns his or her chronology into narrative, writing a story that expresses an "experiential sense of what it felt like" to live through the events. We tell participants that the story should capture the cognitive and emotional details of what happened as well as the dramatic tension they recall experiencing. After each partner independently finishes, we bring them together finally to exchange and read each other's version of the epiphany. We have asked some couples to tape their conversations during this session as they confront differences in their accounts and attempt to construct together one story out of two. In this stage of the process, partners collaborate in the coproduction of a text that re-presents their experiences, negotiating what to include and how, that is, through what narrative devices and forms. The co-constructed story that results is intended to be an empathic and evocative text that incorporates both partners' voices and subjectivities and invites outsiders into the intersubjective world of the narrators. We try to impress on our storytellers the desire to take what they are telling about their experience and make it the experience of the people who will read, or see, or hear their tale (Benjamin, 1936/1969; Richardson, 1994). In this way we encourage a narrative journey that travels from experience to text to reader, where reading reflexively refers to the intertextual interpretive activities of tellers and hearers. Writing, speaking, and listening are thus situated, interactive, interpretive activities.

The exemplar from our project that we describe below is an experiment in the performance of personal narrative. It is our autobiographical attempt to show what Geertz (1983, p. 16) refers to as "a local example of the forms human life has locally taken" in order to see ourselves among others, as a case among cases, an instance that records a difficult passage of lived experience into speech and verbal expressibility (Scarry, 1985). This particular case embodies what Jackson calls "radical empiricism" (after William James), a methodology in which "we make ourselves experimental subjects and treat our experiences as primary data" (Jackson, 1989, p. 4).

AN ABORTION STORY

The tale we describe here is an account of the lived experience of legalized abortion narrated in both the female and male voices (see Ellis & Bochner, 1992, for a complete transcript of the narrative text). It is a "true" story of one couple's intense, chaotic, and disturbing crisis, which, at the time, was so powerfully absorbing that they lacked an interpretive framework to make sense of it. The purpose of writing and subsequently performing the story was to create an "experience of the experience" (Ellis & Bochner, 1992, p. 98) that could reveal the actors to themselves and, perhaps, help others know themselves better by seeing, hearing, and/or feeling what the experience was like to the participants.

"Alice" and "Ted" had been involved in a romantic relationship for only 10 weeks when they discovered that Alice was pregnant. For Alice, who was 39 years old, and Ted, who was 44, it was their first personal experience of pregnancy. Suddenly their relationship was transformed from a state of romantic and lustful bliss into a paralyzing seriousness as they decided whether to terminate the pregnancy. How would this decision be made? What were each person's rights and obligations, and to what extent would these be taken into account? Would the decision be based on political, moral, spiritual, or psychological grounds? How rational would the decision be and how emotional? Who could they consult for help in reaching a decision? How would commitment to the future of their relationship be affected?

As university professors, Alice and Ted had formulated abstract theories and strong convictions about "rights to choose." Now they were faced not with a hypothetical "what if?" but with a real "what now?" For Alice and Ted, the events of the following week were intense and emotionally charged. Each of them knew that this could be their last chance to experience parenthood and each realized the responsibility associated with the birth of a child as well. After an agonizing appraisal of their options, they agreed that Alice should have an abortion. The abortion occurred 10 days after the pregnancy was confirmed.

In the aftermath of the abortion, it became clear that their relationship and their personal lives had been affected profoundly by this experience. The intensity and passion of the relationship had been unwittingly anesthetized. For 2 months after the abortion, they were numb, self-protective, and unable to discuss their experience or express their feelings about it to each other. When they finally broke through their resistance, they realized how much they had been affected by the abortion and how far they had ventured into submerged and private registers of emotion. They were startled to admit that they had not known how to feel about or interpret what was happening and wondered whether others experiencing abortion had these feelings as well.

Alice and Ted reviewed the literature on abortion—as was their habit of mind—only to find that reports and stories about abortion are primarily about the illegal ones performed in back rooms and dark alleys, revealed in generalities, primarily by women, many years after the experience (Bonavoglia, 1991; Messer & May, 1988). Details of the emotional and communicative process of the experience were obscure, leaving readers without a sense of the complexity, confusion, and ambivalence often attributed to the lived experience of abortion (Francke, 1978; Petchesky, 1984; Wasielewski, 1992). On the whole, the emotional trauma of abortion is bleached of its most profound and stirring meanings. The contradictions and ambivalence are bypassed in favor of political ideology or moral indignation. Alice and Ted were virtually certain, however, that other people had been as bruised by the ambivalence and conflicts associated with the constraints of making a choice as they were.

Why didn't the literature on abortion reflect more of the human side of the lived experience of abortion—the meanings and feelings embodied by the experience? Alice and Ted concluded that the absence of narratives that detail the emotional complexities and ambivalence of abortion may be the result of individuals feeling forced to accept and endure these blows of fate passively or being subjected to taboos against sharing these disturbing feelings openly, making it nearly impossible to find the words to talk about what happened.

Alice and Ted were convinced that their story could be helpful to others who might face similar circumstances. Although many aspects of the events seemed unique to them at the time, their story may only have been a replaying of events encountered by many other people. They decided to treat their own experiences as primary data and to transform them into a personal narrative that could be shared with a wider public audience.

Separately, each of them wrote a narrative about the experience. Alice, a sociologist who teaches qualitative methods and ethnography, approached the "data" methodologically as akin to fieldwork. She reconstructed her experience chronologically as a set of field notes. Within a few days, she had finished a 26-page account of scenes, feelings, private thoughts, and conversations that took place, as she remembered them. To recollect the events as accurately as possible, she used her calendar and consulted friends with whom she had shared some of her thoughts and feelings at the time. Alice conceived the project as one in which theory would be build inductively from the recalled details. Her goal, though, was to "show" what happened, as one would in a novel, rather than to "tell" in the usual social science genre.

Ted took several months to construct his 42-page account, which blended descriptions of events and feelings with an analysis of them. There was very little dialogue in Ted's narrative because his experience had taken place mainly in his head and not in conversation with others. He placed less emphasis on recording all the details and more on the manner of telling the story rhetorically. Ted and Alice did not see each other's narrative until both versions had been completed.

While Alice was concerned primarily with producing field notes that represented the experience as accurately as possible, and only secondarily with the "telling" of the story, Ted was primarily interested in formulating a telling that made a point and was intersubjectively sensitive to the audiences that would be seeing or hearing it. Attempting to place the reader in the frame of the abortion as lived in her experience, Alice turned to the abortion and her feelings toward it as what needed to be described, explained, and made intelligible. Ted, on the other hand, placed the abortion within the frame of their intimate relationship. This difference in framing reflected Alice's academic commitment to the sociology of emotions (Ellis, 1991) and Ted's to relational aspects of communication (Bochner, 1984).

Alice and Ted invited other persons with whom they had consulted during the decision-making process to contribute to the narrative and thus provide multiple voices for the telling of the story. Two of Alice's best women friends gave their accounts, and Ted received reports from a close male friend and a female coworker in whom he had confided at the time. Alice's friends disclosed how their conversations had called up memories of their own experiences with abortion and pregnancy and emphasized the emotions they felt regarding Alice. Ted's male friend highlighted the way he had thought through the moral principles involved and how their friendship related to the episode, while his female confidant gave a rational and precise account of the specific conversation in which they had discussed the abortion.

After Alice and Ted exchanged and discussed their narratives with each other, they decided that the best way to tell their story was in the form of a dialogue. The long individual narratives were synthesized into a single "script" that presented, in sequence, critical scenes in which they expressed their self-reflections, feelings, and analysis of the main events. The goal was to produce a collective version of their story that could be performed for a wider audience.

In preparing the final version of the narrative, Alice and Ted agreed that it was important, in certain instances, to keep the separate accounts intact, for example, each person's vivid descriptions of their immediate bodily and emotional reactions to the abortion procedure. When finished, the co-constructed narrative included several episodes in which Alice and Ted describe the same event, each from her or his own perspective and in her or his own words (see Ellis & Bochner, 1992). Shown and performed side by side, these enactments of the same events from each person's point of view provide a striking exemplar of the emotional significance and relativity of different modes of representing events, and point to the complexities and difficulties of voicing experiences of physical and emotional pain (Scarry, 1985).

Alice and Ted performed their personal narrative at a professional social science conference (Ellis & Bochner, 1991). The version they enacted covered the encounters associated with the discovery and shock of the pregnancy, pre- and postdecision interactions, and the abortion procedure as described in both the female and male voice. They intended the performance to be both dramatic and reflective, emotionally expressive, and academically meaningful. The narration shifted between explicit detail and discussion of the utility of dealing with lived emotional experience and its verbal expressibility. Attempting to draw the audience as near as possible to the experience and not to themselves, the narrators decided to use pseudonyms, a decision that provoked considerable discussion among those who witnessed the performance and, later, among those who read the published script. Although these events happened to the authors personally, the use of different names indicates that these experiences could usefully be regarded as typical (Abraham, 1986). Immediately after their performance, Alice and Ted sat close together as two more conventional conference presentations were made. Ted whispered in Alice's ear, "Finally, I feel finished." Alice acknowledged that these words captured her feeling as well.

PERSONAL NARRATIVE AS RESEARCH ON
INTERPERSONAL COMMUNICATION

We began this chapter by calling attention to reflexive qualities of lived communicative experience. Our call for a "radical empiricism" that begins by making oneself an experimental subject and then takes this biographical experience as primary data is one way to take reflexivity seriously and to provide a methodology for bringing lived experience into the center of research on close relationships. Alice and Ted's story—our story—is an exemplar of what we have in mind. The case itself, however, is far less important for our purposes here than the path it is intended to clear, to use Michael Jackson's (1989) phrase, for future generations of students of interpersonal communication. We have emphasized the procedural details of how the narrative was constructed and performed because we think it can be more generally applied to cases in which the empirical field is one of interactions and intersubjectivity as experienced in the epiphanies that so often characterize close relationships.

Langellier (1989) argues that personal narratives intersect the spheres of public and private life "where telling a personal experience is part of a social process of coping" (p. 264). The interpretive world view that we embrace is a pragmatist view that construes knowledge not so much as a way of representing reality as a way of coping with it (Ellis, 1995; Rorty, 1982). The social process of telling a personal story is one meaningful and potentially enlightening way of approaching this goal. As one sociologist said in a letter to Alice after hearing her performance: "Narratives unfold with flesh and blood. . .encouraging empathy, identification and a humanization of content" (Slobin, Personal Communication, February 1991). The goal becomes inviting others—readers, listeners, and so forth—into the story in such a way that they not only know what it was like, they *feel* it (Richardson, 1994).

Although we see our story and the lived events it depicts as part of the same intertextual fabric, we do not see them as one and the same. Telling the events is not identical to living them, yet the story, as we constructed it, cannot be completely detached from the experiences out of which it was formed. The story is tied to the events it displays, but the events have no independent authority by which the story can ultimately be judged. The story reconstructs the events and undoubtedly redefines them *for a purpose*. Often that purpose is to unify the past with an anticipated and hopeful future. The reframed and re-contextualized lived moments are given meanings directed toward a future. Crites (1986) refers to stories that ceaselessly reiterate the past as "hell" because they abandon a hopeful projection into the future; they are confining and despairing. The narrative challenge of Ted and Alice's story is to come to terms with the numbing aspects of their experience so that they can nourish the opportunity of creating a future together. They are not so much reiterating their experience as they are transferring it to a new context that begins to articulate future possibilities.

As a procedural method of inquiry, the exemplar we have described offers a systematic and replicable way of examining some of the most important qualities of interpersonal communication. By first emphasizing autonomously constructed narratives of events that were shared, these procedures can highlight the power and relativity of modes of description. For example, in a metanarrative that Alice and Ted constructed in response to reading each other's narrative, they comment on the graphic differences between his account of grief and her account of worthlessness and on her repeated use of the term "baby" juxtaposed against his repeated references to a "fetus." These descriptive revelations led them to contemplate further the significance of the frames of grief compared to self-contempt, physical pain juxtaposed against emotional pain, and the experience–near female voice in contrast to the somewhat more distanced male voice.

By transforming two separate accounts into a dialogical form of narration, the narrators confront two levels of intersubjectivity. The first requires them to devise a mutually agreeable code, particularly in the instances of apparent disagreement about what really happened. Then, after these differences have been negotiated and/or arbitrated, they must formulate a collective voice, a code in which the point of the story can be made accessible in a public performance. Thus, the process of writing and performing the narrative reproduces and underscores the practices of communication that are played out in the lived world of interpersonal relationships.

Moreover, the reflexivity of performing a personal narrative draws attention to the ways in which communication is used to reveal ourselves to ourselves. As Victor Turner (1986) points out: "This can be in two ways: the actor may come to know himself better through acting or enactment; or one set of human beings may come to know themselves better through observing and/or participating in performances generated and presented by another set of human beings" (p. 81). The point of our approach and its self-conscious reflexivity is to dissolve what Bateson (1972) referred to as the "monstrous" (p. 464) old divisions between subject and object, feeling and intellect, and self and other. The monstrous consequences of these divisions have been to privilege a monolithic scientific perspective and to marginalize thick descriptions of lived experience carried out for purposes other than prediction and control. It is time for our social science disciplines to become, as Turner (1982) once said about anthropology, "something more than a cognitive game played in our heads and inscribed in—let's face it—somewhat tedious journals" (p. 97).

REFERENCES

Abraham, R. (1986). Ordinary and extraordinary experience. In V. Turner & E. Bruner (Eds.), *The anthropology of experience* (pp. 45–72). Urbana: University of Illinois Press.

Barthes, R. (1977). *Image, music, text.* New York: Hill & Wang.

Bateson, G. (1968). Conventions of communication: Where validity depends upon belief. In J. Ruesch & G. Bateson (Eds.), *Communication: The social matrix of psychiatry* (pp. 212–226). New York: W. W. Norton.

Bateson, G. (1972). *Steps to an ecology of mind.* New York: Ballantine.

Benjamin, W. (1969). The storyteller: Reflections on the works of Nikolai Leskov. In H. Arendt (Ed.), *Illuminations* (pp. 83–109). New York: Schocken Books. (Original work published 1936)

Berger, P., & Luckmann, T. (1966). *The social construction of reality: A treatise in the sociology of knowledge.* Garden City: Doubleday.

Bochner, A. P. (1984). The functions of human communication in interpersonal bonding. In C. Arnold & J. Bowers (Eds.), *Handbook of rhetorical and communication theory* (pp. 544–621). Boston: Allyn & Bacon.

Bochner, A. P. (1990). *Embracing contingencies of lived experience in the study of close relationships.* Keynote Lecture to the International Conference on Personal Relationships, Oxford University.

Bochner, A. P. (1994). Perspectives on inquiry II: Theories and stories. In M. Knapp & G. R. Miller (Eds.), *Handbook of interpersonal communication* (pp. 21–41). Thousand Oaks, CA: Sage.

Bochner, A. P., & Kelly, C. (1974). Interpersonal competence: Rationale, philosophy, and implementation of a conceptual framework. *The Speech Teacher, 23,* 279–301.

Bonavoglia, A. (1991). *The choices we made: Twenty-five women and men speak out about abortion.* New York: Random House.

Brody, H. (1987). *Stories of sickness.* New Haven, CT: Yale University Press.

Crites, S. (1986). Storytime: Recollecting the past and projecting the future. In T. Sarbin (Ed.), *Narrative psychology: The storied nature of human conduct* (pp. 152–173). New York: Praeger.

Denzin, N. K. (1989). *Interpretive interactionism.* Newbury Park, CA: Sage.

Denzin, N. K., & Lincoln, Y. S. (1994). Introduction: Entering the field of qualitative research. In N. K. Denzin & Y. S. Lincoln (Eds.), *Handbook of qualitative research* (pp. 1–17). Thousand Oaks, CA: Sage.

Ellis, C. (1991). Emotional sociology. In N. K. Denzin (Ed.), *Studies in symbolic interaction* (Vol. 12, pp. 123–145). Greenwich, CT: JAI.

Ellis, C. (1995). *Final negotiations: A story of love, loss, and chronic illness.* Philadelphia: Temple University Press.

Ellis, C., & Bochner, A. P. (1991). *Multiple voices, metanarratives, and lived experience: A case study of choice and constraint.* Paper presented at the Society for the Study of Symbolic Interaction Stone Symposium, San Francisco.

Ellis, C., & Bochner, A. P. (1992). Telling and performing personal stories: The constraints of choice in abortion. In C. Ellis & M. Flaherty (Eds.), *Investigating subjectivity: Research on lived experience* (pp. 79–101). Newbury Park, CA: Sage.

Francke, L. (1978). *The ambivalence of abortion.* New York: Random House.

Geertz, C. (1973). *The interpretation of cultures.* New York: Basic Books.

Geertz, C. (1983). *Local knowledge: Further essays in interpretive anthropology.* New York: Basic Books.

Jackson, M. (1989). *Paths toward a clearing: Radical empiricism and ethnographic inquiry.* Bloomington: Indiana University Press.

Langellier, K. M. (1989). Personal narrative: Perspectives on theory and research. *Text and Performance Quarterly, 9,* 243–276.

Marcus, G. E. (1994). What comes (just) after "post"? The case of ethnography. In N. K. Denzin & Y. S. Lincoln (Eds.), *Handbook of qualitative research* (pp. 1–17). Thousand Oaks: Sage.

Messer, E., & May, K. (1988). *Back rooms: An oral history of the illegal abortion era.* New York: Simon & Schuster.

Petchesky, R. (1984). *Abortion and woman's choice.* New York: Longman.

Richardson, L. (1994). Nine poems: Marriage and the family. *Journal of Contemporary Ethnography, 23,* 9–13.

Rorty, R. (1982). *Consequences of pragmatism (Essays: 1972–1980).* Minneapolis: University of Minnesota Press.

Scarry, E. (1985). *The body in pain: The making and unmaking of the world.* New York: Oxford University Press.

Shotter, J. (1987). The social construction of an (us): Problems of accountability and narratology. In R. Burnett, P. McGee, & P. Clarke (Eds.), *Accounting for relationships: Explanation, representation, and knowledge* (pp. 225–247). London: Methuen.

Stone, E. (1990). *Black sheep and kissing cousins: How our family stories shape us.* New York: Penguin.

Turner, V. (1982). Dramatic ritual/ritual drama: Performative and reflexive anthropology. In J. Roby (Ed.), *A crack in the mirror: Reflexive perspectives in anthropology* (pp. 83–97). Philadelphia: University of Pennsylvania Press.

Turner, V. (1986). *The anthropology of performance.* New York: PAJ.

Wasielewski, P. (1992). Post abortion syndrome: Emotional battles over interaction and ideology. *Humboldt Journal of Social Relations, 18,* 101–129.

White, H. (1980). The value of narrativity in the representation of reality. *Critical Inquiry, 7,* 5–27.

Part V

Conclusion

CHAPTER 12

Practical Theory and the Tasks Ahead for Social Approaches to Communication

VERNON E. CRONEN

ooking at the work collected here, and considering the view of human communication the collection presents, I think of a comment by American humorist and storyteller Garrison Keillor (1987): "Life is complicated and not for the timid" (p. xv). In the the 1970s it did not seem so complicated to most researchers who studied interpersonal communication. The humanists seemed quite confident that with sufficient empathy, trust, and self-disclosure things could go on swimmingly well. Most rhetoricians still had faith that the ancients left us a descriptive and prescriptive core of writings that would guide us to good practice. Perhaps most confident and optimistic were the behaviorists. Their faith was that statistical studies would provide data that could be organized into timeless theorems, axioms, and a covering law—a neat logical system giving us the substantial truths about communication. Things have not worked out as we thought in our or in other social disciplines.

However, the number of new and exciting ideas about communication has never been so large. Young scholars entering the communication discipline have a rich background of reading and sense of social responsibility that is a joy to see, particularly for those of us who were struggling to introduce some of the ideas now summarized under the rubric "social approaches" back in the 1970s.

In this chapter I hope to contribute to this volume in three ways. First, I will emphasize the magnitude of departure from traditional communication studies entailed in the work collected here. Second, I will identify certain issues that arise in the course of the foregoing chapters and offer some ideas about how to move forward the development of social approaches. Finally, I will attempt to further unify the movement by offering some ideas about what we distinctively mean by theory. Here I will introduce the term "practical theory" and further specify its character.

THE QUEST FOR CERTAINTY

The work in this book turns away from what Dewey (1929/1960) called the "quest for certainty" (p. 3). Much of the book reflects Dewey's original arguments against the philosophical traditions that lead to this quest in the first place. Dewey (1920/1957) argued that the West's quest for certainty began in ancient Athens. There, in the 5th century B.C.E., serious political misjudgments led people to seek some "intelligent substitute for blind custom or blind impulse as guides to life and conduct" (p. 126). Unfortunately, argued Dewey, the path chosen was to seek a method that would uncover the real substance behind mere fleeting appearances.

Such a quest, of course, presumed that there must be such primary substances to find. The early Greek thinkers argued that in order to have truth, the objects of study must be stable. Otherwise, we could only have fleeting glimpses of things as they were. That would not provide a certain guide as to what we should do next. Thales, Pythagoras, and Parmenides all connected the possibility of truth to the stability of phenomena (Reale, 1987). Later, in a marvelous bit of circular reasoning, Plato argued that basic "forms" must exist behind the flux of phenomena in order for there to be something substantial to be known without doubt.[1]

In various venues I have likened this quest for certainty to the story of a ragged boy from Chelm who amazed a traveling nobleman with a display of targets exhibiting a musketball strike at the center of every one. Asked how he did it, the boy said it was easy. "You just fire at the barn wall and where the ball strikes you draw a target around it." Determined upon a particular view of knowledge and a technology for getting it, philosophy and social theory drew a picture of the world to fit the kind of knowledge desired. It is from an account of the world, generated in the service of a quest for certainty, that we derived many of the now commonplace notions challenged in most of this book.

The quest for certainty has taken several forms. Newton thought that his work, resting on that of Kepler and Galileo, uncovered the reality of nature behind appearances. The philosophical traditions of enlightenment metaphysics and epistemology surely clashed with the Newtonians' empiricism, but philosophers and scientists were equally embarked on a quest for certainty (Dewey, 1929/1960).

HOW THINGS GOT COMPLICATED

The results of the quest for certainty have been far from successful in social research. It led to assumptions about the world of human experience that were as necessary for the pursuit of certainty as they were implausible. In order to carve out "mind" as an object that could be known with certainty, the mind had to be populated with a strange but by now commonly assumed set of hidden inner processes with thing-like qualities. Mind, for example, was populated with "ideas" that could be represented in language (see Stewart's discussion of representationalism in Chapter 2, this volume). Consciousness became an inner power that could bring about an inner state. In his devastating attack on that idea, James (1904/1977, 1905/1975a) observed that if this were so, it would be possible to have, of all things, empty consciousness! However, the positivist revolution in psychology shoved James and his followers aside as unscientific. Dewey had offered a powerful critique of the reflex arc in 1896, but it was not until the rise of cybernetics in the wake of positivism's failures that Dewey's critique was taken seriously.

Perhaps most peculiar, if closely examined, is the still present tendency among the most "scientifically" minded to follow Descartes's notion that "mind" is a separate object of study, distinct both from brain and the material conditions of social interaction. The confusions this produces are numerous and well documented by many contemporary writers cited in the foregoing chapters (see especially Harré, 1984; Harré & Gillett, 1994; Rorty, 1979; Taylor, 1985a, 1985b). Of course, the Cartesian view of mind in supposedly scientific social research is completely at odds with the the the data that show learning and thinking to involve chemical changes in the brain.

Slippery Meanings

What distinguishes most of the foregoing chapters in this book is that they treat what had been counted as mental objects or states as conjointly created abilities that arise and change *in*, not simply by, communication (Dewey, 1916/1966).

Contrast the approaches taken by the various authors to the central issue of meaning in language. In earlier views borrowed from analytical philosophy or psychology, meaning was a point in n-dimensional space found by factor analysis (Osgood, Suci, & Tannenbaum, 1957), the fulfillment of criteria for well-formed speech acts (Searle, 1969), or an individual's self-report of what utterances mean to him or her.

Most authors of the preceding chapters in this volume take a very different approach to the problem of meaning. Stewart (Chapter 2), following the later Wittgenstein (1953), argues that meaning is a conjoint creation always in process. Indeed, as an episode of action develops, the meaning of a past utterance changes as it is now part of actions that have developed in a new way. Because conversation is not under the control of a single conversant, asking an individual what she or her "really meant" will not get us anywhere.

Stewart's arguments are consistent with those of Jorgenson (Chapter 8) and are representative of others writing in the field (see Cronen, Pearce & Xi, 1989/1990; Sanders, 1987; Shotter, 1994). Steier's (Chapter 4) emphasis on reflexivity and temporality also implies commitment to meanings as emergent, always-in-process phenomena that cannot be captured by unsituated synthetic propositions. If meanings are, to paraphrase Dewey, "values in the running," that obviates the possibility of capturing meaning and swallowing it whole. In communication, as in other social disciplines, the quest for certainty led to a faith that we could find technologies that would determine the real meaning of social action and replace fallible judgment. The social approaches challenge that faith.

Today, the quest for certainty is finding fewer adherents and more critics. In science, Kuhn's (1970) *Structure of Scientific Revolutions* marked a watershed. That book showed the problem of translation across scientific paradigms to have important affinities with the problem of translation across cultures. We can compare our own position to an incommensurable one using a variety of means for acting into the grammar (ethnographers would prefer "code") of that position (Bernstein, 1985).

ENTER THE SOCIAL APPROACHES

It was Dewey's argument that the quest for certainty is not the only response to our need to find an alternative to custom and impulse. The alternative for Dewey and the pragmatist philosophers who followed him was to develop ways of studying social phenomena that take human experience seriously. Rather than looking for hidden mechanisms, Dewey (1916/1966) understood selfhood, institutions, culture, and ways of thinking as created in communication. He challenged us to value what is in process and fraught with possibility as much as what is finished and perfected, and warned against taking socially constituted phenomena for natural facts or powers. He and others worked out a grammar for talking about social action. For example, Dewey admonished us not to work in terms of "ends." That leads to cutting up human action into a set of little jerking movements that come to a stop, requiring some mystical force to start them up again. Instead, he argued for talking about "ends in view" (Dewey, 1922, p. 226). Ends in view are not prior to communication; rather, they are constructed and reconstructed in communication. Another example is Dewey's gambit of switching nouns for verbs and gerunds. He shows what happens when we stop talking about "identity" and start talking about "identifying" (Lamont & Redmer, 1959).[2] Each of us working in what Leeds-Hurwitz (Chapter 1, this volume) terms a "social approach" attempts to develop a vocabulary for talking about situated conjoint action and then to develop that vocabulary further into methodologies and traditions of work.

When the Search with Gun and Camera Fails

Much of the quest for certainty in social theory has been a little like a safari, searching with gun and camera for the real entities in the jungle of fleeting phenomena. Scholars set out to find the real mental illnesses and kill them off, or provide pictures of variable relationships with statistics and data displays. The social approaches deny the possibility of such quests. They are much closer to Dewey's (1922) critique of psychoanalysis, which anticipated the systemic therapy movement's position by more than 30 years. Here is what Dewey had to say about stalking mental illness:

> The treatment of sex by psycho-analysts is most instructive, for it flagrantly exhibits both the consequences of artificial simplification and the transformation of social results into psychic causes. Writers, usually male, hold forth on the psychology of woman, as if they were dealing with a Platonic universal entity, although they habitually treat men as individuals, varying with structure and environment. They treat phenomena which are peculiarly symptoms of the civilization of the West at the present time as if they were the necessary effects of fixed native impulses of human nature. Romantic love as it exists today, with all the varying pertubations it occasions, is as definitely a sign of specific historic conditions as are big battle ships with turbines, internal-combustion engines, and electrically driven machines. (p. 153)

Dewey's point was not that persons could not be helped by professionals. Rather, it was that the kind of work psychoanalysts do misses the character of the problems professionals must address.

The Inescapability of Judgment

Dewey (1929/1960) was critical of Aristotle's tendency to "glorifying the invariant at the expense of change" (p. 17). This is surely a correct estimate of much of Aristotle's work. However, Dewey (1932/1980) was also influenced by Aristotle, particularly Aristotle's avoidance of the ragged marksman's mistake. Aristotle did separate out types of arts on the basis of their subject matter and then discussed the kind of knowing appropriate to each.

Chen and Pearce (Chapter 7, this volume) encourage us to reexamine Aristotle's way of classifying the arts. To develop my argument, I want to recapitulate just a bit of their discussion because that is crucial for the new emphasis on judgment in the social disciplines.

Aristotle did not consider rhetoric, politics, economics, or any of what we call the social disciplines to be *theoretical* arts. Nor did he think the study of them would yield *epistēmē*, or true knowledge of real objects. "Theory" has the same root as the Greek word for "theater." In both cases the phenomenon to be studied is separated from the observer. The "theater of the heavens" will go its way regardless of the astronomers' ideas, just as the play will go on according to its script regardless of how profoundly the audience understands the play. What Aristotle did was acknowledge that there were arts (i.e., phenomena that could be explained by principle) that were neither stable nor separate from the human knower. He called them the arts of *praxis* because they concerned neither the physical world nor the ability to fabricate but rather the way people act together. As Chen and Pearce rightly argue, the result of studying these arts is the attainment of *phronēsis* or practical judgment.

However, technique must be used to inform practical judgment, not to replace it. Let me use my own work on the coordinated management of meaning (CMM) to illustrate.[3] I can teach people the heuristic models of CMM and the principles that inform them. However, that alone will not make anyone a sophisticated researcher or consultant in any domain of human endeavor. That will require using CMM in relevant situations. Knowing the theory cannot replace detailed work with a family, immersion in the way mediation sessions work, or a cultural sensitivity. The social approaches value the search for newer and richer methodologies to inform practical judgment. However, they view methodology as an important means of informing practical judgment, not replacing it.

Emergent Theory

The undermining of foundations for the scientific study of communication continues with the methodologically oriented chapters. Carbaugh and Hastings (Chapter 9, this volume) use ethnography in a somewhat different spirit than that which animated the earlier work of Philipsen (1989). I particularly like the phrase an "adequately ambulatory" theory of communication, which Carbaugh and Hastings take from Hymes (1990). They affirm the importance of offering statements about communication that have generality beyond a particular human group. However, they believe that more general understanding must and will emerge in the continuing study of situated communication. Moreover, they stress methods that must be sensitive to the richness and uniqueness of situated cultural activity. Notice the contrast between Carbaugh and Hastings's view and the traditional idea that the best theory does not require *post hoc* addenda. Implied in their view, and in the case study approach of Chen and Pearce, a perspective that is not emergent is a dead end.

To be accurate, traditional approaches to theory building are also emergent, but only with respect to the accumulation of additional findings and the deduction of some new theorems. However, the basic covering law(s) and axioms are supposed to remain fixed in a sound theory. If we look to the kind of approaches to communication that fit Leeds-Hurwitz's description, the most basic statements themselves emerge in the course of the work. Approaches such as CMM ethnography, and others are identifiable as evolving traditions of work.

The Researcher in the Process

What of the relationship of the researcher developing and exercising practical judgment to the fluid communication phenomena? Jorgenson (Chapter 8, this volume) raises this issue in her discussion of empathy (a topic about which I will have more to say later) and Chen and Pearce discuss the issue in terms of the Aristotleian distinction between *theoria* and *praxis*. I suggest particular attention to their argument that the kind of knowing that one attains working in the the domain of *praxis* is not usefully reduced to technique.

The implications for what it means to know something in the domain of *praxis* are extended when we consider Wittgenstein's arguments about the limits of expression. Wittgenstein (1953) made a clear distinction between the ability to use a rule and a rule formulation. The ability to use a rule always includes more than what can be formulated in a linguistic expression because m meaning involves pointing beyond the moment. By playing chess against very talented opponents, a chess master not only learns to use a number of sophisticated rules for play but also develops a feel for how to use and alter such rules in new situations. Similarly, a consultant or researcher, like a good conversationalist, develops flexible, expanding abilities that cannot be reduced to technique (see also Angus, 1984; Barrett, 1979; Shotter, 1993; Wittgenstein, 1953).

The foregoing argument means that all research is reactive by its nature, including questionnaires (Cronen, 1995; Weaver, 1991). The difference is that the authors in this volume (see especially Steier, Chapter 4) recognize the researcher as participating in a conversation and thus lift the veil from the issue of what obligations researchers and participants have to each other. The interviewers and participants (spouses, work colleagues, etc.) not only learn but also learn how to learn (Bateson, 1972).

Where are we in this new and complicated, but very promising, work? Some issues suggested in the foregoing chapters deserve prompt attention.

WORK THAT IS NOT FOR THE TIMID

I want to suggest an agenda for getting our houses in better order. It is not that we must all agree, but rather that we need to work more on these matters.

The Boundaries of Methodological Pluralism

Bavelas (Chapter 3, this volume) has done a fine job of clearing the air of some confusions that bedevil the debate about quantitative and qualitative methods. I agree with many of the arguments she has made, and yet I think she has not raised the two most troublesome points. The first is that she does not talk about the difference between the two models of the social world that animate much qualitative and quantitative work. Jacobs (1990) developed this point in his response to Cappella (1990). Jacobs observed that there is a difference between conceiving of the social world as patterns of coherent action or as redundancies set against a background of randomness. This difference is accentuated by the position taken by authors in this volume who argue that those patterns are intrinsically unfinished. Counting their partial reoccurrence does not tell us very much, though it might give us a clue to what requires further study.

This reverses the usual role of the case study in relationship to the large-scale "data collection" as Chen and Pearce (Chapter 7) have cogently argued. When there is a great deal of redundancy in a lived social setting, we raise questions such as these: Is the social unit "stuck" in a recurrent pattern that no one likes? How does the ritualized reenactment help the people involved to deal with the *changing* world in which they live? Is repetition of the pattern stultifying the abilities of the social group or is it a deeply enriching ritual? By contrast, the positivist rejoices at finding something stable enough to study.

The viability of the large data collection study rests on the notion of the variable, and this is the second large issue that must be raised. The notion of the variable is inconsistent with the notion of co-created meaning as Stewart (Chapter 2) discusses it, and with reflexivity as Steier (Chapter 4) develops it. A variable is a concept that can take on different values. Recall my own and Stewart's arguments about the import of Wittgenstein's claim that language is not a representation of ideas in the mind. Stewart discussed how Wittgenstein's view meant meaning was always in process and unfinished in a much more profound way than change in quantitative value. If "data points" are interdependent with previous and subsequent actions, the independence assumption underlying statistical procedures is undermined.

Failure to appreciate that the meanings of terms such as "individuality" or "privacy," for example, are matters of *use* in situated, conjointly created practices (not mental or physical entities) leads to to the worst distortions of old positivism. It is a bad question to ask whether one culture or another has more of a "collectivistic" or "individualistic" orientation. We need ask how these terms are used in practice. A good question would be: What is the grammar of individualism for certain episodes in middle-class, second-generation Chinese Americans? Another good question is: What grammars of individualism, if any, are present in the stories told by members of the X family, and how do these inform and become informed by their family's conjoint practices?

In a landmark study, Gadlin (1977) showed how the term "privacy" has a very different meaning for us than it had under the conditions of early colonial life. It is not that we now have *more* of "it." Rather, the term "privacy" means something *different* to us because the grammars of social action in which it appears are now different.

It is not enough to gloss the problem by saying that this is simply the issue of context again. In the social approaches, context returns to its original Latin source as a *verb* meaning to weave together. Thus, context and utterance reflexively evolve and inform one another.

I want to be clear that I do think quantitative work can sometimes be a useful adjunct to other methods. I find some of Bavelas's work, and that of Averill (1989), who also uses some quantitative methods, helpful for my own endeavors. However, the problem of translating the variable analytical concept of meaning and the randomness–redundancy view into terms that make sense with meaning as use requires further careful work.

THE POSITION OF THE RESEARCHER/CONSULTANT

Steier has done a great deal of important work on this matter under the rubric of reflexivity. His work begins by rejecting the idea that social researchers have the same "objective" relationship to the phenomenon of interest as do astronomers. Moreover, if the view of meaning that is explicitly or implicitily present in several of the forgoing chapters is taken seriously, the meaning that emerges in an interview or in fieldwork cannot be simply internal to the participant/client or to researcher/consultant. Here, I simply do not agree with Bavelas that at the point of interpretation we are alone.[4] Consider these matters: Would we be involved in a particular problem of interpretation had not the people studied responded in a particular way to our method of inquiry? Would we be able to interpret or train the coders without cultural knowledge and professional conversations? Would our inquiries be the same had it not been for our prior inquiries and the responses people gave us? Do we recognize the voice of a valued colleague or mentor in our own utterances as we work on problems of interpretation?

To say that the interpreter is alone at the moment of interpretation seems to gloss over the different kinds of positions one can take in conversations (Davies & Harré, 1990)—including those involving research and consultation. Does the researcher position him/herself as the objective voice of the scientific community, or as a sympathetic fellow participant in social process? This is surely important when a researcher is studying a gender-related issue. How is the other cast? As the voice of "you male students," as a unique personal voice, or what? Finally, has the other any opportunity to renegotiate the relationship? If the other does not, as in the case of a questionnaire, does the other change the way he or she positions him- or herself in the process of responding, and how does the other know to do so? These positionings of self and other influence the kind of data obtained because different moral obligations, affordances, and constraints are created by the way people are positioned (Cronen, 1994; Shotter, 1984). The importance of the position of the researcher in the process is particularly problematic in Chapter 11 (Bochner & Ellis, this volume). If Bochner and Ellis are themselves the subjects, they need to tell us how this makes a difference as compared to using the same technique with others. Of course, I also have reservations about resting claims on one case with the authors as subjects.

If we cannot treat interpretation as an individual matter and must treat it as a conjoint process, how do we take account of our own position as researchers in the research process? My own view is that a sound practical theory, recognized as a grammatical ability, ought to provide some better means of describing the role of the researcher. In CMM we have begun to do this by including in our heuristic models the interviewer. The stories that the interviewer can potentially tell include his or her use of CMM theory, but that is not all. For example, some of my graduate students also tell how their knowledge of cultural-depth grammars leads them to modify their use of the interview method. For example, Chinese persons are sometimes insulted by the use of conterfactual conditionals as in questions such as this one: "How do you think your son *would* have responded last year if you had done X instead of Y?" This seems to the Chinese like a game for children. Other stories the interviewer could tell include the kind of relationship she or he has developed with the subjects of study, and perhaps some autobiographical stories that bear on how the interviewer works.

Instrumental and Consummatory Aspects of Communication

It is not all talk. That is not what communication is like. Indeed, talk itself has esthetic qualities that are rarely considered, even in the social approaches as thus far developed (including CMM).

Earlier in this chapter I briefly discussed the limits of expression. Here I want to expand on that theme and to do so using the problem of rapport that Jorgenson (Chapter 8, this volume) explores. Hers is the one chapter that takes seriously the fact that feelings matter in communication.

Unfortunately, the long-standing traditional approach distinguishes emotion from reason, or sets it against reason along the same lines as did the theory of the faculties in Francis Bacon's time. When emotion is taken seriously, it is often treated as another mental object. More recent work, particularly that of Averill (1980), has argued that emotions are *abilities* that arise in coherent ways in patterns of social action.

Averill has been much influenced by Dewey. Dewey distinguished between instrumental aspects of communication and consummatory aspects. Dewey stressed the idea that people learn to have esthetic moments in which things seem to fit together in a beautiful way or form an unpleasant ugliness. Similarly, we learn how to have emotional experiences, both positive and negative. Emotional and esthetic moments are cultural products. Emotions are not the same in every culture or in every historical period (Harré, 1984). Similarly, we must learn how to appreciate music or painting that has a place in the practices of another culture. Dewey (1934a) was careful to note that having an emotional or esthetic experience is an ability learned in coherent action and used in coherent practices.

These aspects of experience are not proofs of the truth of our experience but aspects of experience (Dewey, 1934a). However, without these experiences we are not talking about a human life worth living. Such experiences must be included in our ideas about reflexivity as well. As Dewey observed, the ability to have a profound esthetic experience impacts upon our ability to have further experiences and reflects upon our stories about ourselves, our relationships to others, and even our relationships to the cosmos (Dewey, 1934b). Thus, we may inquire into the grammar of emotions and other feelings.

Now let us turn to rapport. I appreciate Jorgenson's work on this concept, and I think she has done much useful work. However, I also think she could go farther if she thought about rapport as an experience one learns to have in the course of practice. Two related practices are involved which need to be discriminated. One is the practice of reading and writing academic work about rapport, and the other is the reported experience of it in various kinds of conversations. At times, Jorgenson gets close to asking the old question, "What really is rapport?"

What she might do next, if she follows the notion of meaning that Stewart, Chen, Pearce, and I espouse, is to look at the *grammar* of rapport in conversational practice. In her examples of questions drawn from an interview intended to get an understanding of rapport, she does not seem to situate the experience in episodes of social life. In circular questionning as I know it (Fleuridas, Nelson, & Rosenthal, 1986; Tomm, 1987a, 1987b, 1988), the situating of experiences in time and place is crucial. I would want to be asking questions such as these: What was going on in your professional activity around the time you found yourself becoming able to establish rapport with your interviewees? What were you saying and what were they saying just before you began to have this feeling? What was going on at the point you started to experience it? How did things go differently (for you, for them) as a result of your having this feeling? What did the others say or do that helped you to know you were having rapport with them? After the interview was over, what did you do and how did you feel?

I might also ask comparison questions such as these: Who among those interviewed seemed to have the most rapport with you, who the next most, who the least? What do you think they would say about who had the most rapport? How was this similar to or different from the last time you felt you had established rapport with interviewees?

The point of these questions is to get an idea of the grammar of rapport. As part of a grammar, it is a way to go on in conjoint experience. Could it be that rapport is experienced more strongly after episodes in which we have doubts about the importance of our work and our relationship to our subjects? What is happening when the feeling is manifest, and how is it a *conjoint* product of the interaction? We might get an idea by finding out what responses of others are part of manifesting the feeling. Of vital importance is how having the feeling plays a role in what we are able to do in a particular episode and in further episodes.

Critical-Cultural Theory and Reductionism

Lannamann (Chapter 6, this volume) does much thoughtful work in calling our attention to issues of voice. These are similar to the questions I raised earlier when I questioned whether we are as isolated at the point of interpretation, as Bavalas argues. Lannamann, however, emphasizes the notion of politics and the presence of politically powerful formations in the utterances one uses.

His argument carried thus far is important. However, when he applauds the critical–cultural studies tradition for its way of attending to political matters I must part company with him. The difficulty with the critical–cultural studies tradition is that it does not touch the ground of situated action. The study by Willis (1977) of British working-class schoolboys is about the only example I can find of scholars from that tradition looking closely at the situated practices of actual people. Even in the case of that study, the method of interviewing does not stress the temporal character or detail of lived experience. The critical–cultural tradition seems to have no way of connecting the patterns of practice in economic relationships or media texts with the lived experience of embodied persons. Although many in that tradition are Marxists, critical–cultural studies fail to to make good on Marx's (1888/1959) famous fifth thesis on Feuerbach in which he takes his opponent to task for failing to recognize "sensuousness as practical human-sensuous activity" (p. 244). The point Marx was making was that real materialism has to take into account how social relationships are manifest in the felt experience of embodied persons.

Influenced by the critical–cultural studies tradition, Lannamann tends to reduce communication to its political dimension and then offers no way of studying how political–economic factors impact upon situated conjoint action. The social approaches discussed herein have the potential for doing so without losing sight of the political aspects of life. By using the notion of rules constituting grammars of practice, they can describe grammatical features of situated joint action that are learned from episodes of economic practice, media stories, and the like.

The social approaches, however, do not have to make the political reduction or treat persons as merely pulled and pushed by some outside economic forces. In the social approaches, bits of grammar from, say, commercial television may be studied as *parts* of *some* of the stories that make up the grammatical abilities actors *bring to episodes of conjoint action.* We could then study how those bits of grammar are reflexively reconstituted, extended, or changed in communication and how they make a difference as part of the emergent grammar. We would then attend to how they play a role in stories about intimate relationships, parenting practices, friendships and so on. We would not presume at the start of a study that the politically loaded bits of grammar are necessarily dominant in particular episodes, and we would not have to appeal to some sort of causation from a distance, such as economic forces. These studies would be especially enhanced if, in the social approaches, unlike most of the critical cultural approach, the researchers' relationship to those studied was also made an explicit part of the research.

THEORY OR PRACTICAL THEORY?

What kind of theory can we make of a study in which the phenomena evolve, the principles that guide our studies evolve, and the knowledge of researchers cannot be fully reduced to formulations? Moreover, the work impacts upon the phenomena of interest, the persons whose practices are studied, and researchers' own practices and abilities? Clearly, this is complicated and not for the timid.

Nothing said here argues for the abandonment of professional study and practice in communication. Although practical judgment, or learning *from within* practice (Shotter, 1993) cannot be reduced to a technology, the use of formulations and other guides is important for informing judgment, as I have argued earlier. However, the approaches we are developing look less and less like theory as it is usually understood.

I am tempted to call the enterprise that engages contributors to this volume, the development of a "practical art." By "art" I mean what Aristotle did; a way of working informed by principles derived from the study of that art. However, there are obvious educational–political dangers in adopting such a phrase. It might suggest that we are endorsing a literary as opposed to a social perspective on communication, and that we do not properly belong with the other social disciplines. For that reason I have been suggesting the phrase "practical theory" (Cronen, 1994), even though it seems like an oxymoron.

John Shotter introduced the phrase "practical theory" in his 1984 book, *Social Accountability and Selfhood.*[5] I think it is reasonable to retain the word "theory" if modified by the term "practical." Many fundamental ideas about how to refine and develop our work owe a debt to the modern scientific tradition of theory building. This debt includes an "empirical emphasis" (in Bavelas's correct use of the term). This is reflected in attention to the careful collection and recording of data and concern for the relationship of observation to theoretical orientation. Our way of inducing principles is very non-Aristotleian and much in debt to Newton's way of working (Goodman, 1983). Perhaps we owe the most profound debt to quantum physics for demonstrating the inseparability of the means of observation and the nature of the data.

Our newfound interest in the ancients' notion of practical arts must not blind us to the fact that, detached from science, these practical arts tended to become near catechisms—endless lists of distinctions to be memorized and passed on to the next generation of students. A look at Cicero's *De Inventione* or his later *Partitiones Oratoriae* should illustrate my point. It was modern science that insisted on a continuing relationship of observation to a body of knowledge. Science deemphasized the passing on of traditional ways of thinking in favor of empirical work and the right to call older ideas into question. For these reasons retaining the term "theory," modified by the term "practical," seems justified even though the differences between theory in the hard sciences and in social disciplines are profound.

If I am correct that this volume presents a distinctive kind of work that is unlike traditional theory, yet rigorous in its own way, we need to get our house in better order. What is a practical theory? Earlier (Cronen, 1994), I offered a preliminary definition of practical theory and here I want to refine that effort. I suggest that a practical theory may be defined by five features:

1. Practical theory is concerned with the way embodied persons in a real world act together to create patterns of practice that constitute their forms of life.
2. A practical theory provides an evolving grammar for a family of discursive and conversational practices. The grammar of practical theory should be internally consistent and defensible in light of data.
3. These practices constitute a family of methods for the study of situated social action wherein professionals join with participants and clients. As such, practical theory respects the centrality of the grammatical abilities of persons in conjoint action.
4. Practical theories are assessed by their consequences. They are developed in order to make human life better. They provide ways of joining in social action so as to promote (a) socially useful description, explanation, critique, and change in situated human action; and (b) emergence of new abilities for all parties involved.

5. A practical theory coevolves with both the abilities of its practitioners and the consequences of its use, thus forming a tradition of practice.

I next want to expand on the key terms used above.

Embodiment and the Real World

Leeds-Hurwitz (Chapter 1, this volume) has already discussed the importance of regarding persons as embodied beings in a real world and not as texts or the points of textual intersection. This, however, raises the issue of how to regard the materiality of the world without falling into the trap of some form of determinism. I suggest we take seriously Shotter's (1993) idea that the brute phsyicality of the world be treated as a set of "sensory topics." He means "topics" in a sense roughly like that in Aristotle's *Rhetoric*. That is, a sensory topic is a place to look that is open to a variety of possible elaborations under particular conditions. For example, we may take it as given that humans are born with a response to a loud sudden noise such as thunder. This response can be, and has been in some cultures, elaborated as cowardliness in males to be overcome by training but the natural response of females. It could also be part of a cultural grammar in which such reactions are said to be the reverberation in men and women alike of the gods' voices. How the sensory topic is realized such that it counts in social life depends on the conjointly created grammar in which the brute fact is given meaning by the way we carry on together about it. So far, few studies using social approaches have focused on sensory topics from the vantage point Shotter suggests.

The emphasis on embodied practices also distinguishes practical theory and the social approaches from the literary approach distinguished by Leeds-Hurwitz (Chapter 1, this volume).

Episodes and Forms of life

The terms "episode" and "forms of life" indicate that human life is made up of multiple, varied patterns. Episodes are not little monads of practice but, rather, have multiple relationships to each other. Together, they produce what Wittgenstein (1953) called forms of life. I choose these terms to call attention to the need to see human action in larger terms than the single episode or single relationship. Lannamann (Chapter 6, this volume) and Sigman (Chapters 10, this volume) are making the same point.

Grammars of Practice

I am choosing the term "grammars of practice" as a way of doing what any approach to the social world must do—offer a way of talking about coherence and incoherence, sense and nonsense. CMM theory was originally infamous in the communication discipline because of its insistence that the coherence of conversation was a matter of rules that emerge and are reconstituted in situated conjoint action (Cronen & Pearce, 1981; Pearce & Cronen, 1980). Stewart has returned to this argument in his chapter. To talk about rules in Wittgenstein's sense as he does and as my colleagues and I have done (Cronen, Pearce, & Xi, 1989/1990) is to reject the idea that there is an underlying formal logic of conversation to be found. Neither Stewart nor the CMM team is saying that the rules of conversation are remade from nothing each time people meet. We are born into a preexisting social world and we learn our rule-using abilities by acting into the practices of others in that world.

In CMM, we have argued that the emergent rules of human interaction are intrinsically moral in character. That is, they have to do with what we can do, must do, or must not do at particular situated moments. They also have to do with distinguishing that for which we are and are not responsible. This moral approach distinguishes CMM's notion of rules from those based on probability terms. It has long seemed to me that Aristotle was right to argue that the world of human *praxis* is distinguished by this intrinsically moral character (Cronen, 1994; Cronen & Pearce, 1981; Pearce & Cronen, 1980). However, whether or not we agree with the CMM position, we must somehow come to terms with the character of grammar in which social action attains coherence.

For practical theory, a grammar of practice refers to the abilities a professional brings to a situation, joining with the abilities of others. These professional abilities are informed by a coherent way of going on—the practical theory. However, that grammar is not isolated from the fuller human experience of the professional person, nor from the way that professional acts into others' behaviors.

Family of Discursive and Conversational Practices

A practical theory must, obviously, lead to practices. These practices may take many forms as is amply illustrated by the foregoing chapters. Some of these are more formalized than others, and indeed more or less formalized methods can be combined as Bavelas has argued. That is why I refer to a family of practices. These together constitute methodology, not just method. Consider ethnography. Fieldwork usually includes some observation, some participant observation, and some kinds of interviewing. Doing consultation with CMM we have used our special form of circular questioning, reflecting teams, and even techniques with some similarities to that reported by Bochner and Ellis in their chapter (Pearce & Cronen, 1980). In other words, we employ a family of methods.

A consequence of stating "up front" that practical theory generates conversations and discourses is to clarify the idea that theory is a story about phenomena that informs communication in and out of its academic discipline. Theory is not simply or primarily a disembodied set of beliefs. We sometimes think of science as a set of propositional statements about the world. However, even in disciplines where the subject matter is independent of the person's activities, knowing correct propositions is not enough. We would not call someone a chemist if that person could memorize and repeat what is in a chemistry book but could not do original work, justify what he or she does, interpret his or her results, defend his or her claims for other chemists, and so on.

When describing practical theory as generative of communication abilities, I have distinguished the terms "discursive" and "conversational." This is to make the point that some of our practices have the character of discourse in Foucault's (1972) sense. That is, they are formalized practices, strongly instantiated, that require particular relationships among the participants to fulfill their felicity conditions. Other practices are more fluid and open to change in these relationships. Because we regard what we are doing in social theory as carrying on *in* social conversations and not merely *about* them, we are alert to choosing and negotiating the kind of relationship we want to have with those we study.

Joining and Respecting the Centrality of Others' Grammars

Chen and Pearce (Chapter 7, this volume) have elaborated the idea that in practical theory we join with those whose activities are of interest and may do so from a variety of positions. Here I want to talk about respect for the centrality of others' grammars.

I will again use the practical theory of CMM to illustrate this idea and the connection it has with the idea of a practice. When one of my graduate students or I conduct an interview based on CMM, we bring to the situation certain grammatical abilities attained by the study of it including a technique adapted for CMM, "circular questioning." This technique was also discussed by Jorgensen. Attempting to understand a problem among people in a business setting, we might ask questions such as these: (1) How would episodes of decision making go if you [Mr. *Y*] did not "stand up" [Mr. *Y*'s words] to Mr. *X* when he says _____? (2) If you did not have episodes in which you "stand up" to Mr. *X*, would anything else in your working relationships change?

The first question above is informed by several aspects of CMM grammar. These include the CMM admonition to explore the *clients'* grammar. Thus we use the clients' own metaphor of "standing up" to someone (Cronen, 1994). The second question is informed by the CMM position that some of the clients' stories are influential for their other stories. When we consider that influence among stories, we are exploring the grammatical connections of one story to others. For example, Mr. *Y* might respond, "The other guys look up to me, they know they can count on me to put up with no guff." Here we get an idea of the possible connection between the episodic story and the relationship story.

To say that we respect the centrality of others' grammars is not to say that we approve of any grammar of practice we encounter. If so, we would have to approve of the grammar of the wife beater and child molester. What we are saying is that for the activity of exploration, we take a stance of curiosity (Lang, 1994).[6]

The reader should also be aware that this and other features of my proposed description differentiate practical theory from critical cultural studies. As I have argued earlier, critical–cultural studies are not directly concerned with with the situated, conjoint activities of embodied persons. They usually focus on cultural texts, particularly the mass media and rock music lyrics. In this way they have an affinity with the literary tradition. Moreover, the conception of meaning usually at play in that tradition is the semiotic one critiqued by Stewart (Chapter 2, this volume), not a conception based on meaning as use.

Internally Consistent and Defensible

Here I am making a move that sets practical theory off vis-à-vis some forms of social constructionism. Following Dewey, I am saying, I think in accord with the other authors in this volume, that we need not claim that we have the *Truth* on our side to argue that our practical theory is more useful than another. We can offer a variety of arguments to that point and we must crucially point to evidence of our theory's use in various studies. This claim is very different than the position argued by Gergen (1994) that each approach is simply another voice and that no voice has any right to argue that it should be privileged over another.

Whereas the idea in commensurability does lead to the conclusion that we cannot often find a simple common yardstick to "prove" one approach better than another, that does not mean good reasons cannot be offered for working one way instead of another (Taylor, 1985a). Any of us who has worked in consultation or with family therapists knows how important it is to develop working stories that integrate what has been learned in interviews and then to find out which stories are more useful guides for carrying on the work.

Consequences and Social Use

Practical theory seems consistent with the pragmatists' view of theory that its payoff is not truth but consequences (James, 1908/1975c). However, consequence is sometimes read in the street sense or (worse) Republican sense of immediate results for one isolated goal. What James (1907/1975b) wanted was a way of thinking that could guide us well through experience. That is the sense in which pragmatist thinkers used the criterion of consequence in place of truth.

They were influenced by science, but not by the stories told by some scientists about finding final truth. Rather, they were influenced by the stories lived by scientists in the the process of their work. They noticed that scientists were not content that a theory was successful for a particular study. Scientists were concerned with what possibilities the theory opened for science and for the broader explanation of natural phenomena.

Similarly, utility in social thought meant much more for the pragmatists than did the ability of ideas to solve this problem or that. That is why Dewey (1922) placed such heavy stress on deliberation. He said that we are prone to having our ability to judge consequences obscured by this project or that and, as a result, "do not give opposing consequences half a chance to develop in thought" (p. 247). He was concerned for the broader social–political consequences of situated action.

Description, Explanation, Criticism, and Improvement

Aristotle argued that there is no reason to pursue the arts of *praxis* except for the reason of making life better. To that end, a practical theory, like any other kind of theory, should offer guidance about what to look for. Even contemporary positivists rarely claim that the world is made of bits of data simply waiting to be collected. A practical theory indicates what should count as data (description) and then offers a grammar for how to put data together into a coherent explanation informed by the particular practical theory.

Nothing in this guarantees that a practical theory will generate one correct explanation. Indeed, it would probably be a weak theory if all it did was lead to one explanation. However, neither should a practical theory simply leave us with multiple explanations. The grammar of the practical theory should provide ways of cogently arguing for and against different interpretations.

We hear this all the time when therapy teams meet with interviewers and offer different explanations of a family's situation. In my own work, the team behind one-way glass and the interviewer periodically meet and use CMM to construct alternative interpretations. They use these alternatives to decide what information to seek. They also discuss what information might lead to discarding a particular interpretation. Rather than treating this as a problem of interjudge agreement, they treat the variety of interpretations as important for opening new possibilities for investigation and intervention. The presence of alternative interpretations does two things for the interviewer: First, it opens affordances for the interviewer when one line of questioning is unproductive. Second, it militates against the tendency to work single-mindedly from one orientation, ignoring information that does not fit.

I do not want to imply that the the only important way we can employ practical theory is in consultation or therapy. Practical theory can enter the conversation in a number of ways, including the publication of social criticism. However, criticism must come from grappling with real situated action.

Coevolution and New Abilities

A practical theory, unlike a traditional positivistic theory, is moribund if it does not exhibit evolution in fundamental ways. Yet it provides an identifiable tradition of work. Consider the ethnographic tradition in communication. The conception of a "cultural code" in that tradition has undergone a great deal of evolution, even though it is a very central idea for that line of work. In earlier work, code seems to be something "out there" that persons decode. In Carbaugh's hands it is much more like the Wittgensteinian notion of a grammatical ability learned by embodied persons in conversation. CMM's move from hierarchies of beliefs to hierarchies of stories that persons could potentially tell is an equally major shift. While it may seem self-serving to say so, I do not regard these changes as weakness but as demonstrations of the vitality of those traditions.

However, the coevolution of practical theory and forms of practice does not tell the whole story. The use of a practical theory not only should lead to enhanced abilities for those whom we study or with whom we consult but should also enrich us as theorists and practitioners. Its use should lead us to be better and more creative in our work on practical theory development and in our applications of theory.

CONCLUSION: IS THIS PERSPECTIVE A THING OF BEAUTY?

The social perspective is complicated. But those who want to read a book that presents work very different from that which is sanctified by the mainstream are probably not the timid sort. With all its complexity and uncharted ground, the prospect of getting involved in such work may look beautiful or ugly, inviting or repulsive. Many aspects of a scholar's experience in addition to the arguments presented here and elsewhere will influence the choice.

How it looks is a bit like the story of a matchmaker who went to a young woman and said that she had a wonderful match for her.

"It's the son of the baker who moved to town last week, do you know him?"

"No I have not seen him, is he good looking?"

"Good looking? He is so handsome he is like a picture. A work of art he is. I'll take you to meet him next week."

Two days later the young woman happened to see the baker's son. She was so shocked by what she saw she went straight to the house of the matchmaker.

"Handsome, you said, like a picture, a work of art, you said! His eyes are not on the same level, his nose is off to one side, his mouth is crooked, he has no hair! Some picture! Some work of art!"

"So, can I help it if you don't happen to like Picasso?"

NOTES

1. All Greek thinkers did not agree with this. Those who rejected the notion of a static substance behind appearances that could be known by humans included Heraclitus and Gorgias, who argued against the stability of the world and the possibility of knowledge such as Parmenides sought from very different perspectives.
2. See Cronen and Pearce (1991/1992) for a way to elaborate Dewey's idea into a way of working of selfhood and individuality.
3. See Cronen (1994, 1995), Cronen, Chen, and Pearce (1988), Cronen, Johnson, and Lannamann (1982), Cronen, Pearce, and Xi (1989/1990), Pearce (1989), and Pearce and Cronen (1980), for a review of this work. The reader will see two important shifts in the work. The first is the greater emphasis on reflexivity after 1982. The second is the decisive move toward

interview methods along with a recasting of the hierarchy of beliefs as a hierarchy of stories with grammatical relationships.

4. I used to agree with this. Pearce and I used to say that the locus of action was interpersonal but the locus of meaning intrapersonal. Then we would say that meaning is created in action. That was confused and I now think wrong-headed. I have not argued that way for many years, but I, not Pearce, am reponsible for the original confusion.

5. It should be noted that Shotter himself has stopped using these words. Shotter (1993) now says that his work provides a "tool box" of ideas to use for analyzing conversation and thus the results of his work bear little resemblance to a theory. This view may be contrasted to the more systematic organization of ideas in CMM theory and ethnography of speaking. My own position on Shotter's work is that it is more integrated and systematic than its author claims. However, that integration is not foregrounded in the written work.

6. Lang (1994) argues that this term "curiosity" is a better orienting term for interviewing than the older term "neutrality," which has led some readers to mistakenly think that the consultant, therapist, or researcher must abandon any moral position. That was never the intent of the term "neutrality" in family therapy.

REFERENCES

Angus, I. H. (1984). *Technique and Enlightenment: Limits of instrumental reason*. Washington, DC: Center for Advanced Research in Phenomenology & University Press of America.

Averill, J. R. (1980). A constructivist view of emotion. In R. Plutchik & H. Kellerman (Eds.), *Theories of emotion* (pp. 305–339). New York: Academic Press.

Averill, J. R. (1989). Stress as fact and artifact: An inquiry into the social origins and functions of some stress reactions. In C. D. Spielberger, I. G. Sarason, & J. Strelau (Eds.), *Stress and anxiety* (Vol. 12, pp. 15–38). New York: Hemisphere.

Barrett, W. (1979). *The illusion of technique*. Garden City: Anchor.

Bateson, G. (1972). *Steps to an ecology of mind*. New York: Ballantine.

Bernstein, R. J. (1985). *Beyond objectivism and relativism: Science, hermeneutics, and praxis*. Philadelphia: University of Pennsylvania Press.

Cappella, J. M. (1990). The method of proof by example in interaction analysis. *Communication Monographs, 57*, 236–240.

Cronen, V. E. (1994). Coordinated management of meaning: Theory for the complexities and contradictions of everyday life. In J. Siegfried (Ed.), *The status of common sense in psychology* (pp. 183–207). Norwood, NJ: Ablex.

Cronen, V. E. (1995). Coordinated management of meaning: The consequentiality of communication and the recapturing of experience. In S. Sigman (Ed.), *The consequentiality of communication* (pp. 17–66). New York: Erlbaum.

Cronen, V. E., Chen, V., & Pearce, W. B. (1988). Coordinated management of meaning: A critical theory. In Y. Y. Kim & W. Gudykundst (Eds.), *International intercultural annual: Theories of intercultural communication* (Vol. 12, pp. 66–98). Beverly Hills, CA: Sage.

Cronen, V. E., Johnson, K. M., & Lannamann, J. W. (1982). Paradoxes, double binds, and reflexive loops: An alternative theoretical perspective. *Family Process, 20,* 91–112.

Cronen, V. E., & Pearce, W. B. (1981). Logical force in interpersonal communication: A new concept of "necessity" in social behavior.*Communication, 6,* 5–67.

Cronen, V. E., & Pearce, W. B. (1991/1992). Grammars of identity and their implications for discursive practices in and out of academe: A comparison of Davies' and Harré's views to coordinated management of meaning theory. *Research on Language and Social Interaction, 25,* 37–66.

Cronen, V. E., Pearce, W. B., & Xi, C. (1989/1990). The meaning of "meaning" in the CMM analysis of communication: A comparison of two traditions. *Research on Language and Social Interaction, 23,* 1–40.

Davies, B., & Harré, R. (1990). Positioning: Conversation and the production of selves. *Journal for the Theory of Social Behavior, 20,* 43–63.

Dewey, J. (1922). *Human nature and conduct.* New York: Henry Holt.

Dewey, J. (1934a). *Art as experience.* New York: Minton, Balch.

Dewey, J. (1934b). *A common faith.* New Haven, CT: Yale University Press.

Dewey, J. (1957). *Reconstruction in philosophy.* Boston: Beacon Press. (Original work published 1920)

Dewey, J. (1958). Experience and nature. New York: Dover. (Original work published in 1925)

Dewey, J. (1960). *The quest for certainty.* New York: Putnam. (Original work published 1929)

Dewey, J. (1966). *Democracy and education.* New York: Free Press. (Original work published 1916)

Dewey, J. (1980). *Theory of the moral life.* New York: Irvington. (Original work published 1932)

Fleuridas, C., Nelson, T., & Rosenthal, D. (1986). The evolution of circular questions: Training family therapists. *Journal of Marital and Family Therapy, 12,* 113–127.

Foucault, M. (1972). *The archaeology of knowledge and the discourse on language.* New York: Harper & Row.

Gadlin, H. (1977). Private lives and public order: A critical view of the history of intimate relations in the United States. In G. Levinger & H. Raush (Eds.), *Close relations: Perspectives on intimacy* (pp. 3–72). Amherst: University of Massachusetts Press.

Gergen, K. J. (1994). *Remarks at the DISPUK seminar on therapy, education and consultation,* Copenhagen, Denmark.

Goodman, N. (1983). *Fact, fiction, and forecast.* Cambridge, MA: Harvard University Press.

Harré, R. (1984). *Personal being.* Cambridge, MA: Harvard University Press.

Harré, R. & Gillett, G. (1994). *The discursive mind*. Thousand Oaks, CA: Sage.

Hymes, D. (1990). Epilogue to "The things we do with words." In D. Carbaugh (Ed.), *Cultural communication and intercultural contact* (pp. 419–429). Hillsdale, NJ: Erlbaum.

Jacobs, S. (1990). On the especially nice fit between qualitative analysis and the known properties of conversation. *Communication Monographs, 57*, 241–249.

James, W. (1975). The essence of humanism. In A. J. Ayer (Ed.), *Pragmatism and the meaning of truth* (pp. 236–243). Cambridge, MA: Harvard University Press. (Original work published 1905)

James, W. (1975b). Pragmatism. In A. J. Ayer (Ed.), *Pragmatism and the meaning of truth* (pp. 1–144). Cambridge, MA: Harvard University Press. (Orignal work published 1907)

James, W. (1975c). The pragmatist account of truth and its misunderstanders. In A. J. Ayer (Ed.), *Pragmatism and the meaning of truth* (pp. 265–282). Cambridge, MA: Harvard University Press. (Original work published 1908)

James, W. (1977). Does "consciousness" exist? In J. J. McDermott (Ed.), *The writings of William James* (pp. 169–183). Chicago: University of Chicago Press. (Original work published 1904)

Keillor, G. (1987). *Leaving home*. New York: Viking Penguin.

Kuhn, T. S. (1970). *The structure of scientific revolutions* (2nd ed.). Chicago: University of Chicago Press.

Lamont, C., & Redmer, M. (Eds.). (1959). *Dialogue on John Dewey*. New York: Horizon.

Lang, P. (1994). Unpublished remarks at the Kensington Consultation Centre Advanced Workshop for Systemic Therapy. Oxford, England

Marx, K. (1959). Theses on Feuerbach. In L. S. Feuer (Ed.), *Marx and Engels* (pp. 243–245). Garden City: Anchor Books. (Original work published 1888)

Osgood, C. E., Suci, G. J., & Tannenbaum, P. H. (1957). *The measurement of meaning*. Urbana: University of Illinois Press.

Pearce, W. B. (1989). *Communication and the human condition*. Carbondale: Southern Illinois University Press.

Pearce, W. B., & Cronen, V. E. (1980). *Communication, action, and meaning: The creation of social realities*. New York: Praeger.

Philipsen, G. (1989). An ethnographic approach to communication. In B. Dervin (Ed.), *Rethinking communication vol. 2; paradigm exemplars* (pp. 258–268). Newbury Park, CA: Sage.

Reale, G. (1987) *From the origins to Socrates: A history of ancient philosophy*. Albany: State University of New York Press.

Rorty, R. (1979). *Philosophy and the mirror of nature*. Princeton: Princeton University Press.

Sanders, R. E. (1987). *Cognitive foundations of calculated speech*. Albany: State University of New York Press.

Searle, J. (1969). *Speech acts: An essay in the philosophy of language*. Oxford: Oxford University Press.

Shotter, J. (1984). *Social accountability and selfhood*. Oxford: Basil Blackwell.

Shotter, J. (1993). *Conversational realities*. London: Sage.

Taylor, C. (1985a). *Philosophy and the human sciences: Philosophical papers (Vol. 1)*. Cambridge: Cambridge University Press.

Taylor, C. (1985b). *Philosophy and the human sciences: Philosophical papers (Vol. 2)*. Cambridge: Cambridge University Press.

Tomm, K. (1987a) Interventive interviewing: Part I. Strategizing as a fourth guideline for the therapist. *Family Process, 26*, 3–13.

Tomm, K. (1987b). Interventive interviewing: Part II. Reflexive questioning as a means to enable self healing. *Family Process, 26*, 167–183.

Tomm, K. (1988). Interventive interviewing: Part III. Intending to ask linear, circular, strategic, and reflexive questions. *Family Processs, 27*, 1–15.

Weaver, D. A. (1991). *Pessimism-related cognitions and depressed mood: A longitudinal study of psychiatric patients*. Unpublished doctoral dissertation, University of Massachusetts, Amherst, MA.

Willis, P. (1977). *Learning to labor: How working class kids get working class jobs*. New York: Columbia University Press.

Wittgenstein, L. (1953). *Philosophical investigations*. New York: Macmillan.

Contributors

Janet Beavin Bavelas is Professor of Psychology at the University of Victoria (Canada). She has written extensively on interpersonal communication, including two of her three books (*Pragmatics of Human Communication*, with Watzlawick and Jackson, and *Equivocal Communication*, with Black, Chovil, and Mullett). Her major research areas include face-to-face interaction, discourse analysis, gestures and facial displays, and a particular interest in alternative research methods. She is currently working on a new book with Nicole Chovil, tentatively titled *Redefining Language: An Integrated Message Model of Language in Face-to-Face Interaction*, which proposes an integration of verbal and so-called nonverbal aspects of communication as well as emphasizing the social aspects of actual language use.

Arthur P. Bochner is Professor of Communication and Codirector (with Carolyn Ellis) of the Institute for Interpretive Human Studies at the University of South Florida. He is the author (with Janet Yerby and Nancy Buerkle-Rothfuss) of *Understanding Family Communication* (Gorsuch) and he has published numerous monographs and chapters on interpersonal relationships and the philosophy of communication inquiry. His current research focuses on local narratives that show the joint interpersonal processes of constructing relationship meanings through talk.

Donal Carbaugh received his Ph.D. from the University of Washington in 1984 and is currently Associate Professor of Communication and Faculty Affiliate in American Studies at the University of Massachusetts, Amherst. His research interests are in developing a communication theory that is ethnographically informed, culturally sensitive, ecologically viable, and attentive to intercultural encounters. His work includes the book *Talking American* (Ablex) and the edited book, *Cultural Communication and Intercultural Contact* (Erlbaum), and has appeared in over a dozen scholarly journals including *Communication Theory*, *Quarterly Journal of Speech*, *Language in Society*, and *Semiotica*.

Victoria Chen received her Ph.D. from the University of Massachusetts, Amherst, in 1988. She is currently Assistant Professor in Communication at Denison University. Her research interests include qualitative analysis of cultural experience/identity and ethnic autobiographical fiction, as well as development of the theory of coordinated management of meaning. She is coeditor of *Our Voices: Essays in Culture, Ethnicity, and Communication* (1994) and has published in *Research on Language and Social Interaction* and *International and Intercultural Communication Annual*.

Vernon E. Cronen is Professor of Communication at the University of Massachusetts, Amherst. He is coauthor with W. Barnett Pearce of *Communication, Action and Meaning* and author or coauthor of a large number of articles and book chapters in communication, psychology, and family therapy. Professor Cronen is an external examiner for the Roehampton Institute's diploma course in systemic management taught through the Kensington Consultation Centre, London. He has also been a regular faculty member of the Kennsington Consultation Centre's Oxford Advanced Workshops for Family Therapists.

Carolyn Ellis is Professor of Sociology and Codirector (with Arthur Bochner) of the Institute for Interpretive Human Studies at the University of South Florida. She is the author of *Fisher Folk: Two Communities on Chesapeake Bay* (University Press of Kentucky), *Final Negotiations: A Story of Love, Loss, and Chronic Illness* (Temple University Press) and coeditor (with Michael Flaherty) of *Investigating Subjectivity* (Sage). Her current work focuses on narrative ethnography, subjectivity, and autobiographical accounts.

Sally O. Hastings is a Doctoral Candidate in the Department of Communication, University of Massachusetts, Amherst. Her research interests are in developing a communication theory of identity and cultural adaptation. Her dissertation research explores ways Asian Indians in the United States use "identity talk about the other" to create a sense both of themselves as East Asians and about the other, the Americans. Her work has appeared in *Communication Theory*.

Jane Jorgenson is a Visiting Assistant Professor in the Department of Speech Communication and Theater Arts at Old Dominion University. She received her Ph.D. from the Annenberg School of Communication at the University of Pennsylvania. She has studied family and relational communication in the United States and Norway and continues to do research on relational approaches to research settings. As a teacher of televised communication courses as well as traditional (face-to-face) classes, she has developed work in distance education, including relational issues and the role of rapport in the televised classroom.

John W. Lannamann is an Associate Professor of Communication at the University of New Hampshire. He joined the faculty in 1982 after receiving his

Ph.D. and M.A. degrees from the University of Massachusetts, Amherst. He is both a critic of the social sciences and an optimist about the possibility of a socially engaged form of communication research. In his recent work he criticizes the underlying ideological assumptions of current interpersonal research and calls for a form of research more closely tied to social and political change. In addition to his critical work, he has focused his analysis of face-to-face communication on the study of domestic violence, family pathologies, and intercultural communication. He has published in *Communication Monographs, Communication Theory, Journal of Communication, Communication Yearbook, Applied Communication Research, Family Process,* and *Journal of Strategic and Systemic Therapies.*

Wendy Leeds-Hurwitz received her M.A. and Ph.D. degrees from the University of Pennsylvania and is Associate Professor of Communication at the University of Wisconsin–Parkside. She is the author of *Communication in Everyday Life: A Social Interpretation* (Ablex), and *Semiotics and Communication: Signs, Codes, Cultures* (Erlbaum). In addition to communication theory, her research interests include the influence of culture on interaction, childhood socialization, the ethnography of communication, and the history of the study of communication, particularly interdisciplinary projects.

W. Barnett Pearce received his B.A. from Carson-Newman College, M.A. and Ph.D. degrees from Ohio University, and studied at Southwestern Baptist Theological Seminary. He is currently Professor and Chair of the Department of Communication at Loyola University of Chicago. His interests range across many of the traditional divisions of the discipline but are grounded in a particular approach to communication theory, which he calls the coordinated management of meaning. Recent publications include *Interpersonal Communication: Making Social Worlds* (HarperCollins), *Reagan and Public Discourse in America* (University of Alabama Press), *Cultures, Politics and Research Programs: An International Assessment of Field Research Methods* (Erlbaum), and *Communication and the Human Condition* (Southern Illinois University Press).

Stuart J. Sigman is Associate Professor and Chair in the Department of Communication at the State University of New York at Albany. He holds a joint faculty appointment to the Department of Linguistics and Cognitive Science. He is also a member of the Core Faculty of the Graduate School, The Union Institute. His doctoral degree was conferred by the University of Pennsylvania in 1982. He is the author of *A Perspective on Social Communication* (Lexington) and serves as associate editor of the journal *Research on Language and Social Interaction*, which he founded in 1987. His main interests are social theory and ethnographic methodology.

Frederick Steier is Associate Professor of Engineering Management and Director of the Center for Cybernetic Studies in Complex Systems at Old Dominion University. He was recently Interim Chair of the Department of

Speech Communications and Theater Arts as well. He received his Ph.D. from the University of Pennsylvania in social systems sciences. He was president of the American Society for Cybernetics from 1989 to 1991. The editor of *Research and Reflexivity* (Sage), his research has focused on relational and systemic approaches to inquiry in diverse domains, from organizations to family therapy to education.

John Stewart has taught communication theory, interpersonal communication, philosophy of communication, and philosophy of interpretive research at the University of Washington since 1969, where he is Professor of Speech Communication. He earned his B.A. at Pacific Lutheran University, M.A. at Northwestern, and Ph.D. at the University of Southern California. His philosophy of communication research has been published in *Quarterly Journal of Speech*, *Communication Theory*, *Western Journal of Communication*, *Communication Education*, and several edited books. He has also edited *Bridges Not Walls: A Book about Interpersonal Communication* and coauthored *Together: Communicating Interpersonally*.

Author Index

Subject Index